THE LOST LITERATURE
OF MEDIEVAL ENGLAND

The Lost Literature
of Medieval England

R. M. WILSON

METHUEN & CO LTD
11 NEW FETTER LANE LONDON EC4

First published 1952 by
Methuen & Co. Ltd
Second edition, revised and reset 1970
First published as a University Paperback 1972

Hardback SBN 416 17000 5
University Paperback SBN 416 18410 3

Distributed in the U.S.A. by
HARPER & ROW PUBLISHERS, INC.
BARNES & NOBLE IMPORT DIVISION

TO
DOROTHY
AND
ANNE

CONTENTS

ABBREVIATIONS

Archiv.	*Archiv für das Studium der neuren Sprachen und Literaturen.*
ASS.	*Acta Sanctorum apud socios Bollandianos.*
Asser	W. H. Stevenson, *Asser's Life of Alfred* (London 1904).
B.M.	British Museum.
Bodl.	Bodleian Library.
Canterbury and Dover	M. R. James, *The Ancient Libraries of Canterbury and Dover* (Cambridge 1903).
C.C.C.C.	Corpus Christi College, Cambridge.
Chronica Majora	Matthew Paris, *Chronica Majora* (RS. 57).
Collectanea	J. Leland, *Collectanea*, ed. T. Hearne (London 1774).
Continuity	R. W. Chambers, *On the Continuity of English Prose* (EETS. 1932).
CS.	Camden Society.
C.U.L.	Cambridge University Library.
De Principis Instructione	Giraldus Cambrensis, *De Principis Instructione* (RS. 21) viii.
Descriptio Kambriæ	Giraldus Cambrensis, *Descriptio Kambriæ* (RS. 21) vi.
EETS	Early English Text Society: Original Series.
EETS. ES.	Early English Text Society: Extra Series.
EHR.	*English Historical Review.*
EHS.	English Historical Society.
Fabyan	R. Fabyan, *The New Chronicles of England and France*, ed. H. Ellis (London 1811).
Florence of Worcester	Florence of Worcester, *Chronicon* (EHS. 13).
Gaimar	G. Gaimar, *Lestorie des Engles* (RS. 91).
Gemma Ecclesiastica	Giraldus Cambrensis, *Gemma Ecclesiastica* (RS. 21) ii.
Gesta Pontificum	William of Malmesbury, *Gesta Pontificum* (RS. 52).

Gesta Regum	William of Malmesbury, *Gesta Regum* (RS. 90).
Hardy	T. D. Hardy, *Descriptive Catalogue of Materials relating to the History of Great Britain and Ireland* (RS. 26).
Hearne	T. Hearne, *Peter Langtoft's Chronicle (as illustrated and improved by Robert of Brunne)* (Oxford 1725).
Higden	*Polychronicon Ranulphi Higden* (RS. 41).
HMC.	*Historical Manuscripts Commission.*
Huntingdon	Henry of Huntingdon, *Historia Anglorum* (RS. 74).
Itinerarium Kambriæ	Giraldus Cambrensis, *Itinerarium Kambriæ* (RS. 21) vi.
Ker	N. R. Ker, *Catalogue of Manuscripts containing Anglo-Saxon* (Oxford 1957).
Langtoft	*Chronicle of Pierre de Langtoft* (RS. 47).
Leland	L. T. Smith, *The Itinerary of John Leland* (London 1907).
Liber Eliensis	E. O. Blake, *Liber Eliensis* (CS. 1962).
Mannyng	*Chronicles of Robert of Brunne* (RS. 87).
Map	M. R. James, *Walter Map De Nugis Curialium* (Anecdota Oxoniensia, part xiv: Oxford 1914).
ME	Middle English.
MHG.	Middle High German.
MLN.	*Modern Language Notes.*
MLR.	*Modern Language Review.*
Monasticon	W. Dugdale, *Monasticon Anglicanum*, ed. J. Caley, H. Ellis, and B. Bandinel (London 1846).
OE.	Old English.
OHG.	Old High German.
ON.	Old Norse.
Ordericus	Ordericus Vitalis, *Historia Ecclesiastica*, ed. A. Le Prevost (Paris 1838–55).
PMLA.	*Publications of the Modern Language Association of America.*
RS.	Rolls Series.
Speculum Ecclesiæ	Giraldus Cambrensis, *Speculum Ecclesiæ* (RS. 21) iv.

SS.   Surtees Society.

STS.   Scottish Text Society.

Symeon of Durham   Symeon of Durham, *Historia Regum* (RS. 75).

Warton   T. Warton, *History of English Poetry*, ed. W. C. Hazlitt (London 1871).

Wendover   Roger of Wendover, *Flores Historiarum* (EHS. 8).

PREFACE

This survey of the lost literature of medieval England is an attempt to provide concrete evidence for the statements often made on the subject. It is hoped that by placing it side by side with the histories of the extant literature a much truer picture of the extent, growth, and development of Old and Middle English literature may be gained. Few of the topics or stories mentioned in the following pages have been dealt with exhaustively – this was inevitable if the study were to be kept within reasonable bounds – but it is hoped that enough indications are given to allow any interested reader to carry out further investigations for himself.

The title is necessarily more concise than correct. At the best such a study could deal only with the literature which has left some trace, and it is obvious enough that much must have disappeared leaving no indication whatever of its former existence. Moreover, even within these inevitable limits, no claim can be made for comprehensiveness. Such a title should include chapters on Anglo-French and Anglo-Latin, and material is available for these, but nevertheless the two literatures have been intentionally omitted. One or two catalogues of monastic libraries, and some collections of medieval wills, although in print, have not been available to me. Moreover, many medieval wills still remain unpublished, as well as lists of books and perhaps the occasional catalogue of a monastic library. Nevertheless, if we may judge from the numerous documents of this type which have been examined, it is unlikely that those which have not been seen would contain much of interest. On the other hand, it is certain that a closer scrutiny of the medieval Latin and vernacular chronicles would bring to light many other stories which must have been current during the Old and Middle English periods. Here it has seemed wiser to limit the selection to those stories for which the available evidence indicates a fairly wide distribution, rather than to attempt an inclusiveness which would in any case be impossible of achievement. The chapter on the lyric is also certainly incomplete, and a wider examination of medieval manuscripts would probably result in the discovery not only of numerous fragments but of some complete poems. Nevertheless it is hoped that, despite such shortcomings, the evidence here presented is enough to justify the conclusions that have been drawn in the final chapter.

Some of the chapters are obviously greatly indebted to earlier works. Chapter I owes much to the edition of *Widsith* by Professor R. W. Chambers, and II to Dr C. E. Wright's *Cultivation of Saga in Anglo-Saxon England*. Some of the translations in Chapters II and IV are taken from the latter work, and for permission to reproduce them I am indebted to the author and to the publishers, Messrs Oliver & Boyd. When such excellent translations already existed it seemed foolish to waste time and effort in producing inferior ones of my own. Chapter V is ultimately based on an article on 'Some Lost Saints' Lives in Old and Middle English', first published in the *Modern Language Review*, xxxvi, 161ff., and I am indebted to the editor for permission to use this article as the basis of my chapter. The original article owed much to Dr R. W. Hunt, Keeper of the Western Manuscripts in the Bodleian Library, both for advice and references, and the revised version remains under the same obligation. The chapters on lyrical and political poetry are inevitably greatly indebted to the various publications by Rossell Hope Robbins, and to Mr G. E. Morris. Similarly Chapter XI necessarily owes much to *The Mediæval Stage* by Sir E. K. Chambers. Some indication of other obligations to individual scholars will be found in the footnotes. In these, whenever possible, I have indicated secondary sources, whether I had derived my original information from them or from the primary source. This seemed the most satisfactory method of showing the earliest publication of the information in question; but I cannot hope to have been completely successful in this, and no doubt some such references have escaped me.

It will be noticed that the title of this book duplicates the title of the article in the *Transactions of the Bibliographical Society* in which Professor R. W. Chambers first pointed out the possible importance of the lost literature. This emphasizes my indebtedness to that great scholar, one of the most humane and inspiring of medievalists. But if the book owes its inspiration to one great scholar, to another, Professor Bruce Dickins, it probably owes the fact that it ever appeared. His wide and accurate scholarship, his generous and kindly assistance, were always ready, and had I availed myself of them to an even greater extent, this book would undoubtedly have been worthier of the two great scholars to whom it owes its existence. Professor A. C. Cawley read the book in proof, and I am grateful to him for numerous corrections and suggestions which have improved it considerably. Finally, to the late Professor A. H. Smith I owe a debt of gratitude for his constant interest in the book, and for his help and guidance in preparing it for the press.

SECOND EDITION

For this second edition the original work has been completely re-written, with numerous verbal changes, many additions, a few omissions, and some re-arrangement of the material. This has made it possible to take account of most of the many references to the lost literature which have appeared since the first publication of the book.

I

HEROIC LEGEND

How much of the heroic poetry of the Germanic peoples has been lost will never be known. In Old English there remains only one complete epic, *Beowulf*, two fragments, *Finnsburg* and *Waldere*, and the short poems *Widsith* and *Deor*; from the continent come the *Hildebrandslied* and the medieval *Nibelungenlied*, together with the Scandinavian poems of the *Elder Edda* which were not written down before the thirteenth century. It is certain that these represent only a fraction of the heroic lays known to the Germanic tribes, the earliest references to such literature dating from the period when the Anglo-Saxons were still on the continent. At the beginning of the Christian era Tacitus had commented on the fact that their heroic lays were the only annals of the Germanic peoples, and referred to the ancient songs in which they celebrated their gods Tuisto and his son Mannus;[1] elsewhere he tells how the deeds of Arminius were still remembered in the songs of his people.[2] Nothing more is heard of such poetry until the fourth century, when the Emperor Julian compared the songs of the barbarians across the Rhine to the croaking of harsh-voiced birds,[3] an opinion clearly shared by the fifth-century bishop of Clermont, Sidonius Apollinaris, who complained that he had 'to bear up under the weight of Germanic words', and to praise 'though with a wry face, whatever the Burgundian, with his hair smeared with rancid butter, chooses to sing'.[4] Similarly, a century later, Venantius Fortunatus, in the introduction to his poems, speaks of the

---

[1] J. G. C. Anderson, *Cornelii Taciti De Origine et Situ Germanorum* (Oxford 1938), p. 6.

[2] J. Jackson, *The Annals of Tacitus* (London 1931–7) ii, 518.

[3] W. C. Wright, *The Works of the Emperor Julian* (London 1913–23) ii, 423.

[4] W. B. Anderson, *Sidonius, Poems and Letters* (London 1936) i, 212. See also the unknown poet in the *Latin Anthology*, ed. A. Riese (Leipzig 1894) i, 221:

> Inter 'eils' goticum 'scapia matzia ia drincan'
> Non audet quisquam dignos edicere versus.

constant buzzing of the harp as it resounds to barbarian lays.[1] This
is practically all that is heard of such literature from non-Germanic
observers, and it is to be regretted that their scorn prevented them
from writing down some of the songs. For further evidence of the
popularity of such poetry among the Anglo-Saxons we are
dependent on later writers.

In Anglo-Saxon England there are occasional general references
to the old pagan and heroic stories. The whole tenor of Bede's
description of the beginnings of Christian poetry in England
suggests that the songs sung at the feast, which Cædmon left when
he saw the harp coming near to him, were of this type, and certainly a contrast appears to be intended between these songs and
the Christian poetry that Cædmon is said to have composed.[2]
Elsewhere the same author tells how the monks of Jarrow, on the
occasion of a visit to St Cuthbert, began to amuse themselves with
stories, to the great distress of the saint who exhorted them to
prayer, having learned in a vision, as the monks afterwards discovered, that plague had broken out in the north.[3] Here again the
indication seems to be that it was the old heroic stories with which
the monks were entertaining each other. St Guthlac, in his youth,
was inspired by songs of the ancient heroes.[4] Asser tells of Alfred's
fondness for such poetry – including the well-known story of how
he received from his mother a book of Old English verse – and it
was above all the learning of this poetry that the king recom-
mended to his children.[5] It may have included the Christian epics
of Cædmon or the pious verse of Aldhelm, but references in
Alfred's own works show that he was familiar with the heroes of
the pagan period. Again, it was one of the charges brought by his
enemies against St Dunstan that he had learned the vain songs of
ancestral heathendom,[6] and the canons of King Edgar forbade
monks to sing such songs, even to themselves.[7]

Yet, despite ecclesiastical opposition, there can be no doubt that
many of the old heroes were remembered throughout the Old
English period. Written versions of some of the poems may

---

[1] *Monumenta Germaniae Historica. Auctores Antiquissimi* IV, i, 2.
[2] C. L. Wrenn, *The Poetry of Cædmon* (Oxford 1948), p. 10.
[3] B. Colgrave, *Two Lives of St Cuthbert* (Cambridge 1940), p. 247.
[4] *ASS., April.*, ii, 39ff.   [5] Asser, pp. 20, 59, 58.
[6] *Memorials of St Dunstan* (RS. 63), p. 11.
[7] B. Thorpe, *Ancient Laws and Institutes of England* (London 1840) ii, 256.

perhaps have been known to Alfred, but most of such poetry probably survived only by oral transmission. Exactly what this oral heroic poetry was like we can never know. It could be known today only from written versions, and when these were made sophistication of the older material was inevitable. All that later references can give are vague hints of the heroes whose names and deeds were longest remembered, and occasionally, if we are fortunate, some garbled version of the deeds themselves.

The Goths were apparently the earliest of the Germanic peoples to leave their northern homes. Their wanderings, and the later glories of the Gothic kingdoms, provided subjects for many heroic lays. It may even be, although there is no real proof of this, that the development of such poetry among the Germanic tribes was to some extent the work of Gothic minstrels. Certainly Jordanes tells of songs about the early wanderings of the Goths,[1] and in later times a surprising number of the characters of heroic poetry were Gothic in origin, even amongst the northern tribes who had long been separated from them. In England one of the best known of these figures was that Eormenric who had established a great Gothic empire stretching from the Baltic to the Black Sea. When this was attacked by the Huns Eormenric, according to Ammianus, committed suicide. But Jordanes has a different story; the Rosomoni having revolted against him, Eormenric caused a woman of that people to be torn asunder by wild horses. In consequence he was attacked by her brothers and wounded in the side so that he became sick and infirm. The Huns took advantage of this to move in battle array against the Ostrogoths, and in the midst of these troubles Eormenric died.

References to Eormenric occur in three of the existing examples of Old English heroic poetry, but they are too brief to give much information about the stories connected with him that were known in this country. The author of *Widsith*,

> in the company of the gracious lady Ealhild, from Angel in the East, sought the home of the Gothic king Eormenric, fierce and faithless (5–9).[2]

[1] C. C. Mierow, *The Gothic History of Jordanes* (London 1915), p. 62.

[2] R. W. Chambers, *Widsith* (Cambridge 1912), p. 189. The introduction to this edition contains by far the best account of those pagan heroes known in this country. See also C. Brady, *The Legends of Ermanaric* (California U.P. 1943), and K. Malone, *Widsith* (Copenhagen 1962).

Later references in the same poem (88–92, 109–10) are followed by a list of Gothic heroes in the household of Eormenric: Hethca, Beadeca, the Herelings, 'Emerca and Fridla, and Eastgota, wise and good, the father of Unwen'. Secca and Becca, Seafola and Theodoric, Heathoric and Sifeca, Hlithe and Incgentheow. Chambers and Kemp Malone would identify Ealhild with Swanhild, the wife of Eormenric in Scandinavian tradition whom he ordered to be torn apart by wild horses, a deed from which sprang all his later misfortunes. However, even if the identification be accepted, the tone of the references here would indicate that this story of her death was unknown to the English poet. The mention of the Herelings and Sifeca as members of the household may suggest that the story, found in the greatest detail in Middle High German tradition, telling how Eormenric caused the death of his nephews, the Harlungs, through the wicked counsel of Sibka, was known also in England. But the deed seems to have been attributed to Eormenric only at a comparatively late date, and there appears to be no particularly close connexion between the various characters in this passage. In *Deor* (21–6) Eormenric is represented as a great and terrible king, but there is no indication of any particular stories connected with him. On the other hand, the reference in *Beowulf* (1197–1201) must have to do with some definite story, though the details of it are unknown:

> I have heard of no better treasure of heroes under the heavens since Hama carried away to the bright city the necklace of the Brosings, the gem and the setting; he fled the treacherous hatred of Eormenric; he chose everlasting gain.

From this it would appear that Hama had robbed Eormenric of the *Brōsinga mene* and had then fled from the court, or possibly died. There is obviously some connexion between this jewel and the Old Norse *Brísinga men* – the necklace of Freyja stolen from her by Loki – but it is impossible to discover the exact relationship. Since Eormenric slew the Harlungs for their treasure, it has been suggested that this may have included the *Brōsinga mene*, and hence that these lines provide a further reference to the Harlung legend, but there is nothing to support such a conclusion. Hama himself appears elsewhere in heroic legend as the enemy of Eormenric. The account of him in *Ðiðriks saga*, which tells how he fled the enmity of Eormenric and later entered a monastery taking with him a great treasure, may perhaps be a Christianization of the unknown story referred to in *Beowulf*.

This is all that the extant literature can tell us about the stories of Eormenric current in this country. On occasion the occurrence, during the later period, of place-names and personal names which can be connected with the characters of heroic legend, has been brought forward as evidence that the legends were still known at the time when the names were given. If such names are of an uncommon type, it is not improbable that the early possessors of them may have been named for one of the heroic characters. But this need not have been the case with later children, and we can never be certain that the parents actually had the legend in mind when they named the child. The continued use of such names may have helped to keep the original legends alive, but we can hardly assume that in every case the name comes from the hero, and therefore that his story is still known and repeated.

So far as Eormenric is concerned, all that is certain is that he was evidently well known in Anglo-Saxon England as a type of fierce and cruel tyrant. It is possible that some version of the Harlung story, known today from Middle High German sources, was in circulation, and there was certainly current some story dealing with Eormenric, Hama, and the *Brōsinga mene*, of which the details are lost.

The longest remembered of all the evil deeds of the legendary Eormenric was the story of his treachery to his nephew Theodoric. The latter was certainly well known among the Anglo-Saxons, though whether as the foe of Eormenric is more doubtful. In *Widsith* (115) he perhaps appears as one of the champions of Eormenric, and if so there is no hint of enmity between the two. The author of *Deor* knew of some story connected with a certain Theodoric, but whether this was the Ostrogoth or the Frank is uncertain:

Theodoric possessed for thirty years the city of the Mærings; that was known to many (18–19).

Such allusiveness indicates that the story was familiar, and the mention of Eormenric immediately afterwards may be an indication that, if this is Theodoric the Ostrogoth, then the hostility between the two was equally well known. Consequently it may perhaps refer to Theodoric's legendary thirty years of exile, but nothing is known of any city of the Mærings in connexion with this. A reference to a different story is to be found in *Waldere*. A speaker, probably Waldere, is referring to a famous sword:

> I know that Theodoric thought of sending it to Widia, and also much treasure with the sword, of adorning much beside it with gold. The kinsman of Nithhad, Widia son of Weland, received the reward for past deeds, because he had delivered him from prison. He hastened forth through the realm of the monsters (ii, 4–10).

This is presumably a reference to the story, found in Middle High German, telling how the hero was rescued from the giants of Duke Nitger by Hildebrand, Widia, and Hama. Other references in Old English indicate a familiarity with Theodoric as a hero of legend. The ninth-century *Old English Martyrology* tells how Theodoric, as an Arian, was cast in torment down the crater of a volcano, and adds 'that was Theodoricus the king whom we call Theodric',[1] obviously identifying the heretic king with the hero of vernacular legend. Elsewhere Alfred's statement, in his translation of Boethius, that 'this Theodric was an Amuling',[2] must be due to the heroic poems of which he was so fond.

There are, then, possible references to two stories extant in Old English concerning Theodoric – his sojourn in the city of the Mærings, and his rescue by Widia – of which the former has been lost entirely or so changed in later tradition as to be unrecognizable. It is possible that the hostility of Eormenric to him was also known, but of the other stories, if any, which were current no trace now remains. A difficulty lies in the fact that there were at least two Theodorics famous in heroic legend: Theodoric the Ostrogothic king of Italy, and Theodoric the Frank, the eldest son of Clovis and through his son Theudebert the slayer of Hygelac. When the exact stories referred to are unknown we can never be certain with which of them we have to deal, and it may be that some of the preceding allusions are to the Frank rather than to the Ostrogoth. Consequently some scholars prefer to identify the Theodoric of *Widsith* and *Deor* with the hero of the later story of Hug-Dietrich and Wolf-Dietrich.

[1] Ed. G. Herzfeld (EETS. 1900), p. 84.
[2] Ed. W. J. Sedgefield (Oxford 1899), p. 7.

Two other Gothic heroes, often mentioned together, are the Wudga and Hama who appear as outlaws in *Widsith* (124–30). Mention has already been made of the reference in *Beowulf* to an unknown story dealing with Hama, and his characterization in later continental literature suggests that he was regarded as the typical outlaw of the period. Wudga, or Widia, was probably an earlier and more important hero who was attracted only at a comparatively late date into the Eormenric cycle. He is usually identified with the Vidigoia, said by Jordanes to have been one of the Gothic heroes, still remembered in song, who had fallen in battle against the Sarmatians.[1] In Anglo-Saxon England he was the hero of a story telling of the rescue of Theodoric; the same reference shows that his legendary descent from Weland was also known. His fame survived the Conquest, and he is mentioned by Laȝamon in his description of the arming of Arthur, where the king's mailcoat, Wygar, is said to have been forged by Witege.[2] Since he is referred to here as a smith, his descent from Weland may be all that is still remembered of him. At a much later date he appears, in company with other Germanic heroes, in a late version of the *Brut*, which tells how 'Hrothwulf and Hunlaf, Unwine and Widia, Horsa and Hengest, Waltheof and Hama, some in Italy, some in Gaul, others in Britain, and the remainder in Germany, achieved fame by their weapons and warlike deeds.'[3] This is the last English reference to Wudga and Hama, and it may be doubted whether the writer really knew anything of the stories to which he so glibly refers.

The same passage in the *Brut* makes also the final mention of another great Gothic hero, Unwine, whose name at any rate was remembered long after the Conquest. He is probably identical with the Hunuil said by Jordanes to have been the son of Ostrogotha, but he did not succeed his father and may have died young. In *Widsith* (114) he appears only as the son of Eastgota; and whilst the mere fact of reference in this poem suggests that he was known as the hero of one or more stories, no other allusion to him is to be found before the fourteenth century. In the *Fasciculus Morum*, written perhaps before 1340, he appears 'in "Elvelond", where now,

---

[1] C. C. Mierow, *op. cit.*, pp. 62, 101.
[2] G. L. Brook, *Selections from Laȝamon's Brut* (Oxford 1963), lines 2828–31.
[3] R. W. Chambers, *op. cit.*, p. 254.

so they say, remain those strenuous warriors Unewyn and Wade'.[1] He is mentioned in the alliterative *Morte Arthure*,[2] and may perhaps appear with Attila in the shorter fifteenth-century Latin version of the romance of *Waldef*:

> At that time (i.e. after Arthur) there reigned in Norfolk a certain king called Attalus. In Suffolk ruled Unwyn, king of Thetford, who fought in single combat against Attalus. But the two were reconciled without the intervention of a mediator.

The difficulty is that in this Latin epitome the proper names of the Anglo-French romance occur in peculiar forms. The Latin Attalus is for the Anglo-French Atle, and in view of the way in which the author of the Latin has treated the other names, the assumed equation of Attalus with Attila may not be well founded. Consequently the suggestion that here we have a dim remembrance of a single combat between Attila the Hun and Unwine the Gothic champion, both now shrunk to petty East Anglian kings, must remain doubtful.[3] Otherwise we have nowhere any hint of the deeds for which Unwine was renowned, though for his name and fame to have lasted so long he must have been an important figure in Anglo-Saxon heroic poetry.

Apart from the Goths, heroes from other nations also provided subjects for Anglo-Saxon minstrels. No doubt the last great battle of the Burgundians, when the bodyguard of Gundahari fell round their king, was as familiar in England as on the continent. The king himself, under the name of Guthhere, was certainly known, though no reference to his last great battle with the Huns has survived. Widsith (65–7) received a ring from him as a reward for his songs, and Guthhere is one of the chief characters in *Waldere*, though the main emphasis there seems to have been rather on the relationship between Waldere and Hagena.

These Gothic and Burgundian heroes were known to the Anglo-Saxons only because of their common Germanic stock. But, as we should expect, they knew too of heroes belonging to their own peoples. One of the most popular of these seems to have been that Offa who ruled over the Angles during the fourth century, whilst

---

[1] *MLR.* xiv, 1ff.   [2] Ed. E. Björkman (Heidelberg 1915), lines 2867–8.
[3] *MLR.* xv, 77, but see also M. D. Legge, *Anglo-Norman Literature and its Background* (Oxford 1963), p. 155.

they were still on the continent.[1] The Old English sources show at least two different stories connected with him. In *Widsith* there is a mention of his famous duel at the river Fifeldor (Eider), a story told at length by Saxo Grammaticus. But the centuries intervening between the two accounts prevent us from assuming that the tale, as known in England, agreed in detail with that which was current in twelfth-century Denmark. In the Old English poem there is only a bare allusion to what was evidently a well-known story:

> Offa ruled Angel, Alewih the Danes: he was boldest of all these men, yet he did not surpass Offa in deeds of valour. But Offa gained, first of men, by arms the greatest of kingdoms whilst yet a youth; no one of his age did greater deeds of valour in battle with his single sword; he drew the boundary against the Myrgings at Fifeldor. Engle and Swæfe held it afterwards as Offa struck it out (35–44).

No direct reference to this story appears elsewhere in Old English, but in *Beowulf* (1931–60) there is a general notice of the bravery of Offa and a bitter attack on the wickedness of his queen Thryth. Yet, despite the lack of references, the story must have lived on, since in the twelfth century a monk of St Albans, in order to glorify the monastery and its reputed founder Offa of Mercia, wrote down the legends concerning the two Offas which were current at the time. In his *Vitae duorum Offarum*[2] the monk tells how Warmundus, the king of the West Angles from whom Warwick takes its name, had an only son, Offa, of great stature and enormous strength, but blind until his seventh and dumb until his thirtieth year. The Mercian nobles, led by Riganus, conspire against Offa and demand the kingdom. Warmundus is too old to lead his army to battle, but in the crisis Offa prays for the gift of speech and, this being granted, volunteers to lead the king's army against the rebels. The two armies meet on the banks of a deep river across which Offa dashes, slays the two sons of Riganus, and leads his army to complete victory. When he returns home his father resigns the throne to him and soon afterwards dies. One day, while hunting, Offa meets a maiden who claims to be the daughter of the king of York and to have fled from the unnatural lust of her father.

---

[1] On the Offa story, see *Modern Philology* ii, 29–76, 321–76.
[2] Ed. W. Wats (London 1640).

Offa marries her and has twin children. Some years later he goes to help the king of Northumbria against the Scots and is victorious. He sends a letter to his nobles telling of his victory, but this is intercepted by the king of York who substitutes a forged letter in which Offa writes that he has met with disaster due to divine wrath at his marriage. Therefore he orders his wife and children to be exposed in the forest and there killed or maimed. Accordingly mother and children are taken away; the children are slain but restored to life by the prayers of an anchorite who hides all three in his cell. On the return of Offa the treachery of the king of York is discovered and punished, but only after a long and weary search are Offa's wife and children restored to him.

Although the locality has been changed it is evident that the story of the duel is still vaguely remembered. This appears to be the reason for an otherwise unexplained hesitation on the part of Offa's army to follow him when he dashes across the river to attack the rebels. Similarly, a reminiscence of the fact that, according to Saxo, the original duel was fought against two opponents, is possibly to be seen in the slaying by Offa of the two sons of the rebel leader. But the stories of his wicked wife, known to the *Beowulf* poet, have either been forgotten or transferred to the wife of the later Offa; instead a common folk-lore theme has been attracted into the legend. On the whole it would seem that ancient tales, antedating the coming of the Angles to this country, have been reinforced and modified by the historic career of Offa of Mercia, though there is nothing to show that these ever had more than an oral existence.

One of the most widely known of the historical references which bulk so largely in the background of *Beowulf* appears to have been the story of Ingeld. Allusions to it are all that remain in Old English, but its probable outline can be gathered from a comparison of the various sources. It seems that the Danish king Healfdene had been slain by the Heathobard Froda. The sons of Healfdene, Hrothgar and Halga, evade the pursuit of Froda and eventually, in revenge for their father's death, burn the hall over the head of his slayer, though hints in *Beowulf* suggest that English tradition may have represented the vengeance as achieved in a pitched battle. Some time later Hrothgar, fearing the vengeance of the Heathobards, attempts to settle the feud by marrying his daughter

Freawaru to Ingeld, the son of Froda. This is the state of affairs reported to Hygelac by Beowulf on his return home. But he considers that the peace obtained in this way will not last. In the retinue of Freawaru will be some Dane who will wear the trophies which his father had won from the Heathobards. Then some survivor of the fight in which Froda fell will urge on his younger comrades to vengeance, and the old feud will break out again. In fact we learn from *Widsith* (45–9) that a later attack by the Heathobards was only repulsed by the combined strength of Hrothgar and Hrothwulf.

Such a theme, the tragic figure of Ingeld hesitating between love of his wife and desire for vengeance, would have an obvious attraction for the heroic poets. In later Scandinavian sources the Heathobards have been forgotten, and Froda and Ingeld are represented as Danish kings. The result is that some authorities regard the struggle as a fight between two branches of the Danish royal house; others retain more of the original story in that the quarrel is still thought of as being between two peoples, but since Ingeld has come to be regarded as a Dane, a different conclusion is given to the story and he is successful in his revenge.

The original version was evidently the one known in England, at any rate during the early period, but the references are so vague that the details are now beyond recovery. Ingeld, however, was apparently so well known that in the eighth century Alcuin could refer to him as a typical character of pagan heroic legend. Writing to the monks of Lindisfarne he reproves them for their continued fondness for the old stories:

> Let the word of God be read in the refectory; there the lector should be heard not the harper, the sermons of the fathers not the songs of the heathen; for what has Ingeld to do with Christ?[1]

The two Germanic heroes who remained longest in popular memory were undoubtedly Weland and Wada. The first of these long remained famous as one of the greatest of smiths, and although only allusions to his fame survive from England, his story is known from the Old Norse *Vǫlundarkviða* and *Điðriks saga*. The first tells how Weland and his two brothers, Egill and Slagfith, married three swan maidens. After seven years Weland's wife leaves him,

[1] P. Jaffé, *Monumenta Alcuiniana* (Berlin 1873), p. 357.

whereupon he forges seven hundred gold rings, one of which is stolen by the men of King Nithhad and given to the king's daughter Beaduhild. Weland himself is then captured, taken to the king's palace, hamstrung, and compelled to work in the smithy. After some time he succeeds in enticing there Nithhad's two sons, kills them, and makes bowls out of their skulls, gems out of their eyeballs, and brooches out of their teeth, presenting these to the royal family as products of his smithy. Beaduhild then breaks her ring and brings it to Weland to repair. He violates her, regains the ring, and with its aid is able to fly away, on his way alighting on the wall of the palace where he proclaims his vengeance. The account in *Điðriks saga*, except for the details of the vengeance, is very different. Weland enters the king's service freely, there is no mention of the swan maidens, and much of the story is taken up with a feud between Weland and the king's smith, and with the forging of the sword Miming. On one occasion, when the king goes out to battle, he leaves behind his stone of victory, and promises half his kingdom and the hand of his daughter to anyone who shall bring him that stone before morning. In the accomplishment of this deed Weland slays the royal chamberlain, and the king, making this an excuse for withholding the reward, drives him away. Weland, intent on vengeance, reappears at court in the disguise of a cook and attempts to poison the king and his daughter. He is detected, lamed, and made to work as a smith. The vengeance is accomplished in much the same way as before, and Weland then makes for himself a garment of feathers and flies away, leaving behind armour and weapons for the son, Widia, to be born to the princess.

The fullest account of the story in Old English occurs in *Deor* (1–12), from which it is clear that Weland's imprisonment and subsequent vengeance were well known, though no indication is given of how he became Nithhad's prisoner. But the earliest reference is probably to be found on the Franks Casket which, according to some scholars, was probably made in Northumbria towards the end of the seventh century, though others would assign it to an English artist in the service of the Frankish king Theudebert (d. 548). On the front of the casket is the representation of a smith at work, two headless bodies lie at his feet, and he holds in his hand a cup made from a skull. Two female figures face

him, and beyond them is a man strangling birds. In all probability
this scene portrays Weland's vengeance; the king's sons have
already been killed, Beaduhild and her maid approach, and Egill
kills the birds from the feathers of which Weland is to fashion his
feather garment. On the top of the casket a man, with the help of
his wife, defends himself and his home by archery against the
attack of assailants armed with shields, swords, and spears. Over
the head of the defender is the name Aegili in runic letters. It is
tempting to connect this scene with the Weland scene on the front
of the casket, and to identify Aegili with Weland's brother Egill.
However, none of the extant versions of the story contains anything that could have served as a model for this picture, so that,
if connected with the Weland legend, it must represent a part of it
which has since been lost.

A mere allusion to Weland's fame as a smith is all that appears
in *Beowulf* (452–5). More interesting are the two references in
Waldere: in the first (i, 2–5) mention is made of the sword Miming,
'the work of Weland', while the second (ii, 4ff.) has the reference
to Theodoric and Widia already discussed, in which the latter is
said to be 'the kinsman of Nithhad, the son of Weland'. These
show that the forging of Miming, and Widia's relationship to
Weland – a detail perhaps hinted at in *Deor* – were known to the
Anglo-Saxons. But whether the feud with Nithhad's smith, of
which in *Điðriks saga* the forging of Miming forms part, was also
known, or whether it was a later development, is a question we
are unable to answer. The only other reference in Old English
shows that Weland's fame as a smith was well known to King
Alfred. In his translation of Boethius *De consolatione philosophiae*,
when he comes to the Latin *Ubi nunc fidelis ossa Fabricii manent*, he
perhaps misinterprets the name of the Roman hero and translates,
'Where are now the bones of Weland, or who knows where they
be?'[1]

Although no complete version of the story of Weland has survived, it was obviously familiar to the Anglo-Saxons. So far as we
can tell from the scanty evidence available, the version known to
them agreed in detail with neither of the Scandinavian ones, but
shared characteristics peculiar to each. The death of the two sons
before the violation of the daughter, and the appearance of Egill,

---

[1] W. J. Sedgefield, *op. cit.*, p. 46; cf. p. 165.

are details shared with *Vǫlundarkviða*; the use of the feather garment, the reference to the sword Miming, and the birth of Widia,
appear only in the Old English and in *Điðriks saga*.

References to Weland in Middle English show that his fame
long survived the Conquest. In Geoffrey of Monmouth's *Vita
Merlini* there is an allusion to the *Pocula que sculpsit Guielandus in
urbe Sigeni*.[1] The hero of *Horn Childe* receives from Rimenhild a
sword made by Weland and the equal of Miming,[2] and similarly
in the fifteenth-century *Torrent of Portyngale*, the king of Pervense
gives to Torrent a sword made by Weland.[3] His fame lasted long in
country districts, especially in Berkshire, as is shown from the
occasional references to the story by local antiquaries, and from its
use in Scott's *Kenilworth*. Nevertheless the Middle English allusions show little knowledge of the actual story of Weland. In all
probability it had already been forgotten by the time of the Conquest, his name and a vague memory of his skill as a smith being
all that had survived.

On the other hand, stories of Wade were certainly known after
the Conquest; in fact we learn more about him from Middle
English than from Old English sources. Originally he may have
been some kind of a sea giant, and many of the early references
still connect him closely with the sea. In *Điðriks saga* he is the son
of King Vilkinus and a sea-wife and the father of Weland, though
otherwise the saga has little to say about him. In the Middle High
German *Kudrun* he has become a type of the faithful retainer,
but his old connexion with the sea is still remembered. The only
reference to him in Old English occurs in *Widsith* (22), 'Wada
ruled the Hælsings', and the first story concerning the hero appears
in the *De nugis curialium* of Walter Map, where he has been
brought into the Offa legend. A certain Gado, son of a king of the
Vandals, from love of adventure leaves his home as a boy and
wanders through the world redressing wrongs. At last he comes
to the court of King Offa who has just married the daughter of the
Roman emperor. On their return home the Roman guests urge
an attack on Offa, but the Romans are deterred by fear of his
friend Gado. But when Gado has been called off to the Indies the

---

[1] Ed. J. J. Parry (Illinois U.P. 1925), line 235.
[2] J. Hall, *King Horn* (Oxford 1901), pp. 183–4.
[3] Ed. E. Adam (EETS. ES. 1887), lines 426ff.

Romans send a mighty army and refuse all Offa's terms for peace. In the meantime Gado, having completed his task, is returning home when his ship, much against his will, carries him to Colchester. He greets Offa there, and accompanied by a hundred chosen knights goes to the headquarters of the Romans in an attempt to make peace but is repulsed. Thereupon he arrays the English forces, placing Offa with the main body in the market-place of the town, Offa's nephew Suanus with five hundred men at one gate, and himself with a hundred men at the other. The Romans avoid Gado and concentrate their attacks on Suanus who, at the third assault, appeals for help. Gado refuses, but as Suanus prepares for the next attack, commands him to fall back. The enemy rush in and are met by Offa in the market-place, whilst their retreat is cut off by Gado. A great slaughter of the Romans follows until quarter is offered to the survivors, who return to Rome with their dead.[1] It is probable that little of the original Wade remains in this very much romanticized story, though the boat which brings him to England against his will is obviously the magic boat of which we hear later.

A reference to another of the stories connected with Wade appears in an early thirteenth-century Latin sermon on humility:

> Ita quod dicere possunt cum Wade:
> Summe sende ylues
> and summe sende nadderes:
> summe sende nikeres
> the bi den watere wunien.
> Nister man nenne
> bute Ildebrand onne.[2]

Here Wade and Hildebrand are mentioned together, though whether this is the hero of the German *Hildebrandslied*, of which only a fragment of sixty-nine lines survives, it is impossible to say. It may be significant that the German poem is said to contain some Old English forms. The fourteenth-century *Fasciculus Morum* places Wade, along with Unwine, in 'Elvelond',[3] and in the alliterative *Morte Arthure* a widow warns King Arthur that it is useless for him to attack a giant, were he more valiant than Wade or Gawain.[4] In *Bevis of Hamton* he is classed with the hero in that

[1] Map, pp. 81ff.   [2] M. R. James, *Academy 1241*, Feb. 1896, p. 137.
[3] *MLR.* xiv, 1.   [4] Ed. E. Björkman (Heidelberg 1915), lines 964-5.

both have slain dragons, perhaps a reference to another lost exploit,[1] and his name is found in a list of famous heroes in the *Laud Troy Book*.[2] In *Troilus and Criseyde* (iii, 614) Panardus 'tolde a tale of Wade', and in the *Merchant's Tale* (E 1423-4) there is a reference to Wade's boat. In Caxton's *Malory* (bk. vii, cap. ix) the damsel Lyonet warns Sir Gareth of Orkney that were he 'as wyghte as euer was Wade or Launcelot' he will not be able to go through the 'Pace Perelus'. It may be significant that the introduction of Wade at this point seems to be due to Caxton, since he does not appear in the corresponding passage of the Winchester manuscript of Malory. It is unlikely that Caxton knew anything more about him than the name, and certainly by the time of Leland the old stories of him seem to have been forgotten, so that when he comes across local traditions of Wade he can find nothing to add to them.[3] Yet a clearer memory of Wade's exploits may have persisted in some quarters, for when Speght edited the works of Chaucer, he was able to add details known from no other source:

> Concerning Wade and his bote called Guingelot, as also his strange exploits in the same, because the matter is long and fabulous, I passe it over.[4]

It has been suspected that Speght himself knew very little of the story – which was why he preferred to 'passe it over'. It is not improbable that by this time most of the deeds of Wade had been forgotten, but at any rate Speght knew the name of Wade's boat, a detail to be found nowhere else.

Tales of Wade had flourished in England for almost a thousand years, yet the only one of them known to us in any detail is that given by Map. And this Latin version may have had very little in common with the vernacular stories of the hero which must have been familiar throughout the Middle Ages.

According to *Widsith* (32), 'Sceafa ruled the Lombards', and although no such king is known to historians, the name was apparently familiar enough to the Anglo-Saxons. He appears at the head of the West Saxon genealogy, and the various references give a good idea of what must have been the general outline of the

---

[1] Ed. E. Kölbing (EETS. ES. 1885-94), lines 2604-5.
[2] Ed. J. E. Wülfing (EETS. 1902-3), lines 20-1.
[3] Leland i, 59.   [4] *The Works of Chaucer, 1598, Annotations.*

story. Sceafa, as a child, was carried alone in a small boat to the island of Scandza, and the people of that land found him asleep, surrounded by weapons, with his head upon a sheaf of corn. He was brought up by them, and eventually became the ruler of the ancient land of the Angles. On his death, in obedience to his command, his people placed him in a boat filled with treasures and weapons, and allowed the sea to carry him away.

It would seem that Sceafa must have been a legendary culture hero whom one or other of the tribes by the North Sea regarded as the founder of their royal family. The author of *Widsith* evidently thought of him as a Lombard, but the tenth-century Æthelweard says nothing of his nationality:

> And this Sceaf arrived with one light ship in the island of the ocean which is called Skaney, with arms all round him. He was a very young boy, and unknown to the people of that land, but he was received by them, and they guarded him with diligent attention as one who belonged to them, and elected him king. From his family King Æthelwulf derived his descent.[1]

William of Malmesbury is the first to connect him with the original home of the Angles, and to tell of his arrival with the sheaf of corn, so that stories of the hero were evidently still current in the twelfth century.[2] In this account Sceafa is said to have been the father of a certain Sceld, known from other sources as the eponymous ancestor of the Danish royal family, and in *Beowulf* (4–52) a similar tale is told of Scyld Scefing. It is perhaps possible that the version in *Beowulf* was the original form of the story; that the name was later misunderstood as 'Scyld, the son of Sceafa', instead of 'Scyld with the sheaf', thereby placing a new ancestor at the head of the genealogy, and that the story was then transferred from Scyld to his supposed father Sceafa. On the other hand, the appearance of Sceafa as a king in *Widsith*, and at the head of the West Saxon royal genealogy, would suggest that the author of *Beowulf* has transferred to Scyld a story that rightly belonged to Sceafa. It may be significant that Æthelweard knows nothing of Scyld, and that William of Malmesbury has a mixed tradition which, whilst ascribing the episode to Sceafa, yet speaks of him as the father of Scyld.

[1] A. Campbell, *The Chronicle of Æthelweard* (London 1962), p. 33.
[2] *Gesta Regum* i, 121.

The various references to these heroes, whether Gothic, Burgundian, or Anglo-Saxon, make it clear that their names and deeds
were widely known in England. It is hardly surprising that not a
word has survived of the Old English narratives, whether in prose
or verse, which must have been current. Many of the stories were
probably never written down, and even if they had been the odds
would still have been heavy against their survival. It is remarkable
enough that three examples should have survived the numerous
accidents that threatened their existence. The manuscript of
Beowulf barely survived destruction in the fire of 1731; the *Finn
Fragment* was printed by George Hickes from a single isolated leaf
found in a volume of homilies in the Lambeth Library. It has not
been seen since, so that the printed vers'on by Hickes remains the
only authoritative source, though had the leaf been lost before
publication, we might have suspected the existence of stories on
the subject from the Finn Episode in *Beowulf*. *Waldere* is known
only from two separate fragments discovered in the Royal Library
at Copenhagen in 1860; without them we should know of the story
from continental sources, but have no reason to suppose that it
had been current in Anglo-Saxon England.

There are other references to heroic stories where the evidence
is even less clear than in the examples already dealt with. When
such allusions are numerous we can be certain that the stories were
widely known; when they are few the matter is more doubtful. Lack
of extant references may be due to accident, and the hero in
question may have been quite as famous as any of those previously
mentioned; on the other hand the comparative absence of them
may be due to the fact that the story or hero never was widely
known and was soon forgotten. Judging from the allusion in
Beowulf (874–97), we should expect some version of *Vǫlsunga saga*
to have been widely known in England:

He spoke everything that he had heard tell of Sigemund's mighty
deeds, much that was unknown, the strife of the son of Wæls, his
far journeys, feuds and crimes of which the children of men knew
nothing – except for Fitela with him, to whom he would tell everything, the uncle to his nephew, for they were always in every struggle
bound together by kinship. Many were the tribes of giants that
they had laid low with the sword. There sprang up for Sigemund
after his death no little fame, when he, bold in battle, had killed the

dragon, the guardian of the treasure. Under the gray stone the son of the prince had ventured alone, a daring deed, nor was Fitela with him. Yet it was granted to him that his sword pierced the gleaming dragon, and stood fixed in the wall, the noble weapon. The dragon lay dead from the murderous stroke. Through his courage the great warrior had brought it about that he might at his own wish enjoy the treasure hoard. The son of Wæls loaded the sea-boat, bore into the ship the bright treasure. The hot dragon melted.

The reference could, of course, have been introduced into the poem at a comparatively late date, and the story have been brought over by the Viking invaders. On the other hand if, as seems possible, an illustration of the death of Sigemund is to be found on the Franks Casket, this would indicate an early knowledge of the story in England.

'Hagena (ruled) the Holmryge and Heoden the Glommas' (*Widsith* 21); the two heroes mentioned here formed the subject of one of the most popular of all the Germanic tales, that which told of the everlasting battle between them. An Old Norse version is given by Snorri Sturluson; a different one is found in the Middle High German *Kudrun*; whilst Saxo appears to have harmonized two originally different accounts. We have no means of knowing which of these versions was current in England, though a closer kinship with *Kudrun* than with Snorri is perhaps suggested by the reference in *Deor* (36-41):

> Once I was a minstrel of the Heodeningas, dear to my lord, Deor was my name. For many years I had a good office, a gracious lord, until now Heorrenda, a man skilful in song, has received the land that the protector of warriors formerly gave to me.

The connexion between the Old English Heorrenda and the Middle High German Horant seems certain, whilst the fact that Wada is mentioned in *Widsith* in the line immediately following the reference to Hagena and Heoden may suggest that he played his part in the Old English as in the Middle High German version of the story.

The lord of Widsith is said to have been Eadgils the Myrging, who may perhaps have been one of the characters in the Offa saga. Saxo tells how Athislus, king of Sweden, was slain by Keto and Wigo in revenge for the death of their father, and it was this attack of two against one which led to Offa's duel with two opponents in an attempt to wipe out the stain on the Anglian name. It seems clear, however, that Saxo has confused the nationality of this Athislus. We know of only one Swedish king of the name, Athils son of Óttar in the *Ynglingatal*, the Eadgils son of Ohthere in *Beowulf*, whose dealings with Hrólf Kraki were a favourite subject of Scandinavian story. But the authorities agree that this Athislus died whilst celebrating a religious ceremony, and not in battle. Possibly Saxo's confusion is due to the fact that the Myrgings were also called Swæfe, and in view of the common medieval confusion of Sweden with Swabia, it is easy to see how a king of the Swæfe might come to be reckoned a king of Sweden. How far Eadgils was connected with the Offa saga as known in England it is difficult to say. *Widsith* speaks of Offa's antagonists as the Myrgings, and such a connexion would certainly help to explain Offa's duel with two opponents, traces of which seem to be apparent in the later English legends.

The only other hero mentioned twice in the extant Old English records is the Breca, son of Beanstan, against whom Beowulf has a swimming match. He is also presumably the Breoca, prince of the Brondings, in *Widsith* (25), though the exact form of the legends concerning him must remain unknown. No doubt he was famous as a swimmer, but the story in *Beowulf* is confused, and that hero is more concerned with glorifying himself than with telling of the prowess of his adversary.

Elsewhere in Old English, and especially in *Widsith*, are to be found the names of many heroes. Only exceptionally do we know anything about them, so that we can never be certain that they were more than names even to the Anglo-Saxon audience. But when we hear from continental sources of stories in which they figured, it becomes not improbable that similar ones were known in England. So, amongst the followers of Eormenric was 'Eastgota, wise and good, the father of Unwen' (*Widsith* 113–14) who in actual fact appears to have been Eormenric's great-great-grand-father. Cassiodorus, in a famous passage on the characteristics of the Gothic kings, seems to hint at some of the stories connected with him, *Enituit enim Ostrogotha patientia*. Jordanes, enlarging on this, tells how Ostrogotha bore patiently the demands of his kinsmen the Gepids until, compelled at last to fight, he utterly defeated them.

Apart from Gundahari two Burgundian kings are mentioned, 'Gifica ruled the Burgundians' (*Widsith* 19), and Gislhere appears as one of the retainers of Eormenric. The Burgundian code of laws, drawn up sometime before 516, contains a reference to 'our ancestors of royal memory, Gibica, Gundomar, Gislahari, Gundahari'. There can be no doubt that the Old English Gifica is to be identified with this Gibica, as also with the Gibeche of Old High German, and the Giúki of Scandinavian legend, whilst Gislhere must be the Gislaharius whom later German tradition represented as the chivalrous younger brother of Gunther (Gundahari).

'Theodoric ruled the Franks' (*Widsith* 24), and this Theodoric became a favourite subject of continental story. Historically he was the son of Clovis and the conqueror of the Thuringians. The late ninth-century Poeta Saxo tells of popular songs in his praise,[1] and in the thirteenth century he appears as the hero of the Middle High German romance of Hug-Dietrich and Wolf-Dietrich. If this is the Theodoric of *Deor* 18–19, the mention there of the city of the Mærings may refer to the Visigoths, and be an allusion to the long period of exile attributed to the hero.

One of Saxo's tales tells how Sygarus, king of Denmark, caused Hagbarthus, the lover of his daughter Sygne, to be slain, and of how Sygne shared her lover's fate. This Sygarus apparently appears as a ruler of the *Sæ-Dene* in *Widsith* (28), but although the story seems to have been popular in Scandinavia, there is no other evidence for its currency in England. Similarly, the Hlithe and Incgentheow, who appear in the catalogue of Gothic heroes, may perhaps be identical with the Hloth and Angantýr of the Old Norse poem and of the *Hervarar saga*. On the other hand, there can be no doubt that the story of King Ongentheow of Sweden was well known in this country. He is the ruler of the Swedes in *Widsith*, and *Beowulf* remembers his death at the hands of Wulf and Eofor, and of how the fierce king's threats to give his enemies 'to the gallows-tree for the sport of the ravens' recoiled upon himself.

If we are justified in equating the Ægelmund, Eadwine, and Ælfwine of *Widsith* with Agelmund, Audoin, and Alboin, it would appear that some of the Lombard kings were known in England. Paulus Diaconus has stories, no doubt taken from oral tradition,

---

[1] *Monumenta Germaniae Historica, Scriptores* i, 269.

of each of these. He tells how Agelmund saved from the water a child whose father was unknown, and caused him to be carefully brought up so that he became the greatest of champions. We hear how Alboin slew in single combat the son of the king of the Gepids, and of how his father Audoin refused him the honour of his deed because he had not received his weapons from the king of some other people. Thereupon Alboin with forty companions betook himself to the king of the Gepids. The latter, after a struggle between the laws of hospitality and his desire for vengeance, despatched Alboin home with the arms of his own dead son. Later Alboin annihilated the Gepids in a great battle, invaded Italy, and was killed by his wife, a Gepid princess, in revenge for the slaughter of her people. However, all that we know of these heroes in Old English comes from *Widsith*, where they figure only as followers of Eormenric.

Two further stories must also have been known, but the extant references are so puzzling that we can make little of them. These are the Mæthhild story in *Deor* and the *Wulf and Eadwacer* fragment. Both present serious difficulties of interpretation; in the former the reference is too brief, in the latter too allusive, for us to be able to do more than guess at the original story:

> We learned that, that the laments of Mæthhild became numberless, the moans of Geat's lady, so that distressing love robbed her of sleep (14–16).

The name Mæthhild is not otherwise known in heroic poetry, and although Geat appears in some of the royal genealogies, this gives little help. Attempts have been made to connect the allusion with some of the known heroic legends, but without any great success. The most likely suggestion is that it refers to the story of Gaute and Magnhild, otherwise known only from a Scandinavian ballad, of which Norwegian and Icelandic versions have been recorded. These belong to a group of ballads about a harp with magic powers; the harper is a bridegroom seeking to recover his bride who has been carried down to the depths of the water by a merman. Such a story would, of course, be relevant enough to *Deor*, especially if there were a happy ending, but there can be no certainty that this is the story intended here. *Wulf and Eadwacer* almost certainly deals with a scene from one or other of the heroic legends, and connexion has been suggested with the Theodoric story or with the *Vǫlsunga saga*. It may perhaps refer to one of the known stories, but equally probably it has to do with one of those which has otherwise entirely perished.

Vague references such as these give allusions to stories which must have been known in England at one time or another. Whether they were at all widely current is a point on which no certainty is possible. Nor can we tell at what date the stories began to be forgotten, though it is probable that most of this type had disappeared long before the Conquest. Nevertheless we have here the Old English references, and we know something of the subjects from continental sources. There is a third type, however, in which the Old English reference consists merely of a name, and we know nothing whatever of any stories which may at one time have been connected with that name. It is impossible to say how many of the otherwise unknown heroes in *Widsith* would have evoked memories of the heroic age in the minds of the Anglo-Saxon audience, and how many were just as much mere names to them as they are to us. Some of the names, Helm, Sceafthere, Wald, Wod, Hringweald, look like conventional names for chieftains and may have been the poet's own inventions. Others, such as Cælic, Oswine, Gefwulf, Hethca, Wulfhere, may have been the names of real people, though if so we know nothing about them. Nor can we say how many of the stories preserved by Saxo, or by other continental writers, were known in this country. The fact that no Old English allusions to them have survived is obviously no proof that the tales themselves were unknown.

2

HISTORICAL NARRATIVE

Subjects from Anglo-Saxon history were evidently common in the literature of the period. Little enough on such themes has survived in Old English, and the probability is that most of it was never written down. *The Battle of Maldon*, together with the poems preserved in the *Old English Chronicle*, of which the best known is *The Battle of Brunanburh*, are the only remains in the vernacular of this type of literature, and of these *The Battle of Maldon*, incomplete as it even then was, survived only long enough to be printed by Thomas Hearne before its destruction in the Cottonian fire of 1731. If, as seems likely, some of the romances of the later Matter of England – notably *Havelok* and *King Horn* – are based on historical events of the Anglo-Saxon period, some form of the legends must have then been current, though no pre-Conquest reference to them has yet been discovered. Nevertheless indications in the later Latin writers make it clear that Anglo-Saxon poets and story-tellers must have drawn much material from the historical events of the time.[1] Thus William of Malmesbury obtained his information for the earlier period 'more from old songs, popular through succeeding ages, than from books written for the instruction of posterity',[2] and he is obviously referring to oral legends still current in metrical form in his own day. Similar sources are referred to by Henry of Huntingdon who says, when approaching his own times, 'Thus far I have treated of matters which I have either found recorded by old writers, or have gathered from common report; but now I have to deal with events which have passed under my own observation or which have been told to me by eyewitnesses of them.'[3] Evidently during the twelfth

---

[1] Many of the stories mentioned in this chapter are dealt with in more detail by C. E. Wright in *The Cultivation of Saga in Anglo-Saxon England* (London 1939).

[2] *Gesta Regum* i, 155.   [3] Huntingdon, p. 213.

century legends, both oral and written, based on Anglo-Saxon history were frequent enough, and a reference in the Latin life of St Æthelberht of East Anglia would indicate that some of them were already in existence during the Old English period. On his journey to the court of Offa, the saint is said to have been preceded by youths singing of the deeds of his ancestors. None of these songs has survived and today most of the East Anglian kings are little more than names to us.[1]

Obviously it would be impossible to deal with all the stories based, however remotely, on their own history which were utilized by Anglo-Saxon minstrels. In any case many of them have probably vanished altogether, and references to others are so slight that we cannot be certain that the story in question was at all widely known. For some of them, however, the evidence is stronger. The legend may appear in such differing forms in the different sources that direct borrowing of the one from the other is unlikely; the earliest written reference may occur so long after the events with which it deals that the story must have been current orally for a considerable time; and lastly, on very rare occasions, there may be an allusion to some actual written work.

In exactly what form most of this literature was current is a question which hardly allows of any definite answer. The songs about the East Anglian kings were obviously in verse, and at that date presumably in alliterative verse. The *cantilenae* known to William of Malmesbury must have been in some kind of metrical form, though this, of course, is no proof that the Old English versions were also in verse. As a rule our authorities say little or nothing about the form of the vernacular tales of which they make use. But since at the beginnings of a literature[2] narrative is almost invariably in verse, it has usually been assumed that all such legends were, if oral, in some free ballad metre, and if written, in the alliterative line. This is no more than an assumption, and it has been shown that there is reasonably good evidence for the existence in Anglo-Saxon times of a narrative prose similar to that which was later developed in Scandinavia. Consequently it is no longer possible to be quite so certain as some earlier

---

[1] *EHR.* xxxii, 214ff.

[2] Most of this literature was presumably extant only orally, but there appears to be no good reason for limiting the term to the written versions alone.

scholars were about the form which these stories assumed in the vernacular. Only if the fact is definitely stated can we be sure that they were in verse. When, as is usually the case, nothing definite is said on the subject, they are as likely to have been in prose as in verse, and it is not impossible that versions in both may have existed side by side.

There must have been in existence numerous legends dealing with the Anglo-Saxon invasions of which little more than vague references remain. The most famous of such stories was probably that of Hengest and Horsa of which the outline appears already in Gildas, though obscured by that author's usual vagueness. Bede, two hundred years later, gives as a tradition the names of the characters, adds the pedigree of Hengest and Horsa, records the slaying of Horsa in battle by the Britons, and declares that his monument is still to be seen in the eastern part of Kent. The *Old English Chronicle* adds to Bede some details concerning the battles between the invaders and the Britons, in which occasional phrases suggest derivation from early stories on the subject. In Nennius the story has been further elaborated and interwoven with a mass of legend dealing with the miracles of St Germanus. Here the vivid and straightforward narrative, in which is preserved a corrupt Old English phrase, has led to the suggestion that the author's ultimate source 'is an English saga in which the deeds of Hengest and his followers were preserved for later generations'.[1] This is the only one of the stories connected with the Anglo-Saxon conquest of which any details have survived. That there were others is suggested by the traditional dates for the foundations of the various kingdoms, and by the preservation of the names of the early kings in the royal genealogies, but all details have been lost.

The only other story obviously belonging to this period of which anything is known comes from Procopius. He tells how an Anglian princess from the island of 'Brittia' was jilted by the king of the Varini, how she led a great army from the island to attack him, of his capture, and of the final reconciliation between them. Procopius apparently heard the story from a Frankish embassy at the Byzantine court, which seems to have included Angles from

---

[1] C. E. Wright, *op. cit.*, p. 29. But F. M. Stenton, *Anglo-Saxon England* (Oxford 1943), p. 16, finds indications that the story of Hengest and Horsa had been handed down in alliterative verse.

Britain.[1] Whether there is any historical basis for it we are unable to say. No other reference to the tale is known, and some of the information concerning Britain which Procopius appears to have derived from the same source is, to say the least, decidedly curious.

It is natural enough that legends and stories dealing with the period before the Viking invasions should be comparatively rare. English works are few, and by the time they become more frequent only the more important stories would be remembered. The *Old English Chronicle*, before the eighth century, is in general much too brief to give more than the merest hints of such tales, and apart from this there is only Bede and an occasional saint's life. Many of the stories in Bede are given on the authority of tradition, or from the testimony of an eyewitness. Among these are the descriptions of Gregory's meeting with the Angli in Rome, and of St Augustine's conference with the British bishops, the stories connected with Aidan, and the tale of Cædmon. Since most of these occur only in Bede, we have no means of knowing how widely spread they may have been, or whether they had in fact become part of the oral literature of the Anglo-Saxons. In only two cases are Bede's stories found also in another early source; the meeting of Gregory with the Angli, and the vision of Edwin at the court of Rædwald of East Anglia, appear in somewhat different forms in the *Vita antiquissima S. Gregorii* of the Monk of Whitby.[2] Yet, in the comparative absence of contemporary works produced in England, this lack of confirmation is not surprising, and it is likely enough that some of Bede's stories were widely known.

Vague hints of another which may go back to this very early date are to be found in the *Gesta Herewardi*. Among a list of the principal followers of Hereward occurs a certain 'Godwin Gille, who was called Godwin because he was not unequal to that Godwine, the son of Guthlac, formerly celebrated in the songs of the ancients'.[3] The only hero of that name now known to us is the great earl, and he was probably the son of Wulfnoth – at any rate there is no other authority for making him the son of Guthlac. It is perhaps possible that Godwine's true descent has been forgotten,

[1] H. B. Dewing, *Procopius: History of the Wars* (London 1914–28) v, 255ff.
[2] B. Colgrave, *The Earliest Life of Gregory the Great* (Kansas U.P. 1968), pp. 90, 98ff.   [3] Gaimar i, 372.

and that he has been provided with a new ancestor. Even so it is unlikely that the author of the *Gesta Herewardi* would speak of one who was contemporary with the father of his hero as having been 'celebrated in the songs of the ancients'. In all probability the reference is to be taken along with the account of the parentage of St Guthlac as given by Ordericus Vitalis. The saint is said to have been the son of Penvaldus and Tetta, and 'after eight days the child was baptized and named Guthlac, that is *belli munus*, from the tribe whom they call the Guthlacingas'.[1] We know nothing more about this tribe. It may have been one that took a prominent part in the invasion, or in the early history of the Anglo-Saxons, and like the Old Norse Vǫlsungar have had a saga dealing with it. If so, the saga has been entirely lost and these two references are all that remain.

Some evidence for the one-time existence of an Old English poem on the famous battles of the period may perhaps be provided by the twelfth-century chronicle of Henry of Huntingdon. For many of the more important battles the chronicler has an appropriate quotation introduced by some such phrase as *unde dicitur*, and many of them, when turned into Old English, seem to fall naturally into alliterative verse. The first refers to the battle in 617 in which Rædwald of East Anglia defeated and killed Æthelfrith of Northumbria. It is said to have been fought on the eastern bank of the river Idle, *unde dicitur; 'Amnis Idle Anglorum sanguine sorduit'*.[2] The elaborate account of the battle which follows was certainly not taken from the *Old English Chronicle*, but just as surely appears to have either a written or an oral source of some kind. The next battle is that of Heathfield (633) in which Edwin of Northumbria was slain by Penda of Mercia and Cadwallon of Gwynedd, *dicitur autem quod Hadfeld rubens undique nobilium fumabat cruore*. A year later Edwin's successor Oswald defeated and killed Cadwallon near Hexham – *unde dicitur: 'Cædes Cedwalensium Denisi cursus coercuit'* – and succeeded to a part of Edwin's power. But he never made an end of Penda who, in 642, descended on him and slew him at the battle of Maserfeld, *unde dicitur, 'Campus Masefeld sanctorum canduit ossibus'*. In 655 Penda

---

[1] Ordericus ii, 269.
[2] A similar phrase is in Wendover i, 116, but it may have been borrowed from the earlier writer.

himself was defeated and slain by Oswy of Northumbria, and the importance of the event is marked by an elaborate description of the battle, as well as by the exceptional length of the quotation referring to it:

> unde dicitur:—In Winwed amne vindicata est cædes Annæ,
> Cædes regum Sigbert et Ecgrice,
> Cædes regum Oswald et Edwine.

After this there is a long interval until the battle of Ellendune (825) by which Ecgberht of Wessex finally cast off the supremacy of Mercia. It was evidently fiercely contested, *unde dicitur*: '*Ellendune rivus cruore rubuit, ruina restitit, fætore tabuit*'.[1] The chronicler nowhere says definitely that he is quoting from a vernacular poem on the subject, though it seems not unlikely. He was himself interested in Old English poetry; he gives a Latin paraphrase of *The Battle of Brunanburh* and knows of the Old English poem on *The Site of Durham*. So far as we can tell, he seems to have been a conscientious if somewhat credulous historian, and it is difficult to believe that he is inventing the quotations merely to give a more authentic air to his history. It is perhaps possible that his original source was in Latin, though if so it would be difficult to account for the ease with which the quotations can be turned into passable Old English alliterative verse. If in fact the chronicler is quoting from Old English, there is nothing to tell us whether he is using a single poem, or whether there were in existence different poems on the various battles. On the whole it seems unlikely that he knew much more about the battles than the quotations he gives; had his originals gone into any detail he would probably have given a florid description of each battle, such as is found only for those of the Idle and Winwedfield. Altogether, the evidence would suggest that, during the twelfth century, there was still in existence an Old English poem on the famous battles of the early period – perhaps a mnemonic poem something after the style of *Widsith*. Some slight confirmation of such a theory is possibly to be found in the chronicle of Peter of Langtoft where reference is made to a still remembered saying on the battle of Ellendune.[2] Peter's translator, Robert Mannyng of Brunne, improves on this

---

[1] Huntingdon, pp. 56, 90, 91, 95, 60, 132.
[2] Langtoft i, 296.

by declaring that in his own time the battle was still celebrated in song by the country people:

> Under Elendoune þe bataile was smyten.
> Men syng in þat cuntre (fele ʒit it witen)
> 'Elendoune, Elendoune, þi lond is fulle rede
> Of þe blode of Bernewolf, þer he toke his dede.'[1]

It is impossible to tell whether Robert Mannyng is here simply adapting his original, or whether he actually did know of songs on the subject. Occasionally he certainly adds further information to his source, more especially from popular songs, but it is difficult to believe that a not particularly important battle, fought in the south of Mercia, should still have been remembered five hundred years later in Lincolnshire and Yorkshire. Most probably Peter of Langtoft is drawing on Henry of Huntingdon, and Robert Mannyng simply paraphrases.

The only one of the Old English stories of which a fairly full account has survived in the vernacular is that of Cynewulf and Cyneheard, as it appears in the *Old English Chronicle* under the year 755. There can be no doubt that the compiler is making use of a story current at the time when he was writing, more than a hundred years after the events being described. This is indicated by the vivid and circumstantial description of the action, with the stress on the ideals of the heroic age, and by the occasional lapse into direct speech:

> And thirty-one years after Cynewulf ascended the throne he wished to drive out a certain prince called Cyneheard; and this Cyneheard was the brother of Sigebriht [the previous king]. And then Cyneheard heard that the king with a small troop was visiting a woman at 'Merantun'. Thereupon he rode there and surrounded the place before the men who were with the king discovered him. When the king perceived this, he went to the door and defended himself boldly until he saw the prince; then he rushed out against him and wounded him severely. They all continued fighting against the king until they had slain him. Then the king's bodyguard discovered the tumult because of the woman's cries, and they ran there as soon as they were ready and as quickly as possible. Then the prince offered to each of them money and life, and none of them would accept it; but

---

[1] Hearne i, 14.

they continued fighting until they were all slain, except for a British hostage and he was badly wounded.

In the morning the king's retainers who had been left behind heard that the king was dead, and they rode there – his aldorman Osric, Wiferth his thane, and the men whom he had left behind. They came upon the prince in that place in which the king lay dead; but the gates were closed against them when they went there. Then Cyneheard offered them treasure and land at their own choice if they would grant him the kingdom, and his men said that amongst them were some of the kindred of the besiegers who would not desert them. But the attackers replied that no kinsman was dearer to them than their lord and they would never follow his slayer; but they offered to allow their kinsman to depart from there unharmed. These last said that the same offer had been made to the companions of the attackers who had been with the king. Then they said that they did not care for it 'any more than your companions who were slain with the king'. And they fought about the gates until they broke in and slew the prince and all the men who were with him except one, he was the godson of the aldorman and so his godfather saved his life, but he was nevertheless severely wounded.

According to a later entry in the *Old English Chronicle* eighty-four in all were killed in the two fights. Everyone who has dealt with this story sees in it one of the oral narratives of the Anglo-Saxons, but without agreeing as to the form in which it was known to the chronicler. Some take it for granted that he is reproducing in prose an Old English poem, though if this were the case we should have expected to find in it some trace of the original metrical form, and more probably it rather provides evidence for the former existence of an Old English prose narrative. The story appears also in later chroniclers, and the occasional inclusion of details not in the *Old English Chronicle* suggests that it may have survived long in oral tradition. Thus Florence of Worcester knows that the sole survivor of the prince's party, whom the Old English calls the godson of the aldorman, was also the son of Cyneheard.[1]

The great Mercian king Offa, and his wicked queen Cynethryth, seems to have been a fruitful source of stories in Anglo-Saxon times, and some of these were still current in the later Middle Ages. In the thirteenth century John of Wallingford refers to the popular

[1] Florence of Worcester i, 61. But this may be due to a misunderstanding of the Old English.

tales concerning Offa which he had taken down from oral narratives. They were apparently of a fictitious, or at any rate of a marvellous character, and the author intends to sift and as far as possible verify them, with a view to embodying the results in a larger work.[1] At an earlier date than this, towards the end of the twelfth century, some of the stories attached to Offa and his queen were written down by a monk of St Albans in his *Vitae duorum Offarum*. In this a common folk tale has been attached to the queen. She is said to have been related to Charlemagne, and because of her wicked deeds was set adrift in a ship without sails or oars, eventually being driven ashore on the coast of Offa's kingdom. She gives her name as Drida and the king, deceived by her story of why she had been cast adrift, marries her, so that henceforward she is known as Cwendrida. However, she continues with her wicked deeds which eventually culminate in the murder of St Æthelberht (see p. 98). The name of Offa's queen was in fact Cynethryth, and since coins were struck in her name she must have been of some consequence. The only contemporary mention of her appears in various letters, written between 786 and 796 by Alcuin to her son Ecgfrith and others. In these he several times alludes to the queen and sends her messages of affection and respect, particularly advising Ecgfrith to imitate her in charity and piety, all of which would indicate that she was known for her good qualities rather than the reverse. There may have been some confusion in later legend with Cwenthryth, the wicked sister of St Kenelm, or Offa's queen may have suffered for the sins of her daughter Eadburh. At the same time there is an obvious connexion between this story and the reference in *Beowulf* (1931–44) to Thryth, the wife of Offa of Angel:

> Modthryth, high queen of the people, did dreadful deeds; no brave man amongst her retainers – except her great lord – dared look openly upon her with his eyes, but he might count on deadly bonds being prepared for him, arresting hands. Soon after his seizure the sword awaited him, that the patterned blade must settle it, proclaim the punishment of death. That is no queenly custom for a woman to practise, though she is peerless, that one who weaves peace should take away the life of a retainer after pretended injury. However the kinsman of Hemming put an end to this.

[1] *Modern Philology* ii, 31–2.

Both tales evidently go back to the same source, and this presumably referred originally to the wife of Offa of Angel. In the *Vitae duorum Offarum* Offa I marries a wife of the patient, innocently suffering type, and the original characteristics of his queen have been transferred to Cynethryth, the wife of Offa II. Possibly her connexion, whether historical or not, with the death of St Æthelberht led to the conception of her as a monster of wickedness, and the identity of the second element of the names led the writer to attribute to the wife of Offa II a story originally belonging to the wife of Offa I.

Some of the odium attached to Cynethryth may perhaps have been due to the character of her daughter Eadburh. The latter was married to Beorhtric of Wessex, and stories concerning her seem to have been in circulation in that kingdom during the ninth century. She is said by Asser to have begun 'to live as a despot in the manner of her father' – perhaps an indication of the West Saxon attitude to Offa. It was 'common knowledge' that she persecuted the favourites of Beorhtric, and eventually, in trying to poison a youth whom he favoured, she poisoned the king too. The further adventures of Eadburh in France, whither she fled on the death of Beorhtric, are then described. There she came before Charlemagne, and on being offered the choice of marrying either the emperor or his son, she chose the latter on the score of his youth. In consequence she got neither, but nevertheless Charlemagne

> gave her a great convent of nuns, wherein, having laid aside the secular dress and taken upon her the habit of a nun, she enjoyed, but only for a short time, the office of abbess. For as she had lived unrestrainedly in her own land (according to tradition), so much the more unrestrainedly was it discovered that she was living among a foreign people, for, having been debauched by a certain man of her own race, she was, at length, openly exposed, and driven from the convent by order of King Charles, and in poverty and misery she lived shamefully until her death. So, accompanied by one slave boy and begging day by day, at last she ended her life wretchedly in Pavia, as we have heard from many who saw her.[1]

Since Eadburh was married in 789 and Asser wrote in 893, it is only just possible to accept the statement that he drew his

[1] Asser, pp. 12–14; Wright, p. 95.

information 'from many who saw her'. But, whether this were the case or not, there must have been extant in ninth-century Wessex a number of stories dealing with the misdeeds of Eadburh.

After the Viking invasions various legends arose which attempted to explain the raids as acts of private vengeance. The most detailed of these stories is that of Beorn Butsecarl and King Osberht of Northumbria. Gaimar tells how Beorn's wife was raped by the king who, after hunting in the Ouse valley, had called at her house for a meal, at a time when Beorn was away guarding the coast from the pirates. The lady falls ill, and her husband on his return asks the reason for her sickness. She tells him everything and asks him to kill her, but is comforted by Beorn who promises vengeance. In the morning he goes to York, defies the king, and leaves, along with many of the lords who support him. They abandon Osberht, make a knight called Ælla their king, and resolve to call in the Vikings. The Vikings duly come and Osberht is defeated and slain by them. In the meantime Ælla is out hunting, and is dining in the forest when a blind man appears and asks for food. The king boasts of his successful hunting, whereupon the blind man interrupts, tells of the capture of York by the Vikings, and of the death of Osberht. As a sign that he is speaking the truth he prophesies that Ælla's nephew Orrum will be the first to fall in the coming battle in which the king himself will be slain. Ælla places his nephew in a high tower for safety and sets out for York, on the way meeting with men fleeing from the previous battle. Orrum, using two shields as wings, manages to fly from his prison, seizes a horse and three javelins, and follows the English army. On overtaking it he gallops to the front and advances first against the Vikings. Two of them he transfixes with his javelins, but an archer then lets fly an arrow which pierces his heart. Mad with grief, Ælla rushes into the midst of the enemy, is killed, and his army defeated.[1] In this story the names of the kings seem to be historical enough, but history knows nothing of the circumstantial story told by Gaimar. Similar accounts, though in a shortened form, are to be found in the fourteenth-century *Eulogium Historiarum* of Thomas of Malmesbury, and in the fifteenth-century chronicle of John Bromton. In these, however, the names of the Viking leaders are given as Hinguar and Ubba, thus connecting the story with another of the

[1] Gaimar i, 104ff.

34

legends of the Viking invasions, one which attributed them to the sons of Ragnar Lothbrog. It has been suggested that Gaimar may have had a written source for the Beorn story.[1] but it seems more probable that the chronicler is drawing on oral tradition, a tradition which, in view of the variations from Gaimar found in the later writers, must have been extraordinarily long-lived. The thirteenth-century *Narratio de Uxore Aernulfi* tells essentially the same story, except that here Osberht's place is taken by Ælla, and the name of the injured husband is given as Ærnulf.

Other legends connected the invasions with the death of the famous hero, Ragnar Lothbrog who, according to Saxo, was captured by Ælla whilst ravaging in Northumbria and cast into a pit of serpents, his sons afterwards harrying England in revenge for the death of their father. However, if this version was known in England no reference to it has survived. Instead we have an entirely different story, found in its most elaborate form in Roger of Wendover, and connecting the death of Ragnar with the martyrdom of St Edmund. Lothbroc, a Danish king, is swept out to sea whilst hunting sea-fowl. After many days he is cast ashore on the coast of Norfolk and taken to King Edmund. He is received with honour, becomes a favourite of the king, and because of this arouses the jealousy of the chief huntsman Beorn. One day, whilst hunting, Beorn secretly slays Ragnar and hides the body, but the king and the court are led to it by a dog which Lothbroc had befriended. Beorn is convicted of the murder and sentenced to be cast adrift in the same boat as that in which Lothbroc had come to England. The boat comes ashore in Denmark, is recognized, and Beorn is carried before the sons of Lothbroc who demand news of their father. After various tortures Beorn confesses that their father had been cast ashore in England, but asserts that he had been put to death by King Edmund. The sons vow vengeance, compel Beorn to act as guide, set out with a great army for England, and eventually succeed in killing Edmund.[2] Much of the story consists of quite conventional folk-lore themes, and its elaboration suggests a long period of development. No doubt there is some relationship between the version in Wendover and the story as it appears in Scandinavian sources. Edmund was known to have been killed by the sons of Lothbrog; this suggested the connexion

---

[1] *MLR.* xxvii, 168–74.   [2] Wendover i, 303ff.

of Edmund with the death of Ragnar, and so he replaced the almost unknown Ælla in popular legend.

English records make no mention of Ragnar's ravages in England, which are so prominent in Scandinavian sources. In this respect he is completely overshadowed by two historical characters, Hinguar and Hubba, who are said to have been his sons, and round whom numerous stories gathered. According to Saxo, Ragnar had four wives and by them eleven sons and two daughters. Most of these are absent from the English traditions which know only of Healfdene (not found in the Scandinavian versions), Iwer/Hinguar (Saxo's Ivarr the Boneless), Hubba/Ubba (the Ubbo of Saxo), and Bærin (corresponding with the Scandinavian Bjorn). The most important of these were Hinguar and Hubba, and the best known of the legends connected them with the martyrdom of St Edmund, but occasional hints of other stories can also be detected. Geoffrey of Wells, in his *De Infantia S. Eadmundi* (1148–56), gives another reason than vengeance for their father's death for the invasion of England:

> On a certain day therefore, when the sons were aiding their treacherous father in mischief and their own wickedness and pride were being triumphantly talked of, their father swelling with poisonous thoughts and raging with disdainful elation said, 'You are puffed up for nothing and cast forth your words to the winds. For what have you achieved worthy of remembrance in the hazards of battle? Forsooth a young man Edmund not many years ago embarked from Saxony, landed on the English shores with a few followers and disposes of the East Anglian realm at will. What have you ever accomplished to compare with that? What kind of offspring have I begotten in you?' They, incensed alike by envy as by their father's reproof, entered upon a joint design against Edmund, making crafty plans. After they had considered for a long time by what scheme they could attack him and had gathered together a great army of partisans for this purpose, they all with one assent determined that with their collected forces they should on a sudden attack his kingdom and destroy the people and the king by treachery and guile.

The same story appears also in the Anglo-French life of St Edmund by Denis Pyramus (c. 1170).[1]

Another tale connected with the sons of Lothbrog concerns the

[1] *Memorials of St Edmund's Abbey* (RS. 96) i, 103; ii, 190ff. Wright, p. 137·

Raven Banner. The B, C, D, and E manuscripts of the *Old English Chronicle* tell of an attack on Devonshire in 878 by 'the brother of Iwer and Healfdene' – presumably Hubba – in which he was slain, 'and there was the banner captured which is called "The Raven" '. Further information is given by the *Annals of St Neots* which tell how the banner had been woven in a single day by the three daughters of Ragnar:

> For it is said that the three sisters of Hynguar and Hubba, the daughters that is to say of Lodebroch, wove that banner, and made ready the whole of it in one noon-tide. People say also that in every battle in which this standard precedes [the warriors], if victory is to be theirs then there appears in the middle of the banner what seems to be a living raven flying; but if they are to be defeated, then it hangs down quite lifeless. And this fact has often been proved.[1]

The A text of the *Old English Chronicle*, which is almost contemporary, has no mention of the banner; the B text comes from the tenth century, the other manuscripts belong to the eleventh, and the *Annals of St Neots* apparently date from the twelfth. In any case the reference to the Raven Banner must go back to the common original of B, C, D, E, and this would indicate a date not later than the middle of the tenth century for the origin of the story. A similar banner possessed by Cnut is described in the eleventh-century *Encomium Emmae*,[2] but the circumstantial account of the weaving of the banner in the *Annals of St Neots* would indicate that it originally belonged to the sons of Lothbrog and was later appropriated by the biographer of Cnut. The banner appears again in the saga of Siward of Northumbria, though there is little beyond the name to connect it with the banner of the sons of Lothbrog. A dragon is ravaging Northumbria and is being sought by Siward. In the course of his search he asks for information from an old man whom he finds sitting on a hillock. The man warns him that his search will be in vain, and prophesies that he will return to his ship, voyage to London, take service with the king, and later receive land from him. Siward expresses doubts about the prophecy, and says that these doubts will be felt also by his companions. Thereupon the old man draws from his bosom a

---

[1] Asser, p. 138; Wright, p. 126.
[2] Ed. A. Campbell (CS. 1949), p. 24.

37

banner which he calls 'Ravenlandeye', and gives it to Siward so that his companions will the more readily believe him. Siward eventually becomes earl of Northumbria, and after various adventures gives the banner to the citizens of York who place it in the ancient church of St Mary.[1] In this story the banner has probably been confused with the 'Landeyða', the banner of Harald Hardrada, though with the ON. *eyða* of the second element replaced by OE. *ege*.

On fo. 1r of MS. 82 in the library of Pembroke College, Cambridge, are preserved, in a twelfth-century hand, two alliterative verses on the sons of Lothbrog:

> Ynguar and Ubbe. Beorn wæs þe þridde.
> loþebrokes sunes. loþe weren criste.

These are followed by a note in Latin telling how Hubba was slain at 'Vbbelaue' in Yorkshire, whilst Beorn, after having destroyed the church at 'Scapeia' and violated the nuns there, was engulfed by the earth as he was riding in full armour and with lance erect at 'Frendesbiri' near Rochester.[2] Probably the two lines are no more than mnemonic verses, and almost certainly the writer of them knew nothing more, but it is possible that they may at one time have formed part of a longer poem on the sons of Lothbrog of which the remainder has been lost. Certainly the Latin note would suggest that the deaths of these famous Vikings had given rise to still more tales. Historically nothing is known of the fate of Beorn; Hubba is said to have been killed in the attack on Devonshire in 878 in which the Raven Banner was captured; Hinguar died in Ireland in 872, and Healfdene was killed in battle there in 877. But such endings were too tame for popular legend, as is shown by the note in the Pembroke College MS., and the possibility that such stories may have been widespread is suggested by the existence of a slightly different version in the *Liber de Hyda*:

> Hynguar was drowned whilst crossing a ford in Berkshire, and the ford, even to the present day, is called 'Hyngarford' by the country-people, from his name. Hubba, indeed, whilst he was riding, the earth suddenly opened and swallowed him.[3]

[1] J. A. Giles, *Vita Quorundum Anglo-Saxonum* (London 1854), pp. 5–9.
[2] Ker, p. 124; M. R. James, *A Descriptive Catalogue of Manuscripts in the Library of Pembroke College, Cambridge* (Cambridge 1905), p. 71.
[3] *Liber Monasterii de Hyda* (RS. 45), p. 10.

Legends of the Viking invasions seem, at a later date, to have been confused with earlier stories of the Anglo-Saxon conquest. In the chronicle of Robert Mannyng of Brunne are references to stories about the founders, real or imaginary, of Scarborough and Flamborough. Scarthe and Flayn are represented as having been the followers of a certain Engle, from whom the country afterwards received its name:

> When Engle hadde þe lond al þorow,
> He gaf to Scardyng Scardeburghe;
> Toward þe northe, by þe see side,
> An hauene hit is, schipes in to ryde.
> Flayn highte his broþer, als seyþ þe tale
> Þat Thomas made of Kendale;
> Of Scarthe & Flayn, Thomas seys,
> What þey were, how þey dide, what weys.
> Mayster Edmond seis, as me mones,
> Þat þe Engle hadde nynetene sones.
> Þyse nynetene, after þe fader deuis,
> Departed þe lond in nynetene partis.
> Of þo parties fond y non wryten,
> But o partie þat y can wyten;
> Þe nynetenþe partie was þat þynge
> Þat langed to seint Edmond þe kynge:
> Þis ys þat oþer skyle y fond
> Why hit was called Engelond,
> Als Maister Edmond þer-of seys,
> & as he seys, y seye þat weys.[1]

From this it would seem that Mannyng knew of two works dealing with the exploits of these heroes, one by Master Edmond, and one by Thomas of Kendal. Both have disappeared, but a summary of the story, as told by Master Edmond, is given by Mannyng. According to this it would appear that Scarthe was regarded as a Briton, and that after Britain had been won by the Angles a British king called Engle laid claim to the land. Fearing Engle and his champion Scarthe, the Angles then made him king of the country. However, Thomas of Kendal evidently told a very different story; he knew a more correct form of the hero's name, and also that he had a brother Flayn. Despite Mannyng there can be no doubt that

[1] Mannyng ii, 514.

39

these legends dealt originally with the Viking and not the Anglo-Saxon invasions. They are evidently to be connected with the account of the foundation of Scarborough in *Kormáks saga*:

> The brothers (i.e. Thorgils and Kormák Qgmundarsynir) fought in Ireland, Wales, England, Scotland, and they were accounted the most splendid men. They first built the fortress which is called Scarborough. They raided into Scotland and took many fortresses, and had much force; there was no one like Kormák in the army as far as strength and courage were concerned.[1]

Elsewhere in the same saga we learn that Skarthi was the by-name of Thorgils, and the two brothers are obviously to be identified with the Scarthe and Flayn of English tradition, the former having given his name to Scarborough, the latter to Flamborough. Presumably the nicknames of the two brothers, Skarthi and Fleinn, were remembered in English tradition when their real names had been forgotten. There is no indication in *Kormáks saga* that the hero had any nickname; but the saga gives little attention to nicknames, and that of Thorgils would also have been unknown had it not by chance been embedded in two of Kormák's verses.[2] Nothing is known about the exploits of Scarthe and Flayn, or of the works by Thomas of Kendal and Master Edmond in which their deeds were celebrated, except for what Mannyng himself tells us. Since this is the case with stories which we know once had a written existence, it is not surprising that others, probably never written down at all, have left even slighter traces. Mannyng also knew of tales about a certain Ynge, but he knew of them only in an oral form:

> But of Ynge saw y neuere nought,
> Neyþer in boke write ne wrought;
> But lewed men þerof speke & crye,
> & meyntene al-wey vp þat lye.

Earlier in his chronicle this Ynge had appeared in legends connected with the Anglo-Saxon invasions, where she is said to have been the daughter of Hengest whom Mannyng knew better as Ronewen.[3] But despite Mannyng there were certainly Middle English writings

---

[1] *Íslendinga Sögur* (Reykjavík 1946–9) vi, 389.
[2] *Acta Philologica Scandinavica* i, 320.
[3] Mannyng ii, 515; i, 264.

of a kind about Ynge. A fragmentary chronicle tells how *wassail* and *drinkhail* came into this land through 'mayde ynge' from whom the country took its name. The story follows closely that of Hengest's acquisition of land as told in Laȝamon, but with the credit usurped by Ynge. Afterwards the country is divided up into Kent, Essex – and here the fragment breaks off.[1] Obviously there can be no historical basis for such a story, and it does not seem possible to connect Ynge in any way with the Ing of the Old English *Runic Poem*. Presumably the whole tale is a comparatively late concoction, with the name Ynge derived from the name of the country, and the exploits of some of the early invaders attributed to her.

It will be seen from this that whilst some of the traditions connected with the Viking invasions appear to have been written down at one time or another, others were probably never more than oral legends. Of the English kings who bore the brunt of these invasions the best known is Alfred, and in later times numerous stories appear to have become attached to him. According to William of Malmesbury, the places where Alfred suffered ill fortune and poverty were still in his time being pointed out by the natives,[2] but the best known of the stories about the king is, of course, that of the cakes. This first appears in the *Annals of St Neots*, where it is given on the authority of a life of that saint no longer extant.[3] No pre-Conquest reference is known, its presence in Asser being due to an interpolation by Archbishop Parker, but it is found in many of the lives of St Neot, as well as in an early twelfth-century English homily. Despite its comparatively late appearance it is likely enough that the story was in circulation during the Old English period. Other stories about Alfred occur in the lives of St Neot, all tending to the glorification of the saint, but there is nothing to suggest that they were at all widely known, and they may have been invented by the compilers of the lives. Similarly Higden, following William of Malmesbury, has a story of Alfred, disguised as a minstrel, entering the camp of the Vikings, and so learning their plans. The same tale is found in the Winchester annals and in the pseudo-Ingulph, and all have apparently

---

[1] T. Hearne, *Robert of Gloucester's Chronicle* (Oxford 1810), pp. 731–3.
[2] *Gesta Regum* i, 129.
[3] Asser, p. 136.

transferred to the king a story told of Olaf Cuaran before the battle of Brunanburh.[1]

There is rather better evidence for the anecdote of how Alfred's ghost walked after his death. It is given on the authority of tradition by William of Malmesbury, according to whom the body of Alfred was first buried in the cathedral, but afterwards,

> because of the folly of the canons, who asserted that the royal spirit, resuming its body, wandered nightly through the buildings, Edward, his son and successor, removed the remains of his father, and gave them a quiet resting-place in the New Minster.[2]

Also connected with Alfred are the stories which seem to have circulated during his reign concerning Denewulf, bishop of Winchester.[3]

The tenth century was the most glorious period of Anglo-Saxon history. Some of the greatest of the West Saxon kings were reigning, and since the *Old English Chronicle* fails us for most of the time, we know comparatively little about most of them. However, some apparently struck the imagination of their contemporaries, with the result that numerous tales grew up round their names. More especially there seems to have been a rich growth of legend concerning Athelstan, though most of the stories have been preserved only by twelfth-century chroniclers. William of Malmesbury tells of the alleged illegitimate birth of the king:

> There was, in a certain village, a shepherd's daughter of marvellous beauty. One night she dreamed that the moon shone from her womb and lit up the whole of England. Next morning she told her dream to her companions, and eventually it reached the ears of a woman who had formerly nursed the sons of the king. Because of the dream she adopted the maiden, and brought her up as her own daughter. One day Edward the Elder, whilst passing through the village, visited his old nurse. He became enamoured of the maiden, passed the night with her, and from this single intercourse was conceived the future king Athelstan.[4]

There is certainly no historical basis for such a story, and equally

---

[1] Higden vi, 376ff., *Gesta Regum* i, 126; cf. *Liber de Hyda* (RS. 45), pp. 45, 47, and H. Savile, *Rerum Anglicarum Scriptores* (Frankfurt 1601), p. 869.
[2] *Gesta Regum* i, 134.
[3] Florence of Worcester i, 97; cf. *Gesta Pontificum*, p. 162.
[4] *Gesta Regum* i, 155ff.

little for that which tells of Athelstan's responsibility for the death
of his brother Eadwine. The first report of this comes from
Symeon of Durham, who simply says that 'King Athelstan ordered
his brother Eadwine to be drowned in the sea', but William of
Malmesbury has fuller details. A certain Alfred is said to have
conspired against the king, and Eadwine was falsely accused of
complicity in the plot. Because of this he was

> compelled to go on board a vessel with a single servant, without a
> rower, without even an oar, and the boat was decrepit with age.
> Fortune laboured for a long time to restore the innocent youth to
> land; but when, at length, far out at sea, the sails could not endure the
> violence of the wind, the young man, sensitive and weary of life
> under such circumstances, put an end to it by a voluntary plunge
> into the water.

The servant eventually brings his master's body to land, and
Athelstan, repenting of his deed, inflicts vengeance on the accuser
of his brother, who brought his own destruction upon himself by
the tactless remark, when he slipped, 'Thus brother assists
brother'.[1] Both these stories of Athelstan are said to have been
taken from ballads 'popular through succeeding times', and legends
of the king and his brother seem to have lingered in some districts
as late as the sixteenth century.[2]

The best known event of Athelstan's reign was the battle of
Brunanburh, and William of Malmesbury tells a vivid story of how
Olaf Cuaran, in the disguise of a minstrel, entered the English
camp on the evening before the battle:

> [Olaf], who perceived how great a danger threatened, cunningly
> undertook the duty of reconnoitring, and putting aside the insignia
> of royalty took a harp in his hands and made his way to the tent of
> our king. Here, singing before the entrance and now and then also
> plucking the resounding strings in pleasing harmony, he was readily
> admitted, professing himself a minstrel who earned a daily wage by
> this kind of art. For some time he delighted the king and his com-
> panions with his melodious entertainment, though during his singing
> he took careful note of all he saw. When the end of the feast had put
> a limit to these pleasures and the talk of the soldiers again became
> full of the serious business of war, he was given a reward for his song

[1] Symeon of Durham ii, 124; *Gesta Regum* i, 156ff.
[2] Leland ii, 86.

and ordered to depart. Loathing to take this away with him he buried it in the ground. This act was noticed by one who had previously served him in war and was immediately reported to Æthelstan, who found fault with him because he had not betrayed their enemy when he was in their presence; but he made answer: 'The same oath which I lately made to you, O King, formerly I made to Olaf; if you had seen me break it against him you would have reason to beware of a similar happening with regard to yourself. But deign to listen to a servant's advice, namely, that you remove your tent from here, and, staying in another place until the rest of your forces come, you will with but a slight delay defeat an enemy now wantonly exulting.'[1]

The advice is accepted, and the place on which the king had been encamped is taken by an unnamed bishop who, during a night attack made by Olaf, is killed in mistake for the king. Although later chroniclers transfer the story to Alfred, there can be no doubt that in Anglo-Saxon times it was current in connexion with Olaf, and probably formed part of the saga of Olaf Cuaran which later contributed much to the Middle English *Havelok the Dane*.

Athelstan's successor was Edmund, and his death in 946 is said to have given rise to numerous legends throughout England:

A certain thief, Leof, whom [the king] had exiled on account of his robberies, returned after six years' absence and, on the Feast of St Augustine, Archbishop of Canterbury, took his place unexpectedly among the royal guests at Pucklechurch, as on this day the English were accustomed to keep festival in joyous manner in memory of their Apostle; and by chance sat down next to a councillor, whom the king himself had considered worthy of a place at his table. This fact was noticed by the king alone, the rest being deep in their wine; and his anger being roused and fate egging him on he leapt up from the table, seized the robber by the hair, and threw him to the ground. [But the robber] secretly drew his dagger from its sheath and with as much force as he could plunged it into the king's breast as he fell above him; of this wound the king died and stories of his death spread over the whole of England. The robber too was immediately surrounded by the retainers and torn limb from limb, but not before he had wounded several of them.[2]

This circumstantial account, which includes the preservation of the robber's name, suggests that William of Malmesbury is making

[1] *Gesta Regum* i, 142–3. Wright, pp. 144–5.
[2] *Gesta Regum* i, 159; Wright, p. 82.

use of one of the *cantilenae* of which he speaks, and in fact he could
have derived his story from no other source. The murder is
recorded, with more or less elaboration, by others of the Latin
chroniclers, and by the thirteenth century it has become in John
of Wallingford one of the legends attached to St Dunstan.[1]

It was only to be expected that later legend should have been
busy with the reign of Edgar, and again, at the time when William
of Malmesbury was writing, ballads concerning the king were still
extant. After telling of the favour shown to foreigners during his
reign, the chronicler continues, 'for this history justly and de-
servedly blames him; but the other imputations of which I shall
tell afterwards, rest upon no better authority than ballads'. Later
three stories derived from these ballads are given. The first tells
how Edgar came to marry Ælfthryth:

> There was a certain Æthelwold, a distinguished nobleman of his own
> age and a close confidant; to this man the king entrusted a task, that
> [he should go] to Ælfthryth, the daughter of Orgar, duke of the
> Devonshire people, whose beauty had impressed his informants to
> such an extent that they praised her in the king's hearing – this man,
> I say, he ordered to go and see her and to propose marriage to her
> [on the king's behalf] if report should prove true. [Æthelwold how-
> ever] hurrying on his way and finding nothing different from his
> expectation hid his errand from the parents and won the girl for
> himself. Returning to the king, [he told] only what was for his own
> interest and alleged that she was but small in form and of vulgar and
> common appearance and in nowise fit for his majesty. Æthelwold's
> detractors made known [to the king] with what cunning this man, led
> astray by and involved in these and other amours, had cheated him. He,
> driving out wedge with wedge, that is to say, parrying deceit by deceit,
> showed a calm countenance to the earl and jocosely named a day on
> which he would visit so much-discussed a woman. [The earl] how-
> ever, beside himself with fright at such dreadful jesting, hastened to
> his wife begging her to consider his safety and as much as she could
> to let her clothes detract from her beauty, then for the first time
> disclosing what he had done. But what did this woman not presume
> to do? She dared to deceive the trust of her unhappy lover and first
> husband and to deck herself out at the mirror, omitting nothing that
> would stir the heart of [this] virile young king. Nor did it happen
> otherwise than was planned, for so inflamed was [Edgar] at the sight
> of her that, concealing his hatred, he slew the earl in Wherwell

[1] T. Gale, *Scriptores XV* (Oxford 1691) iii, 541.

Forest, whither he had been summoned to join the king in hunting. When the bastard son of the slain man arrived at the spot with accustomed familiarity and was asked by the king how he liked such sport, he is said to have replied: 'Very well, [my] lord king, for what pleases thee ought not to be distasteful to myself'; by this reply he so assuaged the mind of the furious [monarch] that the latter treasured nothing more dearly in his life after this than that boy, alleviating the offence of this tyrannical act against the father by royal care towards the son. As an expiation of this crime a community of nuns dwells there in a monastery built by Ælfthryth.[1]

A more elaborate version of the story is given by Gaimar, according to whom Æthelwold persuades the king to become godfather to his son, thus placing Edgar and Ælfthryth within the prohibited degrees, and so leading to the introduction of Dunstan into the story. He may have derived his knowledge from some legend current at Wherwell, and one certainly different from that known to William of Malmesbury, since there are effective touches in the latter which Gaimar omits. Moreover, there are some indications that Gaimar perhaps had a written source for his story, though if so this has long since been lost.[2] Certainly, if he did in fact obtain the story from Wherwell, it would help to explain the different conceptions of Ælfthryth that appear in the two accounts. In William of Malmesbury she deliberately sets out to inflame the king, whereas in Gaimar she plays quite an innocent part. Since the queen was the foundress of the monastery at Wherwell, stories from that district would tend to show her in as good a light as possible. It is probable, however, that William of Malmesbury's version was the earlier and more widespread, at any rate if we are to judge from the fact that other writers have little good to say of the queen. At the best she plays an ambiguous part in the murder of Edward the Martyr, and she is also said to have been responsible for the death of Abbot Byrhtnoth of Ely. The latter of these stories appears in the *Liber Eliensis*, which tells how the abbot, on his way to the king's court, surprised the queen in various magical and unnatural practices. In order to prevent her misdeeds from becoming known she attempted to seduce the abbot, and failing in this plotted with her women to kill him in a particularly

---

[1] *Gesta Regum* i, 165, 178; Wright, pp. 146–7.
[2] Gaimar i, 166.

horrible fashion.[1] This part of the *Liber Eliensis* is said to be based on the work of Richard of Ely, who lived during the early part of the twelfth century, and presumably the story represents some local legend of the death of Abbot Byrhtnoth, though no other authority connects Ælfthryth with it.

The second of William of Malmesbury's tales concerns the carrying off of a nun:

> Hearing of the beauty of a certain virgin who was dedicated to God, [Edgar] carried her off from the monastery by force, ravished her, and frequently made her the partner of his bed. When this circumstance reached the ears of St Dunstan, he was vehemently reproved by him, and underwent penance for seven years, submitting, though a king, to fast and to forgo the wearing of his crown during that time.

Later it appears that the name of the lady was Wulfride, and that she was not a nun, 'but a lay sister who had assumed the veil through fear of the king'. The third story, like the preceding one, appears only in William of Malmesbury:

> They add to this a third [example], in which both vices [namely, lust and cruelty] appear. King Edgar, they say, arriving at Andover, which is a town not far from Winchester, ordered to be brought to him a certain nobleman's daughter, the report of whose beauty had spread abroad. The girl's mother, scorning to allow her daughter to become his concubine, and helped by the darkness of night, substituted in the [king's] bed, her maid, a virgin indeed neither unpleasing nor devoid of charm. When the night had passed and dawn was breaking, the woman began to get up, and being asked why she made such haste replied that it was to carry out the day's work for her mistress; held back though with difficulty by the king, she bewailed on her knees her miserable condition [and begged] that as a reward for lying with him he would grant her her freedom, [adding] that it was not becoming his greatness, that she, after ministering to his royal pleasure, should suffer longer under the commands of her cruel masters. Then he, with a foreboding smile, his anger being moved [and] wavering between pity for the girl and anger against her mistress, as if treating the whole thing as a joke, gave her the fulfilment of her wishes. Soon he raised her with great honour to be mistress of her former masters, whether they wished it or not.[2]

---

[1] *Liber Eliensis*, pp. 127–8.
[2] *Gesta Regum* i, 179; Wright, pp. 153–4.

With the possible exception of Gaimar's source it is probable that these stories were current only orally, and the fact that there are a number of tales dealing with Ælfthryth would suggest that there may once have been in existence a long narrative telling of her evil deeds.

The disasters of the reign of Ethelred seem to have led to the development of as many stories as did the glories of that of Edgar. William of Malmesbury tells how the appearance of seven Viking ships off Southampton in 980 led to the circulation of numerous rumours about them,[1] whilst behind Henry of Huntingdon's story of the brave man of Balsham must lie some local tradition which has otherwise been completely lost:

> [The Danes] burnt Cambridge; and withdrawing thence through the hilly parts [*i.e.* the Gogmagog Hills] of a most pleasant and delightful place which is called Balsham; put to death everyone they found in that place; and tossing the children [in the air] caught them on the points of their spears. A certain man however, worthy of far-flung fame, mounted the steps of the church tower, which to this day stands there; and fortified as much by the position as by his courage, defended himself alone from the whole host.

Memories of the massacre of the Vikings on St Brice's Day, 1002, long survived. Some of the later chroniclers, for example John of Wallingford, give highly-coloured descriptions of it. The earlier ones usually have little to say about the event, though Henry of Huntingdon tells us that, as a boy, he had heard some very old people describe the massacre.[2] Unfortunately he does not say much about these stories which must by his time already have lived for more than a century in oral tradition.

One of the most famous of the battles fought against the Vikings during the reign of Ethelred was that at Maldon in 991 in which Byrhtnoth, aldorman of Essex, was defeated and slain. One of the few surviving Old English poems on historical subjects deals with the battle; in all probability it was composed soon afterwards and appears to be fairly historical. The *Old English Chronicle* passes briefly over it, and the account in the *Vita Oswaldi*, probably written by a monk of Ramsey between 997 and 1005, although it adds a few details unmentioned in the poem, also seems to be

---

[1] *Gesta Regum* i, 186.
[2] Huntingdon, pp. 178, 174; Wright, p. 239.

based on fact. Yet by the twelfth century a number of legends had grown up, and some of them are said to have had a written existence in the vernacular. In the *Liber Eliensis* Byrhtnoth has become aldorman of Northumbria, and is credited with two battles at Maldon against the Vikings. In the first he was victorious, but in the second, which took place four years later and lasted for fourteen days, he was defeated and slain. On his way to the second battle he was refused hospitality by the abbot of Ramsey but welcomed by the monastery at Ely, and it was because of this that he made great donations of land to the latter. After the battle Byrhtnoth's head was cut off and taken away by the victorious Vikings, and consequently the abbot of Ely, who took up the body from the battle-field, buried it in the church with a round lump of wax in place of the head. The writer claims to be drawing some of his information from English works, and, considering his material, these must have been very different from the extant Old English poem, though they may ultimately have been based on it.[1] Similar stories were apparently known to the writer of the Ramsey chronicle (c. 1175) though, mindful of the honour and profit of his own monastery, he made Byrhtnoth leave land to it as well as to Ely. In fact some of the details in the *Liber Eliensis* may well be historically correct. The missing head is mentioned also in the *Vita Oswaldi*, and according to Thomas of Ely the body 'was recognized long afterwards by this sign'. This was presumably in 1154, in Thomas's own time, when the remains of the abbey's benefactors were removed from the Saxon church and re-buried in the Norman cathedral. Moreover, according to a report on the discovery of Byrhtnoth's bones, taken from a letter read before the Society of Antiquaries in 1772:

I apprised those who attended on that occasion, May 18, 1769, that if my surmises were well founded no head would be found in the cell which contained the Bones of Brihtnoth, Duke of Northumberland. . . . [Under the effigy of] Duke Brihtnoth there were no remains of the head, though we searched diligently, and found most, if not all his other bones almost entire, and those remarkable for their length, and proportionally strong; which also agrees with what is recorded by the same historian with regard to the Duke's person, viz. that he was *viribus robustus, corpore maximus* . . . It was estimated

[1] *Liber Eliensis*, pp. 133–6.

49

. . . that the Duke must have been 6 foot 9 inches in stature. It was observed that the collar-bone had been nearly cut through, as by a battle-axe or two-handed sword.[1]

The Vikings at Maldon are said in the *Old English Chronicle* to have been led by Olaf Tryggvason, and whether this were the case or not, it is certain that Olaf was one of the most prominent of the Viking leaders of the period. He became the subject of an Old Norse saga, and there is some slight evidence for a written account of his life and deeds in English:

> King Edward [the Confessor] made it a custom to relate the Saga of King Olaf Tryggvason to his great men and his bodyguard on the first day of Easter; and he chose that day rather than any other for the telling of the Saga, saying that Olaf Tryggvason was superior to other kings as much as Easter day is superior to the other days of the whole year. There was a man named Orm, Thorliot's son, a wise and truthful man, who lived at Dyrness in the Orkneys when Edward was King of England. Orm declared that he had heard King Edward read the Saga of Olaf Tryggvason out of the very book that Olaf himself had sent to King Athelred from Jerusalem. One year when the King had read before his great men and all his bodyguard the account of the battle on the Serpent, with the story of King Olaf's escape, exactly as we have related it; and had told them of his journeys beyond the sea to Jerusalem, and how he had fixed his abode at a cloister in England – he added to the story by announcing the death of Olaf Tryggvason, tidings of which had lately been brought to England by travellers from Syrland.[2]

No doubt many of the chief men at Edward's court were of Scandinavian descent, but it is unlikely that many of them would be able to understand Norse, and almost certainly Edward himself would not. Consequently, if we can believe the story, and the evidence is not particularly convincing, a written English version of the saga of Olaf Tryggvason would seem to have been once in existence.

Ethelred's reign ended in disaster, but the death of the king removed one of the chief reasons for defeat, and under his son Edmund, despite treachery amongst the English magnates, the Vikings were fought to a standstill and peace made on the basis

---

[1] E. V. Gordon, *The Battle of Maldon* (London 1937), pp. 20–1.
[2] *Fornmanna Sögur* (Copenhagen 1827) iii, 63ff.; Wright, p. 67.

of a division of the kingdom. Edmund had apparently just suffered a crushing defeat at Ashingdon, and had fled westwards pursued by Cnut, when the war ended suddenly in this way. Such a dramatic and unexpected end inevitably led to the growth of legend, and before long we find a story telling how Cnut and Edmund had fought in single combat for the possession of England. The *Encomium Emmae* and William of Malmesbury both refer to a proposal, of which nothing comes, that the issue should be settled in this way. Henry of Huntingdon is the first to give a detailed description of the fight, which is said to have taken place on an island in the Severn.[1] Gaimar apparently knew only of the earlier story in which a duel is arranged but the idea abandoned in favour of a peaceful settlement. Moreover in his version the proposed duel was to have taken place on a ship, not on an island as in all the other accounts. But towards the end of the twelfth century Walter Map knows of a legend in which appear circumstantial details of the fight, and later writers tell much the same story:

Matters having been arranged with the due solemnity which befitted them, a time having been fixed and guards armed, [the combatants] carried in two boats from opposite shores met on an island in the Severn, equipped with excellent and most valuable arms and horses, as their honour and defence required. On their failures and successes after the beginning of the combat we are not able to dwell (but must pass on to other things), and [tell] how for a long time both sides in silence and throughout varying chances were agitated in turn by sad fears and joyful hopes, as the motionless army watched breathlessly. And this gave rise to a memorable saying; since their horses were slain they fought on foot and Cnut, tall and slim, wearied Edmund, who was heavily built and fleshy (that is to say, rather stout), with such blows good and bad that in an interval of rest, while Edmund was standing panting quickly and breathing heavily, Cnut said (in the hearing of those surrounding them): 'Edmund, you are too short breathed.' He blushing with shame was silent and in the next assault came down on his helmet with such a mighty blow that [Cnut] fell on his hands and knees, but [Edmund] springing back did not overwhelm the fallen man nor hold him down thus smitten, but in revenge returned word for word, and said: 'Not too short breathed if I can bring so great a king to his knees'. The Danes, therefore, seeing that Edmund had spared their lord in a combat of such great

---

[1] Huntingdon, p. 185.

purpose and had forborne to vanquish him in so easy a victory, with many prayers and tears urged them to make a treaty to the effect that for the rest of their lives they should possess the kingdom equally divided between them, and the survivor should succeed to the whole on the death of the other.[1]

It is clear that, on whatever historical foundation it may have been based, there was extant in Map's time a story which told in detail of this single combat, one moreover which was so well known that the words of Cnut and Edmund had become proverbial.

The most notorious of the English magnates during the reign of Ethelred was Eadric Streona, and judging from the evidence it would seem that his evil deeds were remembered, and perhaps added to, long after his death. Florence of Worcester connects him with the death of the aldorman Ælfhelm:

> The deceitful and faithless Edric Streona plotting treachery against the noble Duke Ælfhelm prepared at Shrewsbury a great banquet for him, at which when his guests came Edric received him as his particular friend; but having prepared his snares, on the third or fourth day of the entertainment he took him with him hunting in the forest, where, everyone being occupied in the chase, a Shrewsbury butcher, Godwin Porthund, that is, Dog of the Town, whom Edric had bribed beforehand with large gifts and many promises to commit the crime, suddenly leapt on him from ambush and evilly slew Duke Ælfhelm.[2]

No other evidence for this is known, but the whole business, considering the character of Eadric, is not improbable. He next appears, in connexion with the death of Earl Uhtred, at a time when his treacheries had apparently gone astray and he had fled to Cnut. Uhtred remained faithful to Edmund, but a northward advance by Cnut drew him away to protect York. He found Cnut too strong, had to surrender, and the *Old English Chronicle*, under 1016, notes that 'he was nevertheless slain by the advice of the aldorman Eadric'. The *De Obsessione Dunelmi* says that he was killed by a certain *Turebrand cognomento hold*, and Florence of Worcester gives a similar account, neither of them mentioning Eadric. In the last campaign against Cnut Eadric was again with Edmund, and it was his treachery that led to the final defeat of

---

[1] Map, pp. 212ff.; Wright, pp. 195–6.
[2] Florence of Worcester i, 158; Wright, pp. 142–3.

the English. The *Old English Chronicle* merely says that at the battle of Ashingdon, 'then the aldorman Eadric acted as he had done so often before, began the flight with the Magesæte, and so betrayed his royal lord and the people of the whole of England'. Later writers give more detail. William of Malmesbury places the occurrence at the battle of Sherston:

> After the Feast of St John, having joined battle with [the Danes] at Sherston, he parted company with the issue undecided; the English initiated the flight at the instigation of Eadric, who standing in the enemy's ranks and holding a sword in his hand, which he had stained with blood in the fight by cutting down quickly a certain peasant, cried out: 'Flee, wretches, flee; behold your king has been killed with this sword!' The English would have fled forthwith had not the king, perceiving the act, rushed to a prominent spur of land and taking off his helmet shown his features to his followers. Then, with as much strength as he could launching an iron spear he hurled it at Eadric; but, perceived and avoided by [Eadric], it pierced instead a soldier standing near, so far that it transfixed another also.[1]

Florence of Worcester also gives the episode as occurring at the same battle, but he knows the name of the man killed by Eadric, and has a longer version of the speech:

> When the fighting was ardent [Eadric] perceived the English to be the stronger; so, cutting off the head of a man (Osmear by name), similar in feature and hair to King Edmund, and holding it up on high, he shouted out that the English were fighting in vain, saying:—
> 'Do you, O Men of Dorset, of Devon, and of Wiltshire,
> Betake yourselves straightway to flight, now that your leader is dead,
> For the head of your lord, King Edmund,
> I hold here in my hands; so yield you forthwith.'[2]

Henry of Huntingdon transfers it to the battle of Ashingdon and quotes the actual words said to have been used by Eadric – 'Flet Engle, flet Engle; ded is Edmund'.[3] The *Encomium Emmae*, drawing apparently on a different version, ascribes the treachery to Ashingdon, gives Eadric's words in a slightly longer version, declares that he was bribed by the Danes, and makes him speak before and not during the battle.[4]

[1] *Gesta Regum* i, 215; Wright, p. 186.
[2] Florence of Worcester i, 175; Wright, p. 187.
[3] Huntingdon, p. 184.   [4] Ed. A. Campbell (CS. 1949), p. 24.

In later legend Eadric appears to have played a prominent part in the death of Edmund. Some of the early accounts hint at murder, but the first to declare this openly, and to accuse Eadric, is that of Archdeacon Herman in his *De miraculis S. Eadmundi*.[1] William of Malmesbury is more cautious, but he too has heard of stories which blame Eadric for the death of Edmund,[2] and a similar tale is found in Henry of Huntingdon, where however the son of Eadric is named as the actual murderer. In Map the death is brought about by a concealed spike, and no mention is made of Eadric. Gaimar agrees with the others in naming Eadric, but he has a much more picturesque account than the usual one, and describes the death as due to a *machine infernale – l'arc ki ne falt*.[3]

Eadric did not long survive Edmund. He was put to death in the following year, and it was natural enough that legend should soon connect the two events. The *Old English Chronicle* gives no reason for his death, whilst in the *Encomium Emmae*, Florence of Worcester, and William of Malmesbury, he is slain by Cnut from suspicion of disloyalty, mainly because of his previous record of treachery. Henry of Huntingdon is the first to connect his death with the murder of Edmund:

> And so Eadric coming to King Cnut saluted him, saying: 'Hail to thee who art sole king'. To whom, when he had laid bare the accomplished deed, the king replied: 'As a reward for so great an allegiance I will set you higher than all the leading men of the English.' He therefore ordered him to be beheaded, and his head to be set on a stake on the highest tower in London.[4]

Gaimar makes Cnut himself the executioner, and has the head and body left on the bank of the Thames whence the tide carried them out to sea, while in Map it is the unnamed slave responsible for the death of Edmund who is put to death by Cnut. There can be no doubt that there must once have been in existence a long narrative, whether in prose or verse, dealing with the career and death of Eadric, of which disconnected parts in later chronicles are all that now survive.

Cnut plays an important part in some of the stories already

[1] *Memorials of St Edmund's Abbey* (RS. 96) i, 39.
[2] *Gesta Regum* i, 217. [3] *Medium Ævum* xxv, 79–83.
[4] Huntingdon, p. 186; Wright, p. 186.

mentioned. In addition he had one that was peculiar to himself, his encounter with the waves. This appears first in Huntingdon and is repeated, with some additions, by Gaimar. There was also another story dealing with the marriage of his daughter Gunhilda to the Emperor Henry. William of Malmesbury tells of the splendour of the wedding, about which ballads were still being sung, and of the false accusations later made against the bride:

> The splendour of the wedding pageant was striking, and is even in our times frequently sung in ballads about the streets . . . Proceeding in this manner to her husband, she preserved for a long time the bonds of marriage. At length, being accused of adultery, she opposed in single combat to her accuser who was a man of gigantic size, a young lad who took care of her starling whom she had brought from England, whilst her other attendants held back in cowardly fear. When therefore they engaged, the accuser, through the miraculous intervention of God was defeated by being hamstrung. Gunhilda, rejoicing at her unexpected victory, renounced the marriage contract with her husband; nor could she be induced either by threats or endearments to share his bed again, but taking the veil of a nun she calmly grew old in the service of God.[1]

A century later Matthew Paris speaks of songs on the subject as still current, and since he gives the name of the page, Mimecan, it is clear that he is not simply quoting William of Malmesbury, whilst Ralph of Diceto knows also the name of the accuser, Rodingar.[2] In one form or another these ballads must have had a life of at least two hundred years, yet none of them has survived.

Earl Godwine of Wessex, the greatest of the eleventh-century English magnates, was probably a descendant of Eadric Streona, but later legend preferred to represent him as the son of poor parents. The fullest account of some of the stories connected with him is to be found in Walter Map. Ethelred, whilst hunting, became separated from his companions, and sought shelter in the house of a peasant. The son of the peasant was so attentive and courteous that the king took him to court, raised him above all the men in the kingdom, and eventually made him earl of Gloucester. In return Godwine cleared the land of Vikings and fought in many battles across the sea, so that 'his name was as famous among

---

[1] *Gesta Regum* i, 229.
[2] *Chronica Majora* i, 514; *Abbreviationes Chronicorum* (RS. 68) i, 174.

the Saracens as among the Christians, and his repute was every-where without rival'. After the accession of Cnut, Godwine fights so successfully against him that the king is forced to come to terms. However, under pretence of further honouring the earl, Cnut sends him to Denmark with a letter of death. Godwine opens the letter, and changes it for one entrusting the government of Denmark to him and granting him Cnut's sister as wife. At this point Map's account breaks off, leaving us with no knowledge of what the legend had to say about Godwine's later life and his death.[1] The story of his humble origin appears also in the *Vita Haroldi*, the *Liber de Hyda*, the Old Norse *Knytlinga saga*, and elsewhere. The earl was also apparently connected in popular story with the betrayal and death of Alfred, the brother of the Confessor, and in some of the chronicles his own sudden death is due to an attempt to prove his innocence. It is unfortunate that Map did not give us more of the vernacular saga on the life of Godwine which was evidently then in existence, but it may be that he himself knew nothing more, and was using a written source of which the end was missing. If so, it would explain the otherwise puzzling fact that the story of the letter of death breaks off at the same point in the *Vita Haroldi*.

Another of the great earls, Siward of Northumbria, also had various stories connected with his name. Two of them are given by Henry of Huntingdon, the first of which tells of Siward's reception of the news of the death of his son in battle:

> About this time [*i.e.* 1054] Siward, Earl of Northumbria, a very brave man, almost a giant in stature, and firm indeed alike of hand and mind, sent his son to reduce Scotland to subjection. When his death in battle was announced to his father, the latter said: 'Did he receive his mortal wound in front or in his back?' And the messengers replied: 'In front'. And he exclaimed: 'I rejoice exceedingly, for no other death would be worthy of me or my son'. Siward thereupon set out for Scotland and waged war upon its king, destroying the whole kingdom and subjecting it, thus chastised, to his rule.

This is followed soon afterwards by an account of Siward's own death:

> In the following year [*i.e.* 1055] Earl Siward the mighty, weakened by a flux, felt death approaching and said: 'How great a shame is

[1] Map, pp. 206ff.

this to me not to have been able to meet death in so many battles, but to be left to die like a cow with dishonour! Clothe me in my impenetrable armour, gird my sword about me, and put on my helmet; put my shield in my left hand and my battle-axe inlaid with gold in my right, so that the boldest of warriors may die in the trappings of a warrior'. So he spoke; and as he had said, clad in his arms breathed out honourably his soul.[1]

It seems clear that these two stories, along with that of the Raven Banner, are only part of the saga of Siward which must have been still current in Northumbria during the twelfth and thirteenth centuries. Apparently at a fairly early date it was incorporated into the Waltheof cycle, and a Latin version of it is to be found in the thirteenth-century *Vita et Passio Waldevi*, extant only in a single manuscript now at Douai. The Siward saga appears there in a section, entitled *Gesta Antecessorum Comitis Waldevi*,[2] containing a good many folk-lore themes both English and Scandinavian. A reference to another written work on Siward occurs in the Anglo-French *Delapré Chronicle*, also from the thirteenth century. According to this:

> Many great deeds and many marvels are told about Earl Siward, as long as he lived, as can be found about him in the book of the English which is in Nottinghamshire, and which Richard the Chanter of Nottingham has, which tells of his life and deeds.

It is impossible to say what the book in question was, nor do we know what language it was in, since the reference to *les lyveress as Engleys* is quite ambiguous. In any case this provides further evidence for the presence in thirteenth-century England of a saga of the deeds of Siward, certainly current in English in an oral form, and perhaps also in writing.[3]

According to the records of the Benedictine monastery of St Swithin, Winchester, under the year 1338,

> a certain minstrel named Herebert sang the song of Colbrond, and of the deeds of Emma, freed from the ordeal by fire.[4]

The 'song of Colbrond' was no doubt a version of *Guy of Warwick*, and the 'deeds of Emma' must have been the famous tale of Queen Emma and the ploughshares. The story first appears in an un-

---

[1] Huntingdon, pp. 194–6; Wright, pp. 127–8. [2] Wright, pp. 129–35.
[3] *Bodleian Quarterly Record* vi, 225–30. [4] Warton ii, 97

printed chronicle by Richard of Devizes (C.C.C.C., MS. 339), and is found in many later ones, including the *Annales de Wintonia*, Robert of Gloucester, Higden, and others. It tells how Emma, mother of the Confessor, is accused by Archbishop Robert of adultery with Aylwin, bishop of Winchester. She is imprisoned, but manages to communicate with her friends, and proposes trial by ordeal to prove her innocence. She is allowed to undergo the ordeal of the nine red-hot ploughshares, and on the appointed day does so successfully in the presence of the assembled magnates. A similar story appears in the Middle English romance of *Athelston*, though what the exact relationship – if any – may be between the two versions is impossible to decide. Nor can we be certain that the song of the dikers and delvers in *Piers Plowman* (Prologue 224), 'Dieu vous saue, Dame Emme', refers to this story, though it is possible enough.

The last of the Saxon kings also had stories connected with him, the most famous of which told how he survived Hastings and lived for a long time as a hermit at Chester. Ailred of Rievaulx has heard the story, or at any rate knows of a rumour that the king had escaped from the battlefield.[1] Giraldus Cambrensis had also heard a report to this effect, and adds a good deal of further information:

> It is also asserted that the remains of Harold are deposited [at Chester]. He was the last of the Saxon kings of England, and, as a punishment for his perjury, was defeated in the battle fought against the Normans at Hastings. Having received many wounds, and lost his left eye by an arrow in that engagement, he is said to have escaped to these parts where, in holy conversation, leading the life of an anchorite, and being a constant attendant at one of the churches of this city, he is believed to have ended his life happily. The truth of [this] circumstance was declared (and not known before), in [his] dying confession.[2]

In the thirteenth century the whole story was elaborated into the *Vita Haroldi*, apparently written with the object of proving that Harold's body was not buried at Waltham. Later chroniclers, such as Higden, Knighton, and Bromton, not only know the story – as they might well have done from the earlier historians – but add details of their own. Indeed so firmly fixed had it become that the *Brut y Tywysogion*, under the year 1332, records with much

[1] R. Twysden, *Historiae Anglicanae Scriptores X* (London 1652), p. 394.
[2] *Itinerarium Kambriæ*, p. 140.

circumstantial detail the discovery of Harold's body in St John's, Chester:

> After the kalends of May the body of Harold king of England was found in St John's church, Chester, having been buried more than 200 years before, and his body was found with his crown and his robes and his leather hose and his golden spurs, as entire and as well odoured as on the day when they were buried.[1]

No attempt has been made to give a complete list of all the stories based on Anglo-Saxon history which were current during the Old and Middle English periods. These are only a selection of those for which we have the best evidence in later writings. It is certain enough that there were others for which there are only the vaguest references remaining, and some of them may have been of strictly local currency. There were evidently tales dealing with Ceadwalla, Guthfrith of Northumbria, Eric Bloodaxe, Swegen, and Leofric of Mercia, to name only a few of them. Nor can we know how many of these legends achieved a written existence in the vernacular. For some we have odd scraps of evidence to suggest that later writers are drawing on written sources, but for most we have no evidence one way or the other. On the whole it is probable that many of them were current only orally, though it is possible enough that others may have formed the subjects of written works in English of which all trace has since been lost.

[1] Ed. T. Jones (Cardiff 1941), pp. 237–8.

3

CHRISTIAN EPIC

In all probability a much greater proportion of the Christian poetry has survived than of the heroic or historical narrative. In contrast with these the Christian poetry was essentially a written rather than an oral literature, and once written down there was every reason why such verse should be preserved in the monasteries. It would still be subject to the accidents of time, more especially during the later Middle Ages when it was no longer easily intelligible, but the natural conservatism of the monastic institutions would help to prolong the life of the manuscripts. Certainly, despite accidents, a written literature such as this would start off with a considerably better chance of survival than would one which was mainly oral.

Even so, there is evidence that a good deal of this type of poetry has disappeared. For our knowledge of it we are mainly dependent on the chance survival of three codices: the *Exeter Book*, the *Vercelli Book*, and the Junius Manuscript. A number of folios are missing from the begining and end of the *Exeter Book*, and we have no means of knowing whether this has also involved the loss of some of the poems once contained in the manuscript. Moreover, all three are collections of mainly religious verse made at approximately the same time, and although the contents of them may have been selected on slightly different principles, even so there is extraordinarily little repetition. A poem on *Daniel* in the Junius Manuscript runs parallel with one on *Azarias* in the *Exeter Book*, while the second of these and the *Vercelli Book* both contain a poem on the *Debate of the Soul and the Body*. The corpus of religious verse available at the end of the tenth century must have been very large to make it possible for three such collections to be made with so little overlapping. Of course it is impossible to prove that the three manuscripts have no connexion at all. One of them could have been originally written for an owner who already possessed one of the others, and so repetition may deliberately have been avoided. But in what little is known of their history there is nothing to indicate such a relationship between any of the manuscripts, and the writing and form make it clear that they were not originally the three volumes of a single collection which have since been separated.

Apart from the contents of these manuscripts, there are extant in Old English about a score of pieces of religious and moral poetry preserved in various ways. In only two instances is there any duplication with the poems in the codices. The inscription on the Ruthwell Cross gives lines which occur, in a different form, in the Vercelli *Dream of the Rood*, and a Northumbrian riddle in a Leyden manuscript appears in a West Saxon version in the *Exeter Book*. On the whole it would seem that quite a large amount of religious verse must have existed in Old English, and that only a small proportion of it has survived.

Such a conclusion is confirmed by evidence of a somewhat different type. According to Bede, the earliest writer of Christian epics in Old English was a certain Cædmon, a monk of Whitby, who received the gift of song by divine inspiration. Bede tells the story in some detail, and also gives information about the subjects of Cædmon's poetry:

> He sang the creation of the world, the origin of man, and all the history of Genesis; and he made many verses on the departure of the children of Israel out of Egypt, and their entrance into the Promised Land, with many other stories from holy writ: the incarnation, passion, and resurrection of our Lord, and his ascension into heaven; the coming of the Holy Ghost, and the preaching of the apostles; also about the terror of future judgment, the horror of the pains of hell, and the delights of heaven; beside many more about the divine benefits and judgments.[1]

Bede was a trained and conscientious historian, living not far from Cædmon's monastery of Whitby, and we may therefore take it for granted that the poet actually did compose verses on these subjects. Now the extant manuscript Bodl. Junius 11 contains poems on *Genesis*, *Exodus*, *Daniel*, the *Temptation*, the *Ascension*, and the *Last Judgment*. Such a list of contents inevitably reminds one of the subjects which Cædmon is said to have dealt with, and it is not

[1] C. Plummer, *Bedae Opera Historica* (Oxford 1896) i, 260.

surprising that earlier scholars should have regarded these poems as authentic works by him. Later research, however, has shown that the manuscript is of composite authorship, and that only part of the *Genesis* and part of the *Exodus* can have been composed early enough for Cædmon to have been responsible for them. The two are in any case almost certainly by different authors, so that of the works mentioned by Bede only one is even possibly extant – and there is no real proof of this. It may be, of course, that the extant poems are ultimately based on the earlier works by Cædmon; if so it is likely that they differ considerably from them in metre and language, if not in treatment. Consequently, of the earliest and, according to Bede, the greatest of the Christian poets, the only work that certainly survives are the nine lines of his *Hymn to the Creation*. Bede himself gives only a Latin translation of this, but an English version, in the Northumbrian dialect, has been inserted by the scribes in some of the early manuscripts of the *Ecclesiastical History*. This could easily enough be the source of Bede's Latin, and we have no reason to doubt its authenticity.

Moreover, although Bede considered that Cædmon was the first and the greatest of the religious poets, he also makes it clear that he was not the only writer of Christian verse in the vernacular, since 'others of the English nation afterwards attempted to compose religious poems, but none could ever compare with him'. But of these other poets who flourished between the time of Cædmon and the death of Bede we know nothing whatever.

While Cædmon was at work in the north Aldhelm, bishop of Sherborne, was beginning a similar school of Old English Christian poetry in the south. Florence of Worcester mentions his fame as a poet,[1] and William of Malmesbury, on the authority of the lost *Handbook*, tells us that Alfred considered Aldhelm the greatest of the Old English Christian poets. He also gives the reasons which led the bishop to compose poetry in the vernacular. Apparently his barbarous flock was accustomed to leave for home as soon as mass had been celebrated, without waiting for the sermon. Thereupon the saint, disguised as a minstrel, stationed himself at a bridge which they had to pass. When, after more than one performance, he had made himself popular, he gradually began to 'mingle words of scripture amid the more entertaining matter'.[2]

[1] Florence of Worcester i, 237.   [2] *Gesta Pontificum*, p. 336.

Many of the Latin works of Aldhelm still remain, and adaptations of some of his Latin riddles into Old English are preserved in the *Exeter Book*. Whether the translator of these was Aldhelm or not we have no means of knowing, but even so these could hardly be the Christian poems of which Alfred speaks. It is possible that some of the extant religious poetry may be the work of Aldhelm, or may perhaps be based on it, though there is no indication that such is the case. On the whole it would appear that none of his verse is now extant, and this despite Alfred's commendation and the fact that, according to William of Malmesbury, one at least of his poems must have survived in popular memory for some five hundred years, since it was still remembered by the country people during the twelfth century.

Undoubtedly the greatest scholar of the Old English period was the Venerable Bede. In addition he was probably the first writer of English prose and also a skilful poet in the vernacular. But we hear of his poetry only because it is mentioned in a description of his death written by his disciple Cuthbert. In the course of it he tells how Bede composed on his deathbed,

> in our own language, since he was skilled in our poetry, speaking of the terrible parting of the soul and the body,
>> Fore them neidfaerae naenig uuiurthit
>> thoncsnottura than him tharf sie,
>> to ymbhycggannae, aer his hiniongae,
>> huaet his gastae, godaes aeththa yflaes,
>> aefter deothdaege doemid uueorthae.[1]

There is no reason to doubt the truth of this account in which has been preserved all that survives of Bede's poetry in Old English. Presumably it was not the only verse he composed, and it is a safe assumption that any poetry written by Bede would have been decidedly Christian in tone and subject. As it is, we are left with these five lines alone, and the strong presumption that they form only a small part of the poetic compositions in his native language.

Alfred the Great is known to have been deeply interested in Old English poetry, and is said by Florence of Worcester to have been himself a notable poet.[2] The evidence is late and Florence gives no authority for his statement, but it is possible that some of Alfred's

---

[1] C. Plummer, *op. cit.* i, clxi; A. H. Smith, *Three Northumbrian Poems* (London 1933), pp. 42ff. [2] Florence of Worcester i, 273.

verse still survives. At the end of his version of Boethius's *De consolatione philosophiae* there is to be found a translation of the *Metres* of the original into Old English verse. Whether this is by Alfred is still uncertain, but the author of it certainly appears to identify himself with the translator of the prose, and Alfred's authorship of the latter has never been questioned.

We have here then two writers whom later tradition considered to have been the greatest of the Old English Christian poets, and two others said to have been skilled in the composition of vernacular poetry. Only nine lines of the works of Cædmon remain, and none of Aldhelm; Bede is represented by five lines only, and whilst it is possible that rather more of Alfred's verse has survived, we have no reason to suppose that the *Metres*, even if by him, represent his entire output of Christian verse.

Such evidence as this makes it fairly certain that a good deal of the Christian poetry has disappeared. But when we come to consider the subjects and titles of this lost poetry we are as much in the dark as ever. Something is known of Cædmon's subjects, but nothing of those of Aldhelm or Bede. Ælfric refers to a poem on *Judith*, probably identical with that which still survives,[1] and elsewhere he mentions a poem on St Thomas (see p. 92), but these are the only subjects alluded to. The narrative and heroic poetry might have comparatively little chance of a written existence, but it could survive in popular memory long enough for reminiscences of it to appear in later Latin writers. The Christian epic, on the other hand, might more easily achieve a written form, but after the Old English period it could survive only in the monastic libraries, there to be forgotten and to moulder away as it became unintelligible.

[1] C. W. M. Grein, *Bibliothek der Angelsächsischen Prosa* (Cassel 1872) i, 11.

4

OLD ENGLISH PROSE

Despite the fact that a comparatively large proportion of the didactic and religious prose probably still remains, there is good evidence to show that much has been lost, though whether its survival would have proved of much interest or value is more doubtful. Certainly a good many of the manuscripts of still extant works must have disappeared, as is shown by the occasional discovery of odd leaves or fragments of them which have survived only because they were later used as fly-leaves, wrappers, or pastedowns for other manuscripts or for early printed books. Many of the manuscripts of Ælfric are now represented only by a few odd leaves while, in addition to the extant more or less complete versions, there are four fragments of the Laws, three of the West Saxon version of the Gospels, and two of the *Martyrology*, as well as two adjacent leaves of the Old English Hexateuch, and part of a leaf of a bilingual version of the rule of St Chrodegang.[1] But all these works are well represented by other copies, and it is unlikely that the survival of the complete manuscripts of which they once formed part would have led to any appreciable difference in the general picture of Old English prose.

One of the earliest of the Anglo-Saxon scholars was a certain Tobias who, round about 697, succeeded Gebmund as bishop of Rochester. According to Bede, he was learned in Latin, Greek, and Anglo-Saxon, though at this date the last probably means no more than that he was well-versed in the old heroic poetry. So far as we can tell Bede was the first writer of Old English prose, and consequently that prose had its beginnings in Northumbria.[2] Bede tells us that he had himself translated the Lord's Prayer into the

[1] Ker, pp. 1, 11, 74, 81, etc.

[2] Apart, of course, from the Kentish Laws of Æthelberht, Hlothere, and Wihtred. But these are found only in the twelfth-century *Textus Roffensis*, and it is impossible to say to what extent the present versions represent the seventh-century originals.

vernacular, and his disciple Cuthbert describes how, even on his deathbed, the saint was occupied with turning into English part of St John's Gospel and passages from Isidore of Seville.[1] None of these has survived, and if any of his successors continued the task of translation from Latin into Old English their work too has been lost.

English prose in Northumbria was apparently still-born. Certainly it did not survive the Viking invasions, so that when Alfred decided to attempt the re-education of his people he had to start again from the very beginning, and apparently knew nothing of Bede's earlier work. Although all Alfred's translations are probably still extant, it is not surprising to find that other works, now lost, have also been attributed to him, though the evidence for this is usually slight or non-existent. The best case can be made out for the *Handbook*, the origin of which is described at some length by Asser. He tells how, one day, he read to the king a passage from a certain unnamed book. It caught Alfred's fancy, and he asked the bishop to write it down in a book containing psalms and prayers which he carried about with him. Since the book was already full Asser obtained a fresh sheet on which he wrote the extract, following it on succeeding days with others until the sheet was full. These passages the king translated into English, along with others from various authors. He then collected them into a single volume which he gradually increased to the size of a Psalter and called his *Manual* or *Handbook*. It may have been extant as late as the twelfth century when William of Malmesbury included it amongst the works of Alfred. But William's description of the book leads to some difficulties; he makes use of it to correct a statement that Aldhelm's father was the brother of King Ine, and he gives it as his source for Alfred's opinion that Aldhelm was the greatest of the Old English religious poets. Material such as this is hardly what we should have expected to find in the *Handbook* from the description of it given by Asser. It has been suggested that William knew of the account by Asser, and consequently when he came across a manuscript which included, perhaps as its first item, the Alfredian work that we know as the *Soliloquies* or *Blooms*, he may have taken this to be the *Handbook*, and his historical material would then come from other sections of the manuscript, perhaps

[1] C. Plummer, *op. cit.* i, 296, 409, clxii.

unconnected with Alfred.[1] In any case, the circumstantial description by Asser leaves little doubt that the *Handbook* was a genuine work by Alfred which has since been lost.

Most of the other ascriptions are probably due merely to a desire to credit Alfred with some Old English work known to the writer, though it is unlikely that this is the sole reason for the statement by William of Malmesbury that Alfred had begun a translation of the Psalter just before his death. The fact that he considered this version by Alfred to be incomplete would suggest something more concrete than this; perhaps he had seen a prose translation of the first of the three divisions into which the Psalter was often divided, something similar to that of the surviving *Paris Psalter*. Since there seems to be no other instance of William claiming a work for Alfred without some kind of evidence, it is possible that the manuscript he saw, whatever it may have been, had something in it which convinced him that it was by Alfred.[2] Ailred of Rievaulx ascribes to Alfred the translation of parts of the Scriptures, but without particularizing, whilst the twelfth-century chronicler of Ely had no doubt whatever that the king had turned into English the whole of the Old and New Testaments.[3] Presumably the last two writers are here ascribing to Alfred the extant Old English versions of the Bible.

Collections of proverbs have also been attributed to Alfred. Ailred of Rievaulx knew of one, and so did the annalist of Winchester.[4] Whether such ascriptions indicate that the writers had come across copies of the Middle English *Proverbs of Alured*, whether they are simply depending on the tradition of his wisdom, or whether Alfred actually did compile such a collection, it is impossible to say, though the last is perhaps unlikely. Certainly the ascription of the Middle English collection to Alfred, as well as that of numerous single proverbs in different Middle English works, seems to be due merely to his reputation.

[1] Asser, pp. 73ff.; *Gesta Pontificum*, pp. 333, 336; *Gesta Regum* i, 132; *Medieval Literature and Civilization. Studies in Memory of G. N. Garmonsway* (London 1969), pp. 90ff.

[2] *Gesta Regum* i, 132; *Medieval Literature and Civilization*, p. 89. J. Bromwich, in *The Early Cultures of North-West Europe* (Cambridge 1950), pp. 290ff., would in fact ascribe the prose part of the extant *Paris Psalter* to Alfred.

[3] R. Twysden, *Historiae Anglicanae Scriptores* (London 1652), col. 355; *Liber Eliensis*, p. 54.

[4] R. Twysden, *op. cit.*, col. 355; *Annales de Wintonia* (RS. 36) ii, 10.

In the twelfth century Marie de France ascribed to Alfred a series of fables, which she claimed to have translated from English into French at the request of a certain Count William. A similar attribution is to be found in a collection of Latin fables, closely connected with that of Marie de France, preserved in the fourteenth-century MS. Royal 15 A. vii. According to the prologue, they were first written in Greek by Aesop, translated into Latin by the Emperor Romulus, and into English by *rex anglie affrus*[1] – obviously identical with the *reis Alurez* of Marie de France – and in fact it is not unlikely that the Latin collection has borrowed the ascription from her. There is no reason to doubt that Marie was translating from an English original, and it is possible enough that the author of it may have been called Alfred, but it is unlikely that he is to be identified with the king. In all probability the work was a Middle English compilation by some obscure Alfred whom later writers have confused with his more famous namesake.[2]

Florence of Worcester, in a discussion on the genealogy of the West Saxon kings, brings forward in support of one of his statements the evidence of the *dicta Ælfredi*. Similarly, the twelfth-century writer of a note in the margin of a Cambridge manuscript of the *Liber Pontificalis* appeals to the same authority as evidence for some of his statements.[3] Exactly what work the writers had in mind it is impossible to say. It may be that a copy of the *Soliloquies* contained also a certain amount of historical material, whether by the king or not. Since Alfred himself, at the beginning and end of Book III calls this work *þa cwidas*, this would explain the Latin title given to it, and also the ascription to the king of any historical material in the same volume. Otherwise, unless perhaps the *Handbook* was a very different compilation from what would have been expected, the quotations can only refer to some historical work, whether by Alfred or not, of which nothing more is known.

The fourteenth-century catalogue of the library of Christ

---

[1] K. Warnke, *Die Fabeln der Marie de France* (Halle 1898), pp. 327ff.; H. L. D. Ward, *Catalogue of Romances in the Department of Manuscripts in the British Museum* (London 1893) ii, 288ff.

[2] This lost English collection of fables probably provided the text, and perhaps also the model, for the illustrations of a series of fables which form part of the design of the Bayeux Tapestry. See *Romania* lx, 1–35, 153–94.

[3] Florence of Worcester i, 272; *Neues Archiv der Gesellschaft für ältere deutsche Geschichtskunde* xxxv, 424–7.

Church, Canterbury, ascribes to Alfred the authorship of a work on falconry. Item 496 of the catalogue contained various medical treatises, and also the *Liber Aluredi Regis custodiendis accipitribus*.[1] We know from Asser that Alfred was a keen huntsman but, though it is likely enough that such a subject would have interested him, at this date the ascription could only have been traditional. Nor is there anything to show that the treatise was in English, as it certainly would have been if Alfred had written it. Nevertheless it is tempting to connect this entry with the *libri Haroldi*, mentioned as an authority on the same subject in a manuscript of the *De Avibus Tractatus*, written c. 1200 and now in the Nationalbibliothek at Vienna. The treatise is probably by Adelard of Bath, and the Harold referred to would presumably be Harold Godwinesson whom we know from the Bayeux Tapestry to have been interested in falconry.[2] If he possessed books on the subject, they would almost certainly have been in English, and it would have been natural enough that the name of King Alfred should later have become attached to them, whether correctly or not. However any connexion between the two, though perhaps possible, is not very probable. Nor is it likely that either of them could have had anything to do with another book on hawks by King Henry of England, mentioned by Daude de Pradas, a contemporary of the Emperor Frederick II. If the Henry referred to were Henry I, it is barely possible that the book could have been in English. But more probably Henry of Anjou is intended, in which case the 'reference is apparently to a lost work in Provençal, whether prepared under the king's direction or merely dedicated to him does not appear'.[3]

For the next work attributed to Alfred there is only the doubtful evidence of the pseudo-Ingulph. In his description of the Doomsday Survey the author goes on to affirm that a similar inquest had been carried out by Alfred, and that the official documents concerning it were still to be seen at Winchester.[4] Historically, of course, there is nothing to be said for such a story. Probably the author has simply invented it, though he may perhaps have seen some of the separate returns from which Doomsday was compiled and taken these to be the remnants of an earlier survey. Whatever

---

[1] *Canterbury and Dover*, p. 60.
[2] *EHR*. xxxvii, 398ff.   [3] *EHR*. xxxvi, 347.
[4] W. Fulman, *Rerum Anglicarum Scriptorum Veterum* (Oxford 1684) i, 79.

the explanation we can be certain that no such work was carried out by Alfred. Similarly, Geoffrey of Monmouth and the annalist of Winchester mention Alfred's *Laws*, along with others of his works, though whether they are referring to the extant revision by Alfred of the Laws of Ine, to other codes which they have mistakenly connected with the king, or simply depending on tradition is impossible to decide.[1]

It is clear that, in addition to the works actually written by Alfred, a number of other writings have at various times been ascribed to him. The evidence for such attributions varies with the different works, but is only really strong so far as the *Handbook* is concerned. We are justified in regarding this as a genuine lost work of the king, and the various indications concerning its contents suggest, if our authorities are not mistaken, that it may have been a more interesting work than would have been expected from the title or from Asser's account of its inception. It is unlikely that any of the other titles represent genuine works by Alfred. Some of them are probably later productions which owe their attribution to the memory of Alfred's achievements, while others may not even refer to actual works at all, but only be the writer's opinion of what the king might or should have written.

Apart from the translations made by Alfred there appear to have been extant in Old English other versions of some of the standard Latin works of the period, and though these are now lost they were apparently still in existence as late as the twelfth century. In one of his works Giraldus Cambrensis speaks of 'all the English works of Bede, of Rabanus, and of King Alfred',[2] which were written in the West Saxon dialect. The English works of Alfred we know, and it is unlikely that Giraldus knew anything of the genuine English works of Bede – in all probability he is merely referring to the Old English translation of the *Ecclesiastical History*. But nothing else is known of any English versions of the works of Hrabanus. The author referred to was presumably Hrabanus Maurus, archbishop of Mainz, a voluminous Latin writer and one of the most famous theologians of his time. The reference here, and its connexion with Alfred's works, would indicate that some of

[1] A. Griscom, *The Historia Regum Britanniæ of Geoffrey of Monmouth* (London 1929), pp. 282, 293; *Annales de Wintonia* (RS. 36) ii, 10.
[2] *Descriptio Kambriæ*, p. 178.

Hrabanus's works had also been translated into English, possibly by one or other of the scholars inspired by Alfred. There is nothing inherently improbable in this; it would surely have been remarkable had Werfrith been the only one of Alfred's bishops to respond to the king's appeal for translators. Certainly many of Hrabanus's works could usefully have been translated, his educational treatises, his encyclopaedic *De Universo*, or more particularly the *De Institutione Clericorum*. This is mere guesswork, but the evidence of Giraldus is clear enough, and whoever the Rabanus in question may have been, it is certain that no Old English versions of his works have survived.

It is unlikely that any of the works of Ælfric have been lost. The frequent references which he himself makes to various of them cannot always be definitely identified, but it is usually possible to make a fairly certain guess at the work intended, and when this proves difficult it is mainly because of the vagueness of the reference. More interesting is the reason which Ælfric gives for writing in English:

> I saw and heard much error in many English books, which ignorant men because of their innocence accounted to be of much wisdom; and I had pity on them that they knew not and had not the teaching of the gospel in their writings, except for those men alone who knew Latin, and except for the books which King Alfred wisely translated into English, which are to be had.[1]

This must surely indicate the loss of a number of religious works in Old English. Before the time of Ælfric the only such literature in the vernacular of which we know are the works of Alfred, the translation of Gregory's *Dialogues* by Werfrith, and the *Blickling Homilies*. Since Ælfric expressly excludes Alfred's translations from his condemnation – and presumably he would include Werfrith's work with these – we are left with the *Blickling Homilies* in which, so far as we can tell, there is little if anything to deserve Ælfric's blame. Unless he is referring to some of the Old English Christian poems, which is perhaps a possibility, the period between Alfred and Ælfric must have produced a number of popular religious works which were suspect in the eyes of the clergy. If so, it is not surprising that they should have disappeared; the ecclesi-

---

[1] B. Thorpe, *The Homilies of Ælfric* (London 1844) i, 2.

astics would see to it that they were replaced by more orthodox works.

After the time of Ælfric and Wulfstan there is little direct evidence for the loss of much contemporary religious or didactic prose, but the indirect evidence is strong enough. A single leaf from an eleventh-century manuscript, used as padding for a later binding, contains part of an Old English version of the Legend of the Cross, and two other fragments of the same work were found in the bindings of Archbishop Parker's printed books.[1] The complete work survives only in a late twelfth-century version, and the discovery of these leaves confirms the opinion of the editor of this that it was a modernized copy of a lost Old English text. Similarly, two strips among fragments removed from the binding of books in the library of Pembroke College, Cambridge, contain an eleventh-century interlinear gloss to a Psalter of the Gallican version, the remainder of which has vanished.[2] It seems not unlikely, too, that an Old English translation once existed of parts or the whole of the medical works of Alexander of Tralles.[3] Again, the author of the *Liber Eliensis* claims to have made use of a lost Old English work which gave a brief account of the restoration of Ely during the tenth century, a record of the lands acquired by St Æthelwold on behalf of the monastery, and of the pleas which arose from these transactions. The work had been preserved at Ely and, according to the chronicler, was translated into Latin at the instigation of Bishop Hervey, hence at some time between 1109 and 1130. Manuscripts of the Latin translation still survive, but the original Old English version has long since disappeared.[4] Apart from these, the volume of extant Old English prose from the reigns of Cnut and the Confessor is certainly small, but 'there are laws, letters and charters, and under the Confessor we find evidence of many writers of great ability. Sometimes we have only two or three pages extant of each, sometimes less.'[5] Obviously these few surviving pages are unlikely to comprise the entire output of such authors.

In historical writing there is little evidence for the loss of much

---

[1] *Speculum* xxxvii, 60–78; *Medium Ævum* ix, 84–5.   [2] Ker, p. 126.
[3] G. Storms, *Anglo-Saxon Magic* (The Hague 1948), pp. 19, 21, 23.
[4] *Liber Eliensis*, pp. xxxiv, 63–4, 369.
[5] *Continuity of English Prose*, p. lxviii.

of importance. Many manuscripts of the *Old English Chronicle* have certainly disappeared, and no doubt some of them may have contained occasional valuable details, but on the whole it is unlikely that they included much that is not to be found in one or the other of the extant texts. William of Malmesbury evidently made use of a lost version of the *Old English Chronicle* of the E type, as also did the author of the *Liber Eliensis*; C.U.L. MS. Hh. 1. 10, a manuscript of Ælfric's *Grammar and Glossary*, formerly contained some Old English annals which disappeared when the volume was illicitly borrowed from Cambridge in the seventeenth century, and these are now lost, unless perhaps they are the extant ff. 30–70 of MS. Cotton Domitian viii.[1] Gaimar mentions a Winchester chronicle as one of his sources. It is unlikely that this could have been the extant Parker manuscript, since this was presumably then at Canterbury, but it may have been the lost one now represented only by the annals for 1113 and 1114, or alternatively a version of which no other trace now remains. Elsewhere Gaimar includes among his

> Liueres Engleis, e par gramaire,
> E en Romanz, e en Latin,

le liuere Walter Espac, le bon liuere de Oxeford/Ki fust Walter larcediaen, the *estorie de Wincestre,* and *de Wassingburc vn liuere Engleis.* The first of these was clearly a copy of Geoffrey of Monmouth's *Historia Regum Britanniae,* while the *estorie de Wincestre* was the version of the *Old English Chronicle* mentioned above. The second and the fourth are more difficult to identify. It is tempting to connect *le bon liuere de Oxeford* with the alleged British book, borrowed from Archdeacon Walter of Oxford, which Geoffrey of Monmouth claimed as his source. However, scholars are inclined to doubt the existence of any such work, nor is the book used by Gaimar said to have been in British. The last of Gaimar's sources evidently had some connexion with the present unimportant village of Washingborough in Kesteven, but its contents must remain uncertain. The description given,

> V il trouad escrit des reis,
> E de tuz les emperurs
> Ke de Rome furent seignurs
> E de Engleterre ourent trev,

[1] Ker, p. 22.

would perhaps suggest a copy of Alfred's translation of Orosius, or of the Old English version of Bede, though it is impossible to say why such a work should have been connected with this Kesteven village.[1]

A fair number of Old English books appear in the extant twelfth-century catalogues of monastic libraries, but these are mostly incomplete, and it is only rarely that their English items sound at all interesting. The twelfth-century catalogue of Rochester Cathedral shows only:

> Pastoralis anglicus in uno volumine . . .
> Sermonalia anglica in duobus voluminibus.[2]

The first of these is underlined, and may already have been lost when the catalogue was drawn up. It is not known to exist today, and does not appear in the catalogue drawn up in 1202, but it can only have been a copy of Alfred's translation of the *Cura Pastoralis*. The two volumes of homilies are MSS. Bodl. 340 and 342,[3] and they duly appear again in the later catalogue, which also includes a *Medicinale anglicum*, apparently lost, but presumably simply a version of one or the other of the extant late Old English medical works.

Similarly the early twelfth-century catalogue of Peterborough shows only two works:

> 54. Vite sanctorum anglice . . .
> 65. Elfredi regis liber anglicus.[4]

The first was probably a copy, not now extant, of Ælfric's *Lives of the Saints*. The second was presumably one of Alfred's translations, though it might have been the Peterborough manuscript of the *Old English Chronicle*, which otherwise finds no place in the catalogue.

The library of the Benedictine abbey at Burton-on-Trent seems to have contained a comparatively large number of works in English when a catalogue of it was drawn up c. 1175:

> 71. Omeliarium anglicum.
> 72. Psalterium anglicum.

---

[1] Gaimar i, 93, 275-6.

[2] *Archaeologia Cantiana* vi, 120ff.; iii, 54ff.

[3] For these and other identifications, see N. R. Ker, *Medieval Libraries of Great Britain* (London 1964).

[4] *Trans. Bib. Soc.*, *Supplement* v, p. 28.

73. Passionale anglicum.
74. Dialogum Gregorii et historiam Anglorum angl'.
75. Apollonium angl'.
76. Evangelistas angl'.
77. Ymnarium angl'.[1]

None of the manuscripts appears to have survived, but other copies of the works are known, and some of these, which show no signs of provenance, may be the ones listed here. Few of the items are of any interest. Volumes of Old English homilies are not infrequent, and it is unlikely that this particular one contained anything out of the way. Similarly with the Old English versions of the Psalter, the Gospels, and the Passional; their interest, if any, would have been linguistic rather than literary. Extant copies are available of the translation of Gregory's *Dialogues*, as also of that of Bede's *Ecclesiastical History*. The Hymnary might have been, and the version of *Apollonius of Tyre* probably would have been more interesting. The latter is extant in a single incomplete text (C.C.C.C. MS. 201), the provenance of which is unknown, but since it seems impossible to connect it with Burton, it is probable that the one referred to here, which could have contained a more complete version of the work, is now lost.

When a catalogue of the library of Durham Cathedral was drawn up early in the twelfth century the following English works were to be found there:

Libri Anglici. Omeliaria vetera duo. Unum novum. Elfledes Boc. Historia Anglorum Anglice. Liber Paulini Anglicus. Liber de Nativitate Sanctæ Mariæ Anglicus. Cronica duo Anglica.[2]

C.U.L. MS. Gg. 3. 28, a tenth or eleventh-century manuscript from Durham, and the most complete surviving copy of Ælfric's *Sermones catholici*, is probably one of the three volumes of homilies noted here, but nothing is known of the other two. The *Elfledes Boc* looks interesting. No indication of the identity of Elfled is given, though a Lady Elfleda, daughter of Offa of Mercia and wife of Æthelred of Northumbria, possibly the same as the Ælflæd referred to in the Lindisfarne *Liber Vitae*, is mentioned by Symeon of Durham, s.a. 792. If this were the Elfled in question, the book was presumably a gift by her to the cathedral library, and no guess

---

[1] *Centralblatt für Bibliothekswesen* ix, 201–2. [2] SS. vii, 5ff.

can be made at its contents, though it would be rather surprising if a book in Old English were in existence at this date. However, there is another Elfled connected with Durham. When the tomb of St Cuthbert was opened in 1827, there were found in the coffin an embroidered stole, a maniple, a girdle, and two golden bracelets. On the reverses of the end of the stole and maniple, in the style of the tenth-century Winchester school, was embroidered AELFLAED FIERI PRECEPIT PIO EPISCOPO FRIÐ-ESTANO. Frithestan was bishop of Winchester from 909 to 931, and the stole may have come into the hands of King Athelstan on the death of the bishop. If so, it may be identical with the *unam stolam cum manipulo* mentioned amongst the donations of Athelstan to the shrine of St Cuthbert during his northern expeditions of 934 and 937. The identity of the names might then suggest that *Elfledes Boc* could also have been one of the gifts of Athelstan to St Cuthbert. Along with the stole and maniple he is said to have presented a missal, two texts of the Gospels, and a life of St Cuthbert in prose and verse.[1] The last of these is probably the extant C.C.C.C. MS. 183, which is in Latin. One of the manuscripts of the Gospels was destroyed in the Cottonian fire, but since it is said to have been written in France it could hardly have been the English book mentioned here. Consequently, if *Elfledes Boc* was one of the gifts of Athelstan, and if we have a complete list of his donations – both doubtful possibilities – then presumably the work in question was an English version of the Gospels, though we know of none in existence as early as this. As for the Elfled in question, it is probably significant that this was the name of Athelstan's stepmother.

The *Historia Anglorum Anglice* was presumably a copy of the Alfredian translation of Bede, but the *Liber Paulini Anglicus* is more difficult to identify. The only Paulinus of whom we know in connexion with Northumbria is the missionary of that name. If he is the man referred to here, the book could perhaps have been a collection of extracts from the Old English version of Bede. There is no record that Paulinus himself ever wrote any books, much less any English ones, though he presumably spoke the language. Perhaps the book contained some kind of elementary religious instruction written for the benefit of his new converts,

[1] W. de G. Birch, *Cartularium Saxonicum* (London 1885–93), no. 685.

or more probably it was some English book traditionally connected with him. The only other writers of the name now known are Paulinus of Nola and Paulinus of Aquileia. A verse account of the martyrdom of St Felix written by the former was turned into prose by Bede, and this could perhaps have been an otherwise unknown English version of Bede's work. The *Cronica duo Anglica* were presumably copies of the *Old English Chronicle*. None of the extant manuscripts was written in the North, but the northern material incorporated in some of them indicates that versions of it were in use there The lost original of D was probably northern, and Symeon of Durham, writing in the first quarter of the twelfth century, seems to have made use of a form of the *Old English Chronicle* closely related to the ancestor of E.

When later catalogues of the Durham Cathedral library were drawn up, in 1391 and 1416, these English books seem already to have been lost. In them the only books given as being in English are:

Regula Sancti Benedicti in Latino, et eadem Regula in Anglico. ii fo. 'Psalterium petri' . . .
Donatus Anglice. ii fo. 'i. de' or hoc milite'.[1]

The first is the extant Durham Cathedral MS. B. IV. 24, while the second is St John's College, Oxford, MS. 154, a copy of Ælfric's *Grammar and Glossary*, the second folio of which begins *ðeos boc mihte*.

A fragmentary catalogue of the library of Christ Church, Canterbury, drawn up c. 1170, contains only a single book in English, item 27 being a *Donatus Anglice*, presumably a copy of Ælfric's *Grammar and Glossary*. But the library must have possessed more than this, since the catalogue of Prior Henry of Eastry (c. 1330) shows at least nineteen manuscripts containing Old English writings, a comparatively large proportion of which still survive. Of these, item 296 is almost certainly MS. Cotton Tiberius A. iii, containing a continuous Old English gloss to the Rule of St Benedict and to the *Regularis Concordia*, but item 297, in which were the following Old English works, appears to have been lost:

Expositiones de Prisciano exposite Anglice.
Locutio latina glosata Anglice ad instruendos pueros . . .

[1] SS. vii, 30, 33, 107, 111.

Regula beati Benedicti glosata, Anglice . . .
Consuetudines de faciendo seruicio diuino per annum, glosate Anglice.

None of these is of any great interest. The first two were presumably versions of Ælfric's *Grammar and Glossary* and of his *Colloquy*, and manuscripts of the Rule of St Benedict with Old English glosses still survive. The last item was perhaps a glossed copy of the *De ecclesiasticis officiis* by Amalarius, a work which was extremely popular in England; it was well known to Æthelwold and Ælfric, who both mention it, while the latter also translated passages from the book.

Much more interesting are items 304–20, headed *Libri Anglici*, in the same catalogue:

304. Genesis Anglice depicta.
305. Liber Passionum et Sermones Anglice.
306. Dialogus beati Gregorii.
307. Boeicius de consolatione.
308. Herbarius Anglice depictus.
309. Liber sermonum catholicorum Anglice.
310. Liber sermonum beati Augustini a.
311. Cronica uetustissima a. (C.C.C.C. MS. 173)
312. Liber de ordine monastico a.
313. Cronica secundum Bedam a.
314. Textus iv Euangeliorum Anglice. (MS. Royal 1 A. xiv)
315. Actus apostolorum Anglice.
316. Liber Sermonum Anglice.
317. Regula Canonicorum a.
318. Cronica Latine et Anglice. (MS. Cotton Domitian viii)
319. Liber Edwini a.
320. Excepciones de Prisciano a.[1]

Three of these certainly remain, and so probably do some of the others. No. 304 may perhaps be MS. Junius 11, the 'Cædmonian' manuscript of Old English Christian poetry. No. 305 cannot now be identified, but appears to have been merely a collection of homilies, as also were 309 – probably by Ælfric – and 316. No. 306 was a copy of Werfrith's translation of Gregory's *Dialogues*, and may perhaps be represented by Canterbury Cathedral, MS. Add. 25, fragments of two adjacent leaves which had been used as wrappers. No. 307 was presumably a copy of Alfred's translation of

---

[1] *Canterbury and Dover*, pp. 8, 50ff.

Boethius, and though 308 has been identified with MS. Cotton Vitellius C. iii, there is nothing to show any definite connexion between that manuscript and the entry here. Nothing is known of any translation of the sermons of St. Augustine (310), but the title could represent a lost manuscript of Alfred's version of the *Soliloquies*. No. 312 was presumably a customary, since lost, while the Old English version of Bede (313) has been wrongly identified with C.U.L. MS. Kk. 3. 18. No Old English translation of Acts (315) is now known, and no. 317 is probably represented by Canterbury Cathedral, Box ccc no. xix*a*, two leaves which had been used as the wrapper for a small book, and containing part of an Old English version of the rule of Chrodegang of Metz. The *Liber Edwini* was presumably one of the works of the early twelfth-century scribe Eadwine whose Bible and Psalter occur later in the catalogue, the second of these being the famous *Canterbury Psalter*, while the last item was probably another copy of Ælfric's *Grammar and Glossary*.

It is unfortunate that no complete catalogue of the library of Bury St Edmunds has survived. It was one of the oldest and most important of the English monasteries, and an examination of the press-marks in the extant manuscripts from the library suggests that it may have contained over two thousand volumes. A fragmentary catalogue from the late twelfth or early thirteenth century shows only two works in English:

169. Magnus liber sermonum in anglica lingua . . .
258. Regula beati Benedicti Latine et anglice.[1]

The first may be MS. Cotton Julius E. vii, which is certainly from Bury and contains some of the homilies of Ælfric, while the second is perhaps the extant C.C.C., Oxford, MS. 197. Another reminder of lost volumes from this library is provided by the discovery on the site of the abbey of 'A leaden tablet inscribed with a portion of one of Ælfric's homilies – probably the front cover of an MS. volume of the Homilies'.[2]

The monastery at Glastonbury might be expected to have been fairly rich in English books, but when the extant catalogue of the

---

[1] M. R. James, *On the Abbey of St Edmund at Bury* (Cambridge Antiquarian Society, Communications, 1895), pp. 30, 32.
[2] C. Fox, *Archaeology of the Cambridge Region* (Cambridge 1923), p. 300.

library was drawn up in 1247–8 little of interest remained. Amongst the *Diversi libri de bibliotheca* were:

> Penthateucum Moysy & Josue & Judicum sine glosa. vetust.
> Item duo Anglica vetusta et inutilia.

The only historical work in English was a copy of Alfred's translation of Orosius – 'old but still legible'. Homiletic literature was rather better represented:

> Liber de diversis sermonibus Anglicis.
> Item sermones Anglici. vetust. inutil.
> Passionale Sanctorum Anglice script. vetust. inutil.
> Item quidem liber Anglice.

In addition there was a *Medicinale Anglicum*. Apparently these were the only English books in the library. None of them sounds particularly interesting, and all seem to have been lost.[1]

Equally disappointing is the inventory of the books of the cathedral library of Exeter drawn up in 1327. In view of the donations of Leofric a fair number of Old English books might have been expected, but the only ones mentioned are:

> Martelogium Latinum et Anglicum quod sic incipit Circumcisio.
> Psalterium interlineare glosatura de Anglico precii 2*s*.
> Penitentiale uetus et alia plura cum anglico in fine quod sic incipit In principio prec' xij *d*.

The first is probably C.C.C.C. MS. 196, an eleventh-century martyrology certainly from Exeter, while the last is C.C.C.C. MS. 190, the second part of which contains various ecclesiastical institutes, etc., in Old English. However, despite the lack of notice of them in the catalogue, it is certain that there must have been other Old English manuscripts at Exeter at this date. An eleventh-century copy of the Old English translation of Bede (C.C.C.C. MS. 41), and the *Exeter Book* of Old English poetry, as well as an eleventh-century version of the Gospels (C.U.L. MS. Ii. 2. 11), are all certainly from Exeter, yet none of them can be identified with any of the entries in the catalogue. In fact, at the end of it there is a brief note to the effect that the library contained also 'many other books, written in French, English, and Latin, wasted with age,

---

[1] T. W. Williams, *Somerset Mediæval Libraries* (Somerset Arch. Soc. 1897), pp. 55–78.

to which no value is assigned since they are thought to be worth nothing'.[1]

The late fifteenth-century catalogue of St. Augustine's, Canterbury, in addition to some Middle English works, contained two in Old English:

> 95. Genesis anglic'. 2° fo. *and sylðus*.
> 991. Boecius de consolacione philosophie in Anglicis. 2° fo. *vtterest*.[2]

The first is MS. Cotton Claudius B. iv, while the second, not now known to exist, was presumably a copy of Alfred's translation.

English works occasionally appear in other lists of books, but though the actual manuscript may no longer survive, the work itself is usually well enough known. So, for example, with the list of books given to the cathedral library of Exeter by Bishop Leofric (d. 1072). This contains the following manuscripts in Old English:

> . . . þeos Englisce Cristes-boc . . . & regula canonicorum, & martyrlogium . . . & scrift-boc on Englisc . . . & Boeties boc on Englisc, & .i. mycel Englisc boc be ge-hwilcum þingum on leoðwisan ge-worht.[3]

The first is C.U.L. MS. Ii. 2. 11, containing the West Saxon translation of the Gospels; the second is probably C.C.C.C. MS. 191, a copy of the bilingual rule of Chrodegang; the *scrift-boc*, a penitential, may be C.C.C.C. MS. 190; while the last volume is the present Exeter Cathedral MS. 3501. In fact the only one of these that has been lost is the translation of Boethius.

On fo. 48v of C.C.C.C. MS. 367 is a short list of English books:

> Ðeo englissce passionale. and ii englissce dialogas. and Oddan boc. and þe englisca martirlogium. and ii englisce salteras. and ii pastorales englisce. and þe englisca regol. and Barontus.[4]

In the same manuscript is a letter from Hubert and Edwius, abbot and prior of Westminister, to the prior of Worcester, so that the manuscript may originally have belonged to the cathedral church of Worcester. If so, the library no longer possesses any of the books mentioned. The list is not particularly interesting. The *dialogas*

---

[1] G. Oliver, *Lives of the Bishops of Exeter* (Exeter 1861), pp. 301–10.

[2] *Canterbury and Dover*, pp. 201, 302.

[3] R. W. Chambers, R. Flower, M. Förster, *The Exeter Book* (London 1933), pp. 10–32.

[4] A. J. Robertson, *Anglo-Saxon Charters* (Cambridge 1956), p. 250.

are two copies of the translation by Werfrith, and since the extant manuscripts of this work – MSS. Cotton Otho C. i and Bodl. Hatton 76 – are from Worcester, they are probably the two referred to here. The *Old English Martyrology* seems to have been written somewhere in West Mercia, but there is no reason to suppose that the copy here is to be identified with any of the extant manuscripts. The *pastorales* are probably MSS. C.C.C.C. 12 and Bodl. Hatton 20. The *regol* was presumably a copy of either the Old English version of the rule of St Benedict or of that of Chrodegang of Metz. The title of *oddan boc* is ambiguous; it may refer to a former owner, or it may have dealt with someone called Odda. Several of that name were connected with Worcester, the best known being Odo the Good, archbishop of Canterbury and uncle of St Oswald. Since the book is not said to have been in English, it may perhaps have been the Latin *Vita Odonis* of Eadmer, or the first part of the anonymous *Vita Sancti Oswaldi*. The last item presumably dealt with the vision of the sixth-century St Barontus of Pistoja, and may have been in Latin; if in English it has certainly not survived.

A short list of books has been entered in a thirteenth-century hand in the lower margin of MS. Cotton Otho C. i. The manuscript suffered in the Cottonian fire, and consequently the list is now imperfect:

> Libri dialogorum gre. . . . . Vitas patrum. Item Beda de gestis anglorum/Item vita et m. . . . . synonima ysydori. Item Boecius/De consola. . . . .[1]

Opposite the second line of the list is the word *Anglic'*, though whether this refers to all the works mentioned, or to one only of them, it is impossible to say. The manuscript itself is a composite one, the first part coming from Malmesbury, the second part – in which the list occurs – from Worcester. The extant C.U.L. MS. Kk. 3. 18, containing an English version of Bede, is from Worcester and could be the book referred to here.

During the sixteenth century, just before the final dissolution of the monasteries, John Leland was commissioned to visit them and to inspect the libraries with a view to the possible transference of their most important works to the King's Library. In the course

[1] Ker, p. 237.

of his journeys he jotted down the titles of any interesting books he came across, and some of these are said to be in English. At Southwick he notes an Old English version of Bede (MS. Cotton Otho B. xi), which was also seen there by Thomas Rudbourne (fl. 1460) who quotes two lines from it in his *Historia Maior*; in the Cambridge University Library there was an English version of Boethius, and the Dominicans in the same town possessed a *Biblia in lingua vernacula*. At Glastonbury he found an *Orosius Saxonice* – probably the copy listed in the extant catalogue – and a *Dictionarium Latino-Saxonicum*. Wells had an English version of Gregory's *Dialogues* and a volume of Ælfric's homilies, whilst Ælfric's *Grammar and Glossary* was at Pershore. There was a *Pars veteris testamenti Saxonice* at Abbotsbury, and a *Leges aliquot regum Saxonice* at Christchurch (Twinham). More interesting is the suggestion of a lost historical work from the Premonstratensian abbey of Tupholme. Leland gives a description of the burial of St Oswald at Bardney taken, he says, *ex veteri chronico, Anglice scripto*, which he found at the abbey. Whether this was in Old or Middle English it is impossible to say; at all events it does not appear to have survived. At Ely a note records the presence in the library there of,

A writen booke of a 20. leves founde in an holow stone, kyverid with a stone in digging for a foundation at Yvy cherch by Serisbyri.

With this may be compared Leland's description of a find at Harlaxton, near Grantham:

a stone, under the wich was a potte of brasse, and an helmet of gold, sette with stones in it, the which was presentid to Catarine Princes Dowager. There were bedes of silver in the potte: and writings corruptid.

Unfortunately in neither case is any information given as to the language of the writings concerned.[1]

Two Old English versions of the Gospels are noted in an inventory of the goods of the monastery of Waltham, dated 31 Henry VIII:

A Gospler of the Saxon Tongue, havynge thone syde plated with sylver parcell gilte with ye ymage of Cryst. . . .

[1] *Collectanea* iv; Leland i, 28.

> An another Gospler of the Saxon Tonge, with the Crusifixe and Mary and John, havyng a naked man holdyng up his hands of sylver gilte.[1]

Purvey, in a treatise written in 1405, mentions a Bible in English:

> Also a man of Loundon, his name was Wyring, hadde a Bible in Englische of northen speche, wiche was seen of many men, and it semed too honndred yeer olde.[2]

This was probably an Old English version, and may have been one of the manuscripts still extant. Tyndale, in his *Obedience of a Christian Man*, claims, 'except my memory fail me', to have seen an account in 'the English chronicle' of how Athelstan caused the scriptures to be translated into Old English.[3] Probably his memory had failed him, and if he saw anything of the kind the king referred to would more likely have been Alfred than Athelstan.

It is evident enough that a good deal of the didactic and religious literature of the Old English period has been lost, but the available evidence suggests that comparatively few of such lost works would have been of any particular interest.

---

[1] *Trans. of the Royal Historical Society* vi, 265.
[2] M. Deanesly, *The Lollard Bible* (Cambridge 1920), p. 441.
[3] J. F. Mozley, *William Tyndale* (London 1937), p. 8.

5

SAINTS' LIVES

Throughout the Middle Ages the lives of saints were popular subjects of literature, if only because many of them combined the merits of devotional reading with the attraction of the marvellous. The lives were usually written in Latin, but popular demand, and the attempts of the church to provide a substitute for more secular literature, soon led to the appearance of versions in the vernacular. Many such lives still survive in both Old and Middle English, but inevitably some have been lost. This type of literature, although free from many of the dangers which threatened the continued existence of more secular works, was not entirely exempt from the ravages of time or the danger of accident. Osbern, a monk of Christ Church, Canterbury, wrote his life of Dunstan because of the loss of many of their books in a great fire, while the author of the *De Sanctis Ecclesiae Haugustaldensis* undertook his task because the library at Hexham, containing numerous lives of the saints, had been completely destroyed during the Viking invasions.[1]

It is particularly fitting that any account of lost vernacular lives of the saints should begin with the protomartyr of Britain, St Alban. During the second half of the twelfth century his life was written in Latin by a certain William of St Albans, who claimed to be making use of an Old English work on the passion of the saint.[2] Homilies dealing with the life of St Alban are still extant, but it seems certain that none of these could have been the source used by William, which must long since have been lost. In fact, if we could trust the chronicler of St Albans, it would seem that this is neither the only, nor even the earliest, life of the saint to have disappeared. In the time of Abbot Eadmer, while various excavations were being carried out, a number of books and rolls were found hidden in a hole in a wall. Most of them contained

---

[1] *Memorials of St Dunstan* (RS. 63), p. 70; SS. xliv, 190.
[2] *ASS. June* v, 129.

pagan rites and invocations and these were immediately destroyed, only a single volume with the life of St Alban, 'written in the English or the British language', being preserved. At the command of the abbot this was translated into Latin by a certain priest called Unwona and, as soon as the translation had been completed, the original immediately crumbled into dust.[1] Despite the circumstantial detail, it is difficult to believe in the former existence of a British version of the life of St Alban, or if it had been discovered in this way that it could then have been read; the propaganda value of the tale is too obvious, and the unfortunate disappearance of the original immediately after it had been translated into Latin is particularly suspicious. The whole account is reminiscent of the discovery at the same monastery, in 1178, of the body of St Amphibalus, a discovery which, according to the chronicler, confirmed the account that had been handed down from ancient times in the book of his martyrdom.[2] But since the saint in question is probably no more than a late personification of St Alban's cloak, it is difficult to believe that the book could have been quite as ancient as the chronicler wishes us to assume.

St Helena – another famous saint whom medieval legend connected with Britain – also appears to have had her life written in an English version no longer in existence. A Latin account of her life was composed during the second half of the twelfth century by Jocelyn of Furness, and this is said to be based on an Old English work, the author of which claims to be translating from the British.[3] We need not, perhaps, take the supposed British original too seriously, but there seems no reason to disbelieve Jocelyn's statement that he is using an Old English life of the saint. The poem by Cynewulf, preserved in the *Vercelli Book*, or Ælfric's homily on the Invention of the Cross, can hardly have been Jocelyn's source, and it must be assumed to be lost.

One of the more obscure saints of the early period is a certain St Lewinna, said to have been a British virgin who was put to death during the fifth or sixth century by the Saxon invaders. She was particularly venerated at her minster at 'Sevordh' (possibly Seaford in Sussex), whence her relics were removed – without the

---

[1] *Gesta Abbatum Monasterii S. Albani* (RS. 28) i, 26.
[2] Roger of Wendover, *Chronica* (RS. 84) i, 115.
[3] MS. Bodl. 240 (2469), p. 801a.

consent of the owners – to the monastery of St Winnoc at Bergues. A description of the translation was written soon afterwards by Drogo, a monk of St Winnoc, in the course of which he tells of a guide to the merits of the saint, written in English and fixed to the wall of the minster at 'Sevordh'.[1] This guide has, of course, long since vanished; the interest of the story lies mainly in the fact that it provides an example of a kind of writing of which we hear little, but which may have been a good deal more common in medieval times than is supposed.[2] Dugdale gives 'the copie of the Table that was hanging in the Priorie of Stone, at the time of the Suppression of the same, in the xxix. yeare of the Raigne of our Soveraign Lord King Henry the VIII', and this included 162 lines of verse describing the foundation and benefactors of the monastery.[3] In the same priory were to be found 382 lines on the lives of St Wulfhad and St Ruffin, written or painted upon a table on the epistle side of the choir, and now known only from a transcript in one of the Cotton manuscripts.[4] An English life of St Wulfstan, comprising 75 stanzas in rhyme royal with an eight-line envoy, copied during the seventeenth century into a manuscript now in the Lambeth Library, was apparently originally written on parchment and attached to a triptych, possibly in Bawburgh Church, Norfolk.[5] In one of the Dodsworth manuscripts in the Bodleian is a catalogue of forty-three miracles of St William of York, said to have been copied 'out of a table in the Revestry in the Cathedrall Church of York'.[6] Similarly, an inventory of the goods of St George's Chapel, Windsor, made in 1384, includes a wooden table containing the passion of St George.[7] However, the most famous of such tables was the *magna tabula* at Glastonbury, now in the Bodleian, which 'told in full the stories of St Joseph of Arimathea and of King Arthur, of St Patrick and his Charter, and of the translation of St Dunstan, and much besides'. The following description shows how it was possible for them to contain so much writing, though no doubt the Glastonbury one was more elaborate than most:

It was a folding wooden frame, 3 ft. 8 in. in height, and 3 ft. 6 in. in breadth when opened flat, containing two wooden leaves some-

[1] *Monumenta Germaniae Historica, Scriptores* XV, 2, 784.
[2] See *Speculum* i, 439ff.   [3] *Monasticon* vi, 230.
[4] G. H. Gerould, *Saints' Legends* (New York 1916), pp. 273–5.
[5] *Proceedings of the Norfolk and Norwich Arch. Soc.* xix, 250.
[6] *Yorkshire Archaeological Journal* iii, 210.   [7] *Monasticon* vi, 1364.

what smaller, so that they may fold within the outer case when closed, like the pages of a book. All the six interior faces are covered with MS. written upon parchment affixed to the surface of the wood. There are three pairs of nail holes in the upper, and four pairs in the lower edges of the frame, upon the left hand only. These seem to show that it was affixed to a wall in such a way that it might be opened out as a book. The whole MS. takes up about sixty pages, clearly written, of ordinary exercise book size.[1]

Numerous lives of Anglo-Saxon saints are still extant in the vernacular, either individually or in collections of various kinds, and there are also references to others which have since disappeared. St Oswald of Northumbria appears to have been one of the most popular of the native saints, and his life and death are described in some detail by Bede. A later biographer, Reginald of Durham, writing in the middle of the twelfth century, claims to have obtained much of his information from English sources. The natural assumption is that he is referring either to the Old English version of Bede, or to Ælfric's life of the king, but the statement is preceded by an interesting and detailed description of Oswald's person such as is found in neither of these sources. The king is said to have been tall, with yellow hair, a long face, bright protruding eyes of bluish-grey, and a sparse beard. His lips were rather thin and wore a kindly smile, while his hands and arms were of great length and strength. This information Reginald had received from a certain Robert, a brother of the hospital at York, who had obtained it from a very old book written in English.[2] The description sounds authentic enough, and there is no reason to disbelieve Brother Robert, but the book used by him is certainly not in existence today.

Thomas of Ely, the twelfth-century author of part of the *Liber Eliensis*, claims to have used English sources, though their precise nature is not always specified. When telling of the miracles of St Etheldreda he refers to 'a small book containing her life written

[1] J. A. Robinson, *Two Glastonbury Legends* (Cambridge 1926), pp. 41–2. Compare also the 100 lines of English verse on a table in the hall of St Helen's Hospital, Culham, set up in 1457 by Richard Fannand in honour of the part taken by Geoffrey Barbour in the building of Culham Bridge (Leland v, 113ff.).

[2] Symeon of Durham i, 349. In addition, Reginald claims to have made use of a very old book for his description of some of the miracles at Bardney (Symeon of Durham i, 372).

in English'. Similarly, a reference to St Felix, bishop of East Anglia, unmistakably indicates an English source for his information, though this may not have been a life of the saint. On the other hand, an equally vague reference to St Sexburg almost certainly is to a life in the vernacular. The author of a Latin life of the saint in MS. Cotton Caligula A. viii claims to be making use of Saxon authorities; and that these included an English life of St Sexburg is shown by the fact that a fragment of it is still extant in MS. Lambeth 427, and this was clearly the work used by the author of the Latin life.[1]

A rather indefinite account of the sources for his life of St Aldhelm is given by Faricius (d. 1117), a foreigner who became abbot of Abingdon. They are said to have included works *barbarice atque Latine*, and the first of these words presumably refers to Old English works. More particularly he mentions a volume, written *lucido stylo*, which had been either lost or badly damaged during the Viking invasions, and again, when giving a list of the works of Aldhelm, he tells us that the account was taken from an ancient volume still in the library at Malmesbury. It is impossible to tell whether the English sources included a life of the saint, and he is hardly likely himself to have had much knowledge of the language. But in the prologue he claims that, in dealing with the Old English material, he had utilized the services of an interpreter, so that works in that language could have been used by him.[2] However, the probability is that his vernacular sources were official documents such as charters rather than any connected narrative of the saint's life.

One of the greatest of the Anglo-Saxon saints was Dunstan, round whose name legends seem to have gathered at a very early date. Various Latin lives are extant, and in that written towards the end of the eleventh century by Osbern of Canterbury, the author tells of a disastrous fire at the monastery which had destroyed a number of saints' lives. In order to supply the deficiency he intends to translate into Latin an English life of Dunstan.[3] Similar statements are found in the life of the same saint by Eadmer, and he may independently have made use of the

---

[1] *Liber Eliensis*, pp. 6, 17, 51; cf. Hardy i, 360.
[2] *Patrologia Latina* lxxxix, col. 64, 71, 65, and cf. *Gesta Pontificum*, p. 331.
[3] *Memorials of St Dunstan* (RS. 63), p. 70.

Old English work, no longer in existence, which had been translated by the earlier writer.

One of the items in the thirteenth-century catalogue of the library of Leominster is a *Rotula cum uita sancti Guthlaci anglice scripta*.[1] St Guthlac was a seventh-century hermit of Croyland whose life was written in Latin soon after his death by Felix of Croyland. Various lives in Old and Middle English still survive, but it seems unlikely that any of them can represent the entry here. The three extant Old English versions – the poem in the *Exeter Book* and prose lives in two Cotton manuscripts – are in codices not rolls, and the three manuscripts containing Middle English versions of the life were all written at a date subsequent to the drawing up of this catalogue. The Leominster roll may perhaps be a lost vernacular life of the saint, but more probably it was merely a copy of one of the extant lives, or perhaps an extract from one of the legendaries.

It is particularly fitting that Bishop Wulfstan of Worcester should have been the last of the Anglo-Saxon saints to have his life written in the vernacular. He did not die until 1095, and his long occupation of the see resulted in the continuation of the Old English literary traditions at Worcester until well after the Conquest. Soon after his death a life of him was written in English by his chaplain Colman. But by this time the knowledge of the Old English literary language must have been dying out at Worcester, and when, in the early years of the twelfth century, William of Malmesbury visited the monastery, he was asked by the monks to translate Colman's work into Latin. It is to this translation which, according to William of Malmesbury, closely follows the Old English original, that we owe our knowledge of Colman's life of the saint. However, the Old English life was apparently still in existence at the beginning of the thirteenth century when negotiations were in progress for the canonization of Wulfstan. The papal delegates, in addition to satisfying themselves about the genuineness of certain miracles reported to have been worked by the saint, arranged that there should be sent to the Pope, under the seals of the bishop and convent, the authentic history of his life written a hundred years before in the English language. There can be little doubt that this was the work by Colman, and the

---

[1] *EHR.* iii, 124.

probability is that it remained in Rome. At any rate there is no record that the book ever returned to England. It is possible, too, that this was not the only saint's life written in English by Colman, since William of Malmesbury claims to have re-translated into Latin passages from the life of St Gregory which, 'together with many others', Colman had turned into English.[1]

It is natural enough that the lives of the great Anglo-Saxon saints should have been written in the vernacular; it is more surprising to find that there was formerly in existence an Old English version of the life of St Quentin, of which only the beginning – nine lines in a late twelfth-century hand in MS. Cotton Vitellius A. xv – now remains. So far as can be judged from this, the Old English life was merely a free translation of the existing Latin *Passio*, and had the complete work survived it would have been of comparatively little interest.[2] In another Cotton manuscript, in an eleventh-century hand, is a somewhat longer fragment of *Jamnes and Mambres*, 'a legend that had been pretty thoroughly destroyed elsewhere than in England'.[3] One of the manuscripts badly damaged in the fire of 1731 – MS. Cotton Otho B. x – apparently contained an Old English version of the *Passio de Sancta Margareta*, but the legend is known from two extant Old English texts, and it is unlikely that this lost one contained anything new.[4] Similarly with the Old English version of the life of St Machutus in MS. Cotton Otho A. viii; this manuscript too was badly damaged in the fire, and only fragments of about half the folios containing the work now remain. Most of what is known about it comes from the description in Wanley's catalogue, and from this it seems clear that the Old English was in the main based on the Latin life by Bili, though with some omissions and additions.[5] In addition there must once have existed an Old English version of the life of St Ninian. The author of a Latin life in the thirteenth-century MS. Cotton Tiberius D. iii professes to be giving a detailed account of the saint, founded on Bede and on a *liber de vita et miraculis eius barbarice scriptus*. According to the title, the Latin version is in fact a translation from the English, and

[1] R. R. Darlington, *Vita Wulfstani* (London 1928), pp. 2, xlvii, 11, but it is doubtful whether the last reference really is to complete lives.
[2] *Neues Archiv* cvi, 258–61; Ker, p. 280.
[3] *Neues Archiv* cviii, 15–28; G. H. Gerould, *op. cit.*, p. 123.
[4] Ker, p. 228.   [5] Ker, pp. 218–19.

although nothing more is known of the English life, there is no reason to doubt its former existence.[1] So too with the anonymous Latin life of St Indract in the early twelfth-century MS. Bodl. Digby 112. The author, whoever he may have been, is careful in his closing words to make it clear that all his statements have the authority of an Old English original.[2]

In one of his homilies Ælfric excuses himself from telling of St Thomas because the account of his death has 'previously been translated from Latin into English verse'. This English poem no longer survives, but an old table of contents to MS. Cotton Vitellius A. xii includes as one of the items in the manuscript, *Fragmentum Saxonicum quod forte continet aliquam partem Historiæ sive Legendæ Thomæ Apostoli*, of which there is now no trace.[3] Elsewhere Ælfric also mentions an Old English account of the martyrdoms of Peter and Paul. Since he is unlikely to be referring to the version in the *Old English Martyrology*, this work too must have been lost.[4]

Evidence for the loss of later vernacular lives of the saints is much slighter. Collections of lives in English are occasionally to be met with in catalogues and wills, but as a rule the description is too vague for any satisfactory identification to be possible. For example, the catalogue of the library of Titchfield Abbey, drawn up in 1400, includes a *Legenda sanctorum dicitur aurea in anglicis*.[5] The only Middle English version of the *Legenda aurea* possibly available at this date would have been John Myrc's *Festial*. It is usually said to have been written c. 1400, but all that is definitely known is that it had certainly been completed by 1415, and the work at Titchfield may be too early for it to have been a copy of Myrc. Perhaps it represented one of the many manuscripts, extant or lost, of the *Southern English Legendary*. On the other hand, when Thomas Berkley in 1415 bequeathes a *legendam sanctorumin Anglicis*, this was no doubt a copy of Myrc;[6] and later references are either to the same work, or else to the version of the *Legenda*

[1] Hardy i, 45.   [2] *Gesta Regum* i, cxviiiff.
[3] B. Thorpe, *The Homilies of Ælfric* (London 1844) ii, 520; Ker, p. 280.
[4] B. Thorpe, *op. cit.* i, 370.
[5] *Proceedings of the Leeds Philosophical Society: Literary and Historical Section* v, part iii, p. 166.
[6] E. F. Jacob and H. C. Johnson, *Register of Henry Chichele* (Canterbury and York Society 1937) ii, 124.

Aurea made in 1438. So, in 1467, Peter Arderne leaves to his wife 'my boke of Legenda Sanctorum in Englissh';[1] in 1480 Ann, duchess of Buckingham, leaves to her daughter 'a book of English called "Legenda Sanctorum" ';[2] and at the time of its dissolution Monkbretton Priory possessed a 'Legenda Aurea in englysche'.[3] Rather more interesting is the 'boke of ye dowts of ye legends, both temporall and of saints' which William Bruyn in 1477 left to the church of St Gregory, Norwich, 'to be schewed in the chauncell for them y^t will leryn thereon y^t is wretyn therein'.[4]

So far as individual lives of saints are concerned the author of the *Ancrene Riwle* refers his readers to 'our Englische boc of Seinte Margarete', almost certainly the vernacular life of that saint in the *Katherine Group*.[5] In the late fourteenth-century catalogue of the library at Peterborough one of the volumes is said to contain a *Vita S. Thome Martyris Anglice*, and in 1467 Peter Arderne possessed a 'booke of ye Lyfe of Saint Thomas of Canterbury'.[6] No Middle English work is known which deals with Becket alone, but in the *Southern English Legendary* his life and death are treated at considerable length, and these may simply have been extracts from one of the legendaries. In 1458 Sir Thomas Chaworth leaves to his cousin Robert Clifton 'a newe boke of Inglisse, ye which begynnyth with ye lyffe of Seynt Albon and Amphiabell and other mony dyvers lyfe3 and thynges in ye same boke',[7] – probably a copy of Lydgate's work, and perhaps the extant MS. Huntington H.M. 40. An inventory of the goods of Elizabeth Siwardby of Sewerby, drawn up in 1468, includes an English version of the *Revelations* of St Bridget; Margaret Purdans in 1481 leaves to the nunnery at Thetford an English book of St Bridget; and in 1495 Cecily, duchess of York, leaves to her daughter Anne, prioress of Syon, 'a boke of the Revelacions of Saint Burgitte'.[8] The will of Thomas Horneby of York (1485–6) mentions a *librum de Vita*

[1] SS. liii, 102 n.
[2] N. H. Nicolas, *Testamenta Vetusta* (London 1826), p. 356.
[3] J. W. Walker, *Chartularies of Monkbretton Priory* (Yorks. Arch. Soc.; Record Series lxvi), pp. 5–9.
[4] *Norfolk and Norwich Archaeological Society* iv, 335.
[5] J. Morton, *The Ancren Riwle* (CS. 1853), p. 244.
[6] *Trans. Bib. Soc.*, Supplement v, p. 72; SS. liii, 102 n.
[7] SS. xxx, 227.
[8] SS. xlv, 163; *Norfolk and Norwich Archaeological Society* iv, 366; *Wills from Doctors Commons* (CS. 1862), p. 3.

Katerinæ, in Anglicis scriptum, which could have been a version of any one of the numerous extant lives of that saint.[1] An inventory of books in English belonging to Sir John Paston, drawn up towards the end of the reign of Edward IV, included a life of St Christopher.[2] The only known Middle English version of that saint's life is the fragmentary one in the Thornton Miscellany.

Rather more definite evidence of a lost work comes from the author of the *Scottish Legendary* (written c. 1400). In addition to this, he claims to have translated some part of the story of Christ and the Virgin.[3] To judge from the description given of it, this work must have been of considerable length, including not only a complete account of Christ and the Virgin, but also a series of sixty-six miracles. There is nothing extant with which this could be identified, and it must be assumed to have been lost. Similarly, many of the saints' legends composed by Osbern Bokenham still remain, but he also claims to have compiled an English version of 'Legenda Aurea and of oþer famous legendes at the instaunce of my specialle frendis', including lives of 'Seynt Cedde, Seynt Felix, Seynt Edwarde, Seynt Oswalde and many oþer seyntis of Englond'.[4] This can hardly refer to any of the extant translations of the *Legenda Aurea,* since none of them contains lives of these English saints.

Finally, the sixteenth-century catalogue of the library of Syon Monastery mentions an English version of the legend of the Three Kings, and of the life of St Jerome, versions of both of which still exist, along with an English life of St Francis which, unless it was merely an extract from one of the legendaries, has since been lost. Moreover, in the original index to the catalogue appears a reference to an English version of the *Revelations* of St Elizabeth of Hungary.[5]

This concludes the evidence for written lives of the saints in English which are not now extant, but it is not improbable that the list is far from complete. Occasionally the authors of the extant Latin lives happen to give precise information about their sources,

[1] SS. xlv, 165, n. 2.

[2] J. Gairdner, *The Paston Letters* (London 1904) vi, 65.

[3] W. M. Metcalfe, *Legends of the Saints* (STS. 1896) i, xxvi.

[4] *Englische Studien* x, 1ff.

[5] M. Bateson, *Catalogue of the Library of Syon Monastery, Isleworth* (Cambridge 1898), pp. 101, 111.

but at other times such references are only very general. Jocelyn of Canterbury, writing towards the end of the eleventh century, tells us, in the prologue to his life of St Edith, that he has made use of both oral and written evidence. Later, when describing how Theodoric, one of the original dancers of Colbeck, was healed at the shrine of the saint, we are informed that a description of it was written down *patriis literis* at the command of the abbess. This may have been one of the English books used by the author, but he has nothing definite to say about his other sources, whether English or Latin.[1] Nor were such vernacular sources confined to English, and Irish and Scottish works are sometimes mentioned. So, for example, Geoffrey, abbot of Burton (1114–51), obtained some of the material for his life of St Modwenna from Ireland and *de lingua barbara*. Adamnan, in his life of Columba, made use of Scottish poems in praise of the saint, and Jocelyn of Furness used a *codiculum stilo Scotico dictatum* for his life of St Kentigern. Occasionally the writer merely claims to have had access to some very early authority, but without specifying the language of his source. The author of the life of St Cyned says that he had seen much more concerning the saint in a manuscript he had met with in Wales which was nearly illegible from age. The extant life of St Gudwal is said to be taken from one more ancient; the author of the life of St Ecgwine tells us that he is relating what he has gathered from ancient writings, and he may in fact be making use of Ecgwine's autobiography.[2] Most of these ancient writings, if they existed at all, were probably in Latin, but that this was not invariably the case is shown by a life of St Mildred. The author of this claims to be making use of an ancient record of her life, and it is in fact based upon an Old English life which survives, though incompletely, in MS. Cotton Caligula A. xiv.[3] Similarly, Laurence, abbot of Westminster, compiled at the request of Henry II a life of the Confessor 'from various ancient treatises', and that some of these may well have been in English is suggested by the extant *Vision of Earl Leofric*.[4]

Moreover, vernacular legends of the native saints existed in

[1] *Analecta Bollandiana* lvi, 39, 292.
[2] Hardy i, 97, 170, 208, 84, 372, 415.   [3] Hardy i, 377; Ker, p. 173.
[4] *Gesta Abbatum Monasterii S. Albani* (RS. 28) i, 159; see also *Transactions of the Philological Society, 1907–10*, pp. 180–8.

other than written accounts, and an oral literature had grown up round the more popular ones. Some of the stories which Bede tells of St Augustine, Laurence of Canterbury, Aidan, and others of the great figures in the conversion of England, appear to be taken from oral legend. Occasionally the stories seem to have remained current for a long time, and although many were eventually incorporated in Latin lives others, connected with some particular locality, apparently remained only in popular memory. The life of St Chad is extant both in Old English and in Latin, but at the very end of the Middle Ages places were still being pointed out which popular legend associated with him.[1]

In addition to the lost life of St Oswald, mentioned above, there seem to have existed during the Old English period a number of stories about the king. Already by the time of Bede his dying words had become proverbial:

> It is also given out, and become a proverb, 'That he ended his life in prayer'; for when he was beset with weapons and enemies, and he perceived that he must immediately be killed, he prayed to God for the souls of his army. Whence it is proverbially said, 'Lord have mercy on their souls, said Oswald, as he fell to the ground'.

It has been shown how easily these last words of the king fall into alliterative verse:

> Dryhtin, miltsa   duguþa sawlum,
> Cwæþ Oswald cyning,   þa he on eorþan sag.[2]

In connexion with this it may be noted that the words of Reginald of Durham (see p. 88) seem to suggest that his lost Old English source may have been in verse.

Another legend which Bede appears to have taken from oral tradition is that of the murder of Oswine, afterwards canonized in popular report, by Oswy of Northumbria:

> Oswy, however, had in the early part of his reign a partner in the royal office, by name Oswine, of the line of King Edwin, his father being Osric, to whom we have referred above, a man of outstanding piety and devoutness, who ruled the province of the Deirans for

---

[1] Leland ii, 51, 99.
[2] C. Plummer, *Baedae Opera Historica* (Oxford 1896) i, 151; *Philological Quarterly* xvi, 214.

seven years in the greatest prosperity, being himself beloved by all. But he [Oswy], who ruled the other and northern part of the people across the Humber, that is to say Bernicia, would have no peace with him [Oswine], nay rather, the causes of their disagreements increasing, he encompassed his death most foully. Inasmuch as each having gathered his army together against the other, Oswine, seeing that he could not wage battle with one who had the greater number of followers, deemed it wiser, putting aside all thought of battle, to reserve himself for a better opportunity. He therefore dismissed that army, which he had gathered together, and ordered each man to return to his home from that place which is called 'Uilfaræsdun,' that is, the hill of Uilfar [? Gariston] and which is a lonely place nearly ten miles west of the village of Catterick. He himself turned aside, keeping only one faithful soldier, by name Tondheri, with him and lay hid in the house of an Earl Hunuald whom he thought to be his very good friend. But alas! grievous to say, it was quite otherwise, for betrayed by this same earl he and his follower aforesaid were by Oswy, through the hands of his councillor Ethiluin, put to a death detested by all. This deed was done on the 20th August in the ninth year of his reign, at a place called Gilling [in Yorkshire], where afterwards a monastery was founded in expiation of this crime.[1]

The murder took place in 651, and the fact that the names of the actors and the localities involved were still remembered eighty years later is strong presumptive evidence that the event had become the subject of popular story.

In 793 Æthelberht, the vassal king of East Anglia, was summoned to the court of Offa and there executed. The fact is certain though the reason for it is unknown. However, there was evidently something particularly atrocious about the whole business, since the young king was reckoned a saint and became one of the most popular names in the English kalendar. Later legend had much to say of the circumstances of his death, the extant sources giving two rather different versions. In Roger of Wendover and in the *Vitae duorum Offarum* the whole blame for the deed is placed on Offa's wicked queen, Cynethryth. Æthelberht goes of his own accord to the court of Offa to beg for his daughter as wife and is kindly received by the king. The queen tries to stir up trouble, but Offa refuses to listen. She then prepares a room for Æthelberht, and near the bed arranges a splendid throne under which a

[1] C. Plummer, *op. cit.* i, 154; Wright, p. 84.

deep pit has been dug. Æthelberht is entertained at a splendid feast by Offa, but when he retires to his room and sits on the throne he is precipitated into the pit and there suffocated by servants of the queen.[1] This presumably gives the story as it was current at St Albans, where Offa, as one of the founders of the monastery, is represented as innocent of any complicity in the deed. But legends of the martyr seem to have flourished also in the neighbourhood of Hereford, and these had not the same interest in sparing the memory of Offa. This different version appears in the lives of the saint by Giraldus Cambrensis and by Osbert of Clare, but the earliest account is that found in the twelfth-century *Passio Sancti Æthelberhti*. According to this, the queen succeeds in poisoning Offa's mind by her insinuations, and because of this he offers a reward to any one who will lure Æthelberht into the royal bed-chamber. The task is undertaken by a certain Winberht, who had formerly been at the court of Æthelberht's father but had committed murder and been forced to flee. He goes to meet the saint, who asks the reason for Offa's absence, whereupon,

> Winberht replied: 'He learned too late by your messenger, O king, of your arrival. He declared it to be a great honour to him that the King of the East Angles should wish to visit the King of the Mercians, and he added: "Whatever he asks of me forthwith he shall obtain it". But today he has been bled'. . . . Then the blessed King Æthelbert said: 'Let us go in and meet King Offa'. Winberht replied: 'It is not fitting that anyone should go in to meet the king with his sword on in time of peace. Therefore, O king, put aside your arms and thus go in with the courtiers.' Then [Æthelbert] in the innocence of his mind discarded the sword that he was carrying and gave it to the guileful Winberht. With a few retainers the holy king went to meet a king steeped in evil. The royal door is closed. At once from all sides treachery springs forth. The blameless king is seized, he is confined in chains, he is made to suffer the greatest wretchedness. At length, with his own sword he is beheaded by Winberht.

It has been suggested that the whole *Passio* is based on a 'homily or poem in the vernacular', although if this is the case the original has disappeared. It seems much more likely that it depends rather

---

[1] Wendover i, 249–51; see also R. W. Chambers, *Beowulf: An Introduction* (Cambridge 1959), pp. 239ff.

'on vernacular traditions current in Hereford and its neighbour-hood in Anglo-Saxon times'.[1]

Legends were also current concerning St Kenelm of Mercia, the supposed son of Coenwulf. That king is said to have died in 821 while on an expedition against the Welsh, and according to more or less contemporary authorities he was succeeded by his brother Ceolwulf. However, a story seems to have arisen telling how Coenwulf left a son Kenelm who, though only seven years old at the time, was nevertheless acknowledged as king. After reigning only a few days the boy was murdered by the contrivance of his elder sister Cwenthryth, abbess of Winchcombe. The tale first appears in Florence of Worcester; Giraldus Cambrensis knew of legends dealing with Kenelm and his wicked sister;[2] and later writers tell how the news of the saint's death was carried to Rome by a white dove which dropped a letter on the altar of St Peter:

> This writing, which was in letters of gold in the English language was, at the Pope's bidding, in vain attempted to be read by the Romans and other ecclesiastics who were present; but fortunately there was among them an Englishman who turned the writing into the Latin tongue, and brought it to pass that a letter from the Roman pontiff made known to the English kings where the martyr of their country lay. The following, among other things, was in the letter, 'In clento cou bathe Kenelm kynebearn lith under thorne hæuedes bereaved'.

The English lines appear also, in a slightly different form, in manuscripts of Matthew Paris, though the earliest occurrence of them seems to be in a note, in a late twelfth- or early thirteenth-century hand, on the first leaf of Pembroke College, Cambridge, MS. 82.[3] A slight emendation would give two reasonably good lines of alliterative verse:

> In clento cou bache   Kenelm kynebearn
> lith under [haȝe] thorne   hæuedes bereaved.

Of course the actual existence of a poem on the subject can hardly be assumed on such evidence as this, but it is obvious that ver-nacular tales of Kenelm must have been widespread, and in the

[1] *EHR*. xxxii, 214ff.; Wright, pp. 96–9.
[2] Florence of Worcester i, 65; *Itinerarium Kambriæ*, p. 25.
[3] Wendover i, 273ff.; Ker, p. 124.

medieval kalendar he was commemorated on the supposed anniversary of his death, July 17. Historically there seems to be no justification whatever for the story, yet Kenelm became a favourite saint of the Middle Ages, and the place where his body was hidden in a brake was a well-known resort of pilgrims.

Although we sometimes have reason to suspect the presence of oral sagas among the Anglo-Saxons, it is only exceptionally that we can see the actual progress of these stories from the oral to the written form. One of these rare occasions occurs in the account of the death of St Edmund as recorded in the *Passio S. Eadmundi* (985–7) of Abbo of Fleury. Asser and the *Old English Chronicle* simply say that Edmund was defeated and slain by the Vikings in 869, but Abbo has a circumstantial and detailed account of the king's death, and gives also the line of descent of the story, which he apparently had at second hand from an eyewitness. He tells how the monks at Ramsey had begged him to commit to writing the passion of the saint, for they

> had heard that those things, which were unknown to many and written down by no one but which had been preserved in an historical manner through the memory of antiquity, your Reverence [*i.e.* Dunstan] had related in my presence to the Lord Bishop of the Church of Rochester and to the Abbot of the monastery called Malmesbury, and to others of the brothers standing round, whom you cease not to nourish, as your custom is, with the food of the Divine Word both in Latin and in your own language. To these, your eyes filled with tears, you were wont to reveal that as a young man you had learned it from a certain very old man, who full of faith related it in simple manner to the most glorious Æthelstan, King of the English, asserting most solemnly that on that very day he had been the armour-bearer of that blessed man in the place where he fell a martyr for Christ's sake. Such faith did you put in his assertion that at the prompting of memory you moulded it afresh in a narrative which some time later you retold in pleasing style to a younger generation; because of this the bretheren began at once to assail my want of courage [urging me] to satisfy their ardent longing and not to allow, so far as my strength permitted, a sequence of such great events to perish.[1]

Here the oral legend has already had a life of over a hundred years before it was written down. At this stage it was probably still fairly

[1] *Memorials of St Edmund's Abbey* (RS. 96) i, 3; Wright, pp. 59ff.

close to historical fact, but it was not long before marvellous stories grew up about the youth of the saint. The early lives know nothing of his origin or early years, but with the increasing popularity of his cult legend soon remedied this deficiency. Writing sometime between 1148 and 1156 Geoffrey of Wells tells how Offa, an otherwise unknown king of the East Angles, set out on a pilgrimage to Rome. On the way he passed through the land of the Old Saxons, and was there welcomed by the king and served assiduously by a number of youths, especially by Edmund the younger son of the king. Offa, on leaving, gave Edmund a gold ring and showed another to him, adding that if it should be sent to him with any command he should obey immediately. Offa then continued to Jerusalem, but on his way back fell ill and died, first naming Edmund as his successor and giving to his councillors a ring which was to be sent to Edmund. They duly deliver their message, and eventually Edmund is allowed to go to England. After some delay he is crowned king of East Anglia, but does not reign long before the Viking invasions begin. According to Geoffrey this story was current among the monks of Bury, and further evidence for the existence in the vernacular of such legends is afforded by *La Vie Seint Edmund le Rey* of Denis Pyramus in which, according to the author,

> Translate lai desque a la fin,
> E del engleis e del latin.

Now so far as we know the sources used by Denis were the works of Geoffrey of Wells and of Abbo of Fleury, both in Latin. The way in which he speaks of his English authorities suggests that they, like the Latin ones, were also in written form. If so all trace of them has long since been lost, unless perhaps they are included among the titles of works on the subject, not now existing, which are written on the margins of MS. Bodl. 240, the 'book of Bliburgh', Nicholaus de Warengford, H. Norwicensis, or *alia Legenda*.[1]

The next royal saint is the Edward who succeeded his father Edgar as king of Wessex in 975. He was slain within a few years of his accession, and the manner of his death evidently gave rise to numerous stories, some of which can be traced in later Latin

[1] *Memorials of St Edmund's Abbey* (RS. 96) i, 93ff.; ii, 228.

works. The *Old English Chronicle* gives the bare fact of his death *æt Corfes geate*, but popular rumour seems to have been less discreet, and either hinted at the complicity of his stepmother Ælfthryth or openly accused her. The nearest contemporary source, the *Vita Oswaldi*, is ambiguous about the queen's part in the murder. Edward is said to have ridden to Corfe to visit his half-brother, and whilst still on horseback was surrounded by soldiers, one of whom

> took hold of his right hand as if he wished to salute him, another caught him roughly by the left hand at the same time wounding him. But [the king], as much as he could, cried out in a loud voice: 'Why are you breaking my right arm?' and suddenly fell from his horse and died. The martyr of God was lifted up and carried to the house of a certain poor man.[1]

The first definite connexion of Ælfthryth with the death of Edward occurs about a hundred years later in Osbern's life of St Dunstan, and Florence of Worcester has no doubt that the murder was committed by her orders. According to William of Malmesbury, Edward was stabbed while drinking a cup of wine offered to him by Ælfthryth, and Henry of Huntingdon has apparently heard of stories in which the queen herself is responsible for the actual murder. Walter Map knows still another version, one in which Ælfthryth gives poison to the king, and when this fails hires soldiers to slay him.[2] But the most elaborate account is that given by Gaimar. Edward's dwarf, Wolstanet, fleeing from the anger of the king, rides off to Ælfthryth's house. The king follows, but Wolstanet has hidden in a thick wood, so the king turns aside to his stepmother's house to ask if anyone has seen the dwarf. He finds few people there, and these hesitate to answer him; then the queen comes, begs the king to dismount, and offers to have a search made. The king refuses, but agrees to accept wine. A horn of wine is brought and half of it drunk by the king, half by the queen. When he returns the horn to her and is about to kiss her, he is stabbed to the heart by an unknown servant. The queen has the body buried on a lonely moor and the place covered over by reeds, but during the night it is revealed by a ray of light shining

[1] *Historians of the Church of York* (RS. 71) i, 450; Wright, pp. 162ff.
[2] *Gesta Regum* i, 183; Huntingdon, p. 167; Map, p. 207.

from heaven, carried to Shaftesbury, and there buried.[1] These different versions show that there must have been in circulation a good many different stories dealing with the death of the king which are known today only from the later Latin writers. Moreover, according to Wulfstan of York, 'Edward was betrayed and afterwards killed and after that burned', but none of the versions known to us says anything about the burning of Edward's body, nor do we know any further details of this particular story.

These are some of the best known of the legends which grew up round the more popular of the Anglo-Saxon saints; and quite certainly stories were current concerning others of them, such as St Neot, Dunstan, and the Confessor. No doubt some of them were due to literary and ecclesiastical influence, but it seems certain that others were of popular origin and current only in the oral vernacular literature. Nor did such stories cease with the Conquest, as is shown by those which developed about the birth and parentage of St Thomas Becket. Moreover, in later times many saints were popularly regarded as such but never officially canonized, and the tales which were told about them were almost certainly in the vernacular. So, for example, with John Schorn, who put the devil into a shoe, and other legends seem to have flourished round the names of Thomas of Lancaster, Edward II, and Archbishop Scrope.

[1] Gaimar i, 168ff.

6

ROMANCE

On the whole it is unlikely that many of the romances of the three traditional Matters have been lost. So far as we can tell, these, at any rate in England, were a distinctively literary development, and so were assured of a written existence. Popular stories concerning Arthur may have been current before the appearance of Geoffrey of Monmouth's *Historia Regum Britanniae*, but the evidence for this is slight.[1] Perhaps some of the Arthurian heroes, Tristram and Gawain for instance, were known at an early date, but it is unlikely that there was ever much in English about Lancelot or the Quest of the Grail, to say nothing of the minor characters of the Matter of Britain.

The story of Arthur seems to have originated in Wales, the earliest evidence for it coming from the *Historia Brittonum* of Nennius, while the *Annales Cambriae* add that Arthur and Medraut fell at Camlan, though whether as enemies or allies is left uncertain. In early lives of the Welsh saints Arthur is seldom conspicuous, but his appearance with Cei and Bedguir in the life of St Cadog, and the allusion there to his chivalrous actions, may indicate the existence at that time of stories about the king. Similarly Caradoc of Llancarfan in his *Vita Gildae* (c. 1100) has two stories about Arthur, an account of the killing in fair fight by Arthur of Hueil, brother of the saint, and a tale of the abduction of Guinevere. Despite this there is comparatively little evidence for the existence of stories about Arthur before the twelfth century. In Geoffrey of Monmouth there is a suggestion of earlier tales about him, but no proof of any considerable cycle. However, the 'British hope' certainly antedates Geoffrey, as is clearly shown by a reference in Herman of Tournai. In 1113 certain canons of Laon

---

[1] See R. S. Loomis, *Arthurian Literature in the Middle Ages* (Oxford 1959), pp. 52–63; J. S. P. Tatlock, *The Legendary History of Britain* (California U.P.), pp. 178–229; *Romanic Review* xxxii, 3ff.

were sent to this country to raise funds for the rebuilding of their cathedral. On the way from Exeter to Bodmin they were shown the seat and oven of King Arthur, while at Bodmin one of their servants fell into a dispute with a cripple who maintained that Arthur still lived, and only with difficulty was bloodshed averted.[1] Similarly William of Malmesbury, writing in 1125, considered Arthur 'a man worthy to be celebrated, not by idle tales, but by authentic history', and what these idle tales were is indicated by a later passage in which he says that Arthur's grave has never been found, and hence the old foolish lies that he will return again.[2]

The *Speculum Charitatis* (c. 1141-2) of Ailred of Rievaulx provides rather more doubtful evidence for the presence of popular stories about Arthur before the appearance of Geoffrey's work. Ailred's treatise contains a dialogue between the author and a novice, in the course of which the latter confesses that he has frequently been moved to tears by the misfortunes of a certain Arthur.[3] It has usually been assumed that a copy of the *Historia Regum Britanniae* could hardly have made its way to the north as early as this, and that consequently the reference must be to tales of Arthur current orally throughout the district. Such stories could perhaps have spread through Yorkshire from the Bretons in the household of the duke of Brittany, holder of the honour of Richmond. But it is equally possible that Ailred had in fact already seen a copy of Geoffrey's work. Walter Espec, founder of Rievaulx of which Ailred was abbot, had received a copy of the history from Robert of Gloucester. This was certainly before 1147, and may have been early enough for Ailred to have seen it before he wrote this particular work. Equally doubtful is the evidence of Alfred of Beverley. It was hearing tales of Arthur that led him to borrow Geoffrey's book and to compile his own unimportant chronicle.[4] This again could suggest the existence of tales of Arthur independent of Geoffrey, but it may merely indicate an early vogue for the *Historia* in Yorkshire.

Consequently, although there is some evidence for the presence in English before 1136 of stories of Arthur, it can hardly be pressed very far, and indeed might indicate that where such tales did occur

---

[1] *Patrologia Latina* clvi, 983ff.   [2] *Gesta Regum* i, 11.
[3] *Patrologia Latina* cxcv, 565.
[4] T. Hearne, *Aluredi Beverlacensis Annales* (Oxford 1716), pp. 2-3.

they were due to exceptional circumstances. After the appearance of the *Historia Regum Britanniae* evidence for the existence of popular stories, unconnected with it, is even slighter. Giraldus Cambrensis tells of the discovery of the tombs of Arthur and Guinevere at Glastonbury, mentions the stories current concerning the death of the king, and gives the inscription on the coffin, *Hic jacet sepultus inclitus rex Arthurus cum Wennevereia uxore sua secunda in insula Avallonia.* This exceptional reference to Guinevere as the second wife of Arthur is mysterious, and may suggest a knowledge of stories which have since disappeared.[1] Elsewhere Giraldus has the story that Arthur had killed the brother of Gildas, and that this led Gildas to fling into the sea the books he had written concerning the deeds of Arthur. In addition, Giraldus attaches the responsibility for a jest about a fishing coracle to a certain *famosus ille fabulator Bledhericus*, known from other references as an authority on the Arthurian legend and one who knew all the secrets of the Grail.[2] However, knowledge of such tales by Giraldus need only indicate an oral tradition in Wales, and is no proof of its existence in England or in English. At a later date there are similar indications of the popularity of Arthur. In 1278 Edward I had the alleged tomb of Arthur at Glastonbury opened and the body translated for safety to Worcester, while the crown of Arthur, one of the spoils of the Welsh campaign, was presented by Edward at the high altar of Westminster Abbey.[3] But in all probability such references merely reflect the later popularity of Geoffrey's work.

A difficulty arises when we come to deal with occasional references to written works on the Arthurian legend – the fact that such allusions are often so general that it is impossible to be certain whether the work in question was an Arthurian story no longer represented in the extant literature, or simply a version of one of the surviving romances. Nor are the references always clear as to the language in which the work was written. MS. 248 in Merton College, Oxford, contains a collection of sermons compiled, c. 1350, by John Sheppey, bishop of Rochester. The sermons are

---

[1] *De Principis Instructione*, pp. 126ff. For variant forms of the inscription see also *Speculum Ecclesiæ*, pp. 47ff.; RS. 9, ii, 363; RS. 66, p. 36; Leland i, 288.

[2] *Descriptio Kambriæ*, pp. 209, 202.

[3] *Annales Monastici* (RS. 36) iv, 474, 489; ii, 401. See also RS. 76, i, 91; *Speculum* xxviii, 114ff.

by different authors, some consisting merely of outlines, and one
of the latter has a tantalizing reference to a *sermo de rotunda
tabula*.[1] The only Round Table of which we know is the Arthurian
one, and although the phrase is frequently used of tournaments in
the thirteenth century,[2] it is difficult to see how it would fit in
here. The reference could be to some lost Arthurian story, and the
general context would perhaps suggest one which in some way
connected the Round Table with the legend of the Holy Rood.

The books presented to Bordesley Abbey in 1305 by Guy de
Beauchamp, earl of Warwick, included *Un Volum de la Mort ly
Roy Arthur, e de Mordret*;[3] Queen Isabel (d. 1358) possessed
unus magnus liber . . . de gestis Arthuri, probably identical with the
Romance de Roy Arthure possessed by Richard II in 1384–5,[4]
while among the goods of Sir John Fastolf in 1450 was a *liber de
Roy Artour*.[5] But all these appear to have been in French, and so
presumably was the 'book called Arthur de Bretagne' left in 1391
to 'my daughter Engaine' by Margaret, countess of Devon, though
it could perhaps have been an earlier version of the extant *Arthur
of Little Britain*.[6]

The most important of Arthur's knights was Sir Lancelot, but
he was apparently never particularly popular in England. The
reference in Chaucer's *Nuns' Priest's Tale* (VII, 3212) to the 'book
of Launcelot de Lake' is probably to a French romance, or perhaps
to an earlier version of the extant *Lancelot of the Laik*. The books
given to Bordesley Abbey by Guy de Beauchamp included *le
premer livere de Launcelot*, and one of his ancestors, William de
Beauchamp, had in 1268 bequeathed to his daughter Joan a 'book
of Lancelot'.[7] In 1380 the will of Elizabeth la Zouche mentions
'books called Tristrem and Lanchelot'; in 1392 that of Isabella,
duchess of York, refers to a 'Lancelot'; and in 1412 Elizabeth
Darcy left to Philip, son and heir to the late Lord Darcy, a book
called 'Lanselake'. A book of the same title was possessed by
Thomas Hebbeden who, in 1435, bequeathed to Isabella Eure

---

[1] *MLN.* xlix, 394.
[2] *Annales Monastici* (RS. 36) ii, 402; iii, 313; *Chronica Majora* v, 318.
[3] *Romania* lxxviii, 511–18.
[4] *Trans. Bib. Soc.* xiii, 144ff.
[5] *HMC., 8th Report*, Appendix, p. 268.
[6] N. H. Nicolas, *Testamenta Vetusta* (London 1826), p. 127.
[7] *Romania* lxxviii, 511–18; N. H. Nicolas, *op. cit.*, p. 50.

unum librum gallicum vocatum Launcelot.[1] This last was certainly in French, and the probability is that the others were too.

In England Gawain was easily the most popular of all Arthur's knights. His fame was known to William of Malmesbury, since in 1087 his grave had been discovered in 'a province of Wales called Ross':

> The grave of Arthur is nowhere to be seen, whence ancient ballads fable that he is still to come. But the tomb of [Gawain], as I have said, was found in the time of King William on the sea coast, fourteen feet long; there, as some relate, he was wounded by his enemies and suffered shipwreck; others say that he was killed by his subjects at a public entertainment.[2]

Queen Isabel, in 1358, possessed a French copy of *Percival and Gawain*, presumably the same as the *Romance de Perciuall & Gawyn* which appears in 1384–5 amongst Richard II's books.[3] According to Andrew Wyntoun the mysterious Hucheon of the Aule Realle had written the *Awntyr of Gawane*, as well as a *gret Gest of Arthure* and the *Pistil of Suet Susane*.[4] The last of these has survived, but it is impossible to tell whether the other two titles represent works still in existence or ones which have since been lost.

On the continent there are early references to the Tristram story in the poems of the famous troubadour Bernard de Ventadour; and Chrestien de Troyes claims to have written *Del roi Marc et d'Ysalt la blonde*,[5] though the work has since disappeared. In addition, there is some evidence for the existence of a version of the story in England during the early Middle English period. The author of the Anglo-French romance of *Waldef* claims that both Waldef and Tristram were famous heroes, beloved by the English both high and low, and the context suggests that, translating as he probably is from an English original, he knew of English poems on Tristram as well as on Waldef.[6] However the

A. Gibbons, *Early Lincoln Wills* (Lincoln 1888), pp. 92, 118; *Trans. Bib. Soc.* xiii, 144ff.; SS. ii, 84.

[2] *Gesta Regum* ii, 342.   [3] *Trans. Bib. Soc.* xiii, 144ff.

[4] F. J. Amours, *Wyntoun's Original Chronicle* (STS. 1902–14) iv, 23, 21.

[5] A. Micha, *Les Romans de Chrétien de Troyes. II. Cligés* (Paris 1957), p. 1.

[6] R. Imelmann, *Johannes Bramis' Historia Regis Waldei* (Bonn 1912), pp. xxxiff.

only extant representative of the legend in Middle English is the fourteenth-century *Sir Tristrem*, and this is probably the one referred to by Robert Mannyng of Brunne in his chronicle:

> þat may þou here in sir Tristrem;
> ouer gestes it has þe steem,
> Ouer alle that is or was,
> if men it sayd as made Thomas.[1]

Among the books of Queen Isabel was one of *Tristram & Isolda*,[2] which was presumably in French, as were probably most of the versions of the romance which appear in wills. This was certainly the case with that in the will of Sir John Lescrop (1405),[3] but in others no definite mention of the language is made. So in 1380 Elizabeth la Zouche leaves 'to my lord le Zouche . . . books called Tristrem and Lanchelot', and in 1390 the will of Margaret Courtenay, countess of Devon, includes a *Tristram* and a *Merlyn*.[4] In 1420 Matilda del Bowes leaves various 'romance' books, and also *unum librum yat is called Trystram*, and here, since the other books are described as being in French, the omission in the case of the *Trystram* suggests that it may have been in English.[5] In 1426 Thomas Beaufort, duke of Exeter, leaves to his sister Johanna, countess of Westmorland, *unum librum vocat' Tristram*.[6]

Comparatively little is extant in English on the Grail legend, and the occasional references are probably to French versions of the story. This is certainly true of the *Volum del Romaunce Iosep ab Arimathie, e deu Seint Grael*, presented to Bordesley Abbey by the earl of Warwick, and also presumably of the *liure appelle Galaath* possessed by Richard II.[7]

One of the earliest references to the Matter of France comes from Ordericus Vitalis:

> Anthony, a monk of Winchester, brought [the legend of William Courtnez] here not long since, and complied with our eager desire to see it. There is indeed a story in verse concerning St. William which is commonly sung by minstrels, but the preference must justly be given to an authentic narrative . . . But as the bearer was in haste

---

[1] Mannyng i, 4. [2] *Trans. Bib. Soc.* xiii, 144ff.
[3] SS. iv, 339. [4] A. Gibbons, *op. cit.*, p. 92; *Trans. Bib. Soc.* xiii, 144ff.
[5] SS. ii, 63ff. [6] J. Nichols, *Royal Wills* (London 1780), p. 254.
[7] *Romania* lxxviii, 511–18; *Trans. Bib. Soc.* xiii, 144ff.

to depart, and the severe winter's frost prevented me from writing, I made a short abridgement on my tablets, which I now hasten to transfer correctly to parchment.[1]

Later in the same century Walter Map complains that 'only the triflings of mimes in vulgar rhymes celebrates among us the godlike nobility of the Charles's and Pepins'.[2] Similarly, a fourteenth-century volume of Anselm and Augustine in the library of Balliol College, Oxford, contains also an anonymous work on the Seven Deadly Sins in which are a good many references to contemporary life, among them a reprimand of those who would rather listen to frivolous stories of Roland and Oliver than to a profitable sermon.[3] None of the extant romances of the Matter of France is earlier than the fourteenth century, so that if Ordericus and Map are referring to English works, they have either been lost entirely or were earlier versions of some of the extant romances. The probability is, however, that the narrative of the monk of Winchester was in Latin and the popular tales known to Map and Ordericus were in French, though the fourteenth-century reference is possibly to English stories. In any case we know of at least one English romance on the subject which existed in a written form before the end of the thirteenth century. In 1286 Bjarni Erlingsson of Bjarkey, one of the Norwegian magnates, was in Scotland looking after the interests of the Maid of Norway. On his return to Norway in the following year he took with him a romance in English which he later had translated into Norwegian. The English original has long since been lost, but the Norwegian version of it remains as part of the *Karlamagnús saga* with the title *Af Frú Ólíf ok Landrés syni hennar*, and it is the introduction to this which tells how the tale became known in Norway.[4] Judging from the Norse version we need not greatly regret the disappearance of the English original. It appears to have been a dull work on the old folklore theme of the slandered wife and the cruel mother-in-law.

When the catalogue of the library of St Augustine's, Canterbury, was drawn up during the fifteenth century, item 1517 contained,

[1] Ordericus iii, 5. [2] Map, p. 203.
[3] R. A. B. Mynors, *Catalogue of the Manuscripts of Balliol College, Oxford* (Oxford 1963), p. 216.
[4] B. Vilhjálmsson, *Karlamagnús Saga og Kappa hans* (Reykjavík 1954), p. 101.

in addition to the *Gesta guidonis de Warewik in gallico*, a *Gesta Guydonis de Burgundia in patria lingua*.[1] Guy of Burgundy was one of the heroes who took part in Charlemagne's legendary conquest of Spain; the romance is still extant in French, but no English version of it appears to be known. The phrase *in patria lingua*, as compared with the *in gallico* of the preceding work, should mean that this was in English, and if so we have here the only surviving trace of an English version of another of the romances of the Matter of France.

An English translation of the romance of *Ferumbras*, from which Robert Bruce, whilst a fugitive, read to his companions,[2] still survives, and elsewhere in wills, inventories, and catalogues there are to be found references to a fair number of romances of the Matter of France, but they are invariably in French or Latin, and provide no evidence for any lost romances in English.

Nor is there much evidence for any lost romances of the Matter of Antiquity, and it is probable that the various references to such stories are to copies of works still in existence. In a letter written in 1284 Archbishop Pecham seems to suggest a popular interest in classical or pseudo-classical tales about the alleged Trojan descent of the Britons,[3] but the letter is to the bishop of St Asaph, and is concerned with stories current amongst the Welsh, not necessarily among the English. On the other hand, Edward I and Henry IV quite seriously put forward the precedent of Locrine in support of their claims to the overlordship of Scotland;[4] the chancellor, Michael de la Pole appealed in Parliament to the legend of Brutus as evidence of the antiquity and absolutism of the royal dignity; and the household ordinances of Edward IV were said to be based on the precedents of King Cassibelaun and King Lud.[5] Romances of the Matter of Antiquity are not infrequent in catalogues and wills. Among the French books given by Guy de Beauchamp to Bordesley Abbey (1305) were *Titus et Vaspasien*, *Romaunce de Troies*, *Romaunce deu Brut e del Roy Costentine*, *Enseignement Aristotle*

---

[1] *Canterbury and Dover*, p. 372.
[2] W. W. Skeat, *The Bruce* (EETS. ES. 1870–7) iii, 435ff.
[3] *Registrum Epistolarum J. Peckham Arch. Cant.* (RS. 77) ii, 741–2. On the legend of Brutus, see *Essays and Studies* ix, 9ff.; *Speculum* ii, 33ff.; and T. D. Kendrick, *British Antiquity* (London 1950).
[4] *Ypodigma Neustriae* (RS. 28) vii, 220ff.; T. Rymer, *Foedera* viii, 155, 157.
[5] *Ancient Ordinances of the Royal Household* (London 1790), pp. 15ff.

enveiez au Roy Alisaundre, Romaunce d'Alisaundre ove peintures,
and another *Romaunce . . . de Alisaundre.*[1] Queen Isabel (d. 1358)
possessed a French version of the *Siege of Troy*, along with other
French romances,[2] and elsewhere when the language is not par-
ticularized it was probably Latin. In 1435 Thomas Hebbeden
leaves a book called *Guydo de Columpna*; the comparatively large
number of books belonging to Thomas Dautree of York (1437)
included at least three of this kind, *de Gestis Trojanorum, de Gestis
Alexandri*, and *de Bello Trojanorum*, the last two appearing again in
the will of his son John Dautree (1459),[3] while Edmund Rede
(1487) left books *de vita Alexandrie* and *de Obsessione Troje.*[4]

No doubt Bodel's classification of the chief subjects of romance
was comprehensive enough at the time he made it, but other
subjects, which developed later, could not easily be included
under one of the traditional matters. In England romances appear
dealing with the history – real or imaginary – of the country, and
throughout Western Europe subjects are borrowed from ultimately
eastern sources. The former are often, on the analogy of the three
great Matters, classified as the Matter of England. Some half-
dozen of these are still extant, but there are references to a much
greater number which have since been lost. Most of them deal
with subjects from Old English history, but here we are concerned only with those whose heroes are post-Conquest, or which
are entirely unhistorical. Belonging to the latter class is the
romance of *Waldef*, a long and complicated work which may
perhaps ultimately reflect conditions in East Anglia during the
tenth and eleventh centuries. It is extant only in an incomplete
and so far unpublished Anglo-French version, the author of which
claims to be translating an English story, well beloved by great
and small before the Conquest, just as were the *Brut, Tristan*, and
Aalof. It is hardly possible that there were ever Old English works
on these subjects, and whether, when *Waldef* was composed, any
Middle English versions either is perhaps equally doubtful. So
far as they are concerned, internal evidence makes it clear that the
author used Wace's *Brut*, Thomas's *Tristan*, and the Anglo-
French romance of *Horn* by Mestre Thomas. The last of these
was apparently intended to be the central story of a trilogy, pre-

---

[1] *Romania* lxxviii, 511–18.   [2] *Trans. Bib. Soc.* xiii, 144ff.
[3] SS. ii, 84; xxx, 59ff., 232.   [4] *Trans. Bib. Soc.* vii, 118.

ceded by a romance of *Aalof*, the father of Horn, and followed by one of *Hadermod* which would deal with the adventures of Horn's son.[1] There is nothing to show that the second of these was ever written, but the former existence of a romance on Aalof can be deduced, not only from the opening words of *Horn*, but also from other references in the story. However, despite the rather ambiguous words of the author of *Waldef*, there is little evidence that Mestre Thomas knew any English, and none to suggest that he made use of any works in that language. On the other hand, the author of *Waldef* certainly had an English original for his story, and this was still in existence as late as the fifteenth century, when John Bramis, a monk of Thetford, made a Latin prose summary of it, using also the Anglo-French text which was apparently then complete. According to Bramis, the romance was first composed in English verse, and later translated into French at the request of a lady who did not understand English.[2]

The story of Hereward is known to us today only from a brief Latin version of his *Gesta*, though additional notices of his deeds appear elsewhere. Already when the *Gesta Herewardi Saxonis* was written there was little left of the English original on which it was partly based, and this during the lifetime of those who had been companions of the hero. In the introduction the author tells how the work came to be written. Being interested in the deeds of the famous outlaw, and hearing of an English book describing his life, he sought for it with the intention of translating it into Latin. His search, however, was almost in vain, and he found nothing but a few mutilated and decayed pages. With difficulty he extracted from them some of the early deeds of Hereward written in English by Leofric the Deacon, one of the companions of Hereward. Nothing more was to be found, and consequently he laid the work aside. Then, apparently, someone in authority heard of the half-finished work and desired to see it. Thereupon the author took up his pen again and completed the book from the personal reminiscences of some of the former companions of Hereward.[3]

[1] See M. K. Pope, *The Romance of Horn* (Oxford 1955).

[2] R. Imelmann, *Johannes Bramis' Historia Regis Waldei* (Bonn 1912); M. D. Legge, *Anglo-Norman Literature and its Background* (Oxford 1963), pp. 143–56. See also the mention of Waltheof in the list of Germanic heroes in a late version of the *Brut* (p. 7).

[3] *De Gestis Herewardi Saxonis* (RS. 91) i, 339.

The present form of the *Gesta* certainly lends some support to this account of its origin. The first part, said to be based on a written source, is full of fantastic stories about the ancestry and early life of the hero, while the second, based on information from those who had known Hereward, is a good deal more restrained.

Nor was the work of Leofric the Deacon the only record of Hereward to have been lost. The author of the *Liber Eliensis* refers to a work on the same subject by Richard of Ely, and unless this is identical with the extant *Gesta* – for we are not told whether Richard's work was in Latin or English – it no longer survives.[1] In addition some details of Hereward's struggle against the Normans are to be found in various of the chronicles, notably the pseudo-Ingulph, John of Peterborough, Gaimar, and the *Liber de Hyda*, but no indication is given of the sources of their information.

Although the written English version of the Hereward story appears to have been lost at a comparatively early date, there is evidence to show that he long continued popular. According to the *Gesta*, his deeds were celebrated by the country people, and women and girls sang of them in their dances.[2] The author of the pseudo-Ingulph, for what he is worth, claims that 'his deeds are still sung to this day on the king's highway',[3] and a reminiscence of one such song can perhaps be detected in the words used by Hereward when, disguised as a potter, he visited the court of the Conqueror, *Ollæ, ollæ, bonæ ollæ et urnæ; omnia vasa hæc fictilia et optima*. It has been shown that these would fall naturally into alliterative verse:

> Greofan, greofan, gode greofan and croccan;
> Eal(le) þas læmenan fatu þa selestan.[4]

However, apart from this, the songs have been lost, and quite probably none of them ever had any written existence. Nevertheless there is definite evidence for the former existence in English

---

[1] *Liber Eliensis*, p. 188.

[2] *De Gestis Herewardi Saxonis* (RS. 91) i, 344.

[3] W. Fulman, *Rerum Anglicarum Scriptorum Veterum* (Oxford 1684), pp. 67, 68.

[4] *Liber Eliensis*, p. 183; H. Paul, *Grundriss der germanischen Philologie* (Strassburg 1900–9) ii, 1088.

of at least one, and possibly two, lives of Hereward, along with a number of songs and ballads.

Another hero of the Conquest who appears to have become the subject of popular stories was a certain Eadric, who for a long time kept up a struggle against the Conqueror in the forests of the West. The *Old English Chronicle* (s.a. 1067 D) tells how a powerful thane, Eadric *cild*, raised the West Midlands against William; he fought against him for some years and did not submit until 1070. Brief notices of him are also to be found in some of the Latin chronicles. Ordericus Vitalis includes his name in a list of those who submitted to the Conqueror after Hastings, and a little later tells of a revolt of the citizens of Shrewsbury in alliance with 'Eadric Guilda, a powerful and warlike man'.[1] Florence of Worcester and Symeon of Durham give the bare facts of his fight against the Normans in almost identical words; we hear of his later submission to William, and he is singled out for mention as accompanying the king on his invasion of Scotland in 1072.[2] So far there is no suggestion that Eadric might become the subject of romance, but Walter Map has a story of which the hero is a certain Eadric Wilde, said to have been the lord of the manor of North Ledbury. One evening, returning late from the hunt, he came to a great house in which he saw a number of beautiful women. He immediately fell in love with one of them, entered the house, seized her, and with some difficulty succeeded in carrying her off. He lived happily with her for some time, but eventually, because in a fit of anger he mentioned the 'sisters' from whom he had snatched her, she vanished and was never seen again.[3] The theme is common enough in folklore, and its use here shows that Eadric has become so well known that tales with which he originally had no connexion can be attributed to him. Some memory of his deeds may perhaps be preserved in the *Monasticon* where, under 'Wygmore Abbey', are given details of his mythical struggle against Ralf de Mortimer.[4] However, except for this short reference, we know only the story attached to his name by Walter Map, and nothing has remained of the works celebrating the deeds by which this Hereward of the west gained his fame.

---

[1] Ordericus ii, 166, 193.
[2] Florence of Worcester ii, 1, 7, 9; Symeon of Durham ii, 185, 194, 195.
[3] Map, pp. 75ff. [4] *Monasticon* vi, 348-9.

Fulk FitzWarin, a romance extant only in a French version, also tells of the hero's adventures as an outlaw in the forests of the west, along with some adventures abroad, but this time during the early part of the thirteenth century. There is no doubt that Fulk was a real person, and so were some of his companions; but numerous elements from other sources – especially from the *chansons de gestes* and from popular tales – have been attracted into the romance. Some version of it was evidently known to Peter of Langtoft, since he compares the outlaw life of Robert Bruce to that of 'dam Waryn' as told in the book:

> Du boyvere dam Waryn luy rey Robyn ad bu
> Ke citez et viles perdist par l'escu,
> Après en la forest, forsenez et nu,
> Se pesceit ove la beste de cel herbe cru.
> Son livre le temoyne luyquels de luy est lu.[1]

However, nothing is said about the language of this book. The extant French version of the romance is in prose, but was evidently based on an earlier one in verse, and one still extant in the sixteenth century when it is referred to by Leland. An English romance on the subject, though apparently already incomplete, was known to Leland and, in his abstract of it, he has to rely on the French for the ending:

> Here lakkid a Quayre or ii. in the olde Englisch Booke of the nobile Actes of the Guarines. And these thinges that folow I translatid owte of an olde French Historie yn Rime of the Actes of the Guarines onto the Death of Fulco the 2.[2]

The English romance does not appear to have been seen again after the time of Leland.

A contemporary of Fulk, who also seems to have become the subject of romance, is Eustace le Moine. Historically he is first heard of as a monk in the abbey of Samer, but apparently returned to secular life on the death of his father. He then entered the service of the Count of Boulogne, and by 1203 had become his seneschal.

---

[1] Langtoft ii, 372.
[2] *Collectanea* i, 230ff. In that part of Leland's account taken from the lost English version some of the phrases suggest that his original may have been in alliterative verse.

However, he appears to have quarrelled with him, and by 1205 was in the service of King John, but later left him. He was admiral to Prince Louis when he invaded England in 1215, and was captured and beheaded in the great English naval victory off Sandwich in 1217, but by this time he had already become famous as one of the ablest commanders at sea of the time. This is reflected by the appearance of a French romance of which he is the hero. In this, although the general outline of his life seems to be fairly accurate, there are numerous additions from folklore and from outlaw legends. This is even more the case with the fourteenth-century English chroniclers such as John of Canterbury and Walter of Guisborough. The former, in his *Polistorie*, has a wild tale full of magic, which nevertheless still remembers the name of Eustace's executioner, Stephen Crabbe. The second, though briefer, is equally extravagant and has even forgotten the name of the main character. It is now the story of a tyrant of Spain, surnamed Monachus, who has resolved to conquer the English at the head of an enormous fleet. Even so it still remembers that the turning point of the battle was the capture of Eustace's ship, after which the rest fled.[1] Evidently stories of Eustace the Monk were well known in this country, but there is nothing to show whether they were in English or in French.

In *Piers Plowman* (v, 402) is a well-known reference to the 'rymes of Robyn hood and Randolf erle of Chestre'. Some of the rhymes of Robin Hood remain, but those of Randolf, earl of Chester, have been completely lost. Langland says nothing more about them, and although Randolf plays an important part in *Fulk FitzWarin* there is no hint in that romance of any stories connected with him. But Dugdale's *Baronage* contains a long unhistorical account, ascribed to an 'old monk of Peterborough', which, in all probability, gives part of the lost romance. It tells in some detail of the deposition of John and the subsequent French invasion. On the death of John the loyalists are rallied, and the invaders completely defeated at Lincoln; their leader, the earl of Perche, is killed by Randolf, and the young Henry crowned king. All this is quite unhistorical, and the fictitious nature of the narrative, together with the fact that the earl of Chester plays throughout the

---

[1] H. Rothwell, *The Chronicle of Walter of Guisborough* (CS. 1957), pp. 159–60; *EHR.* xxvii, 649–70.

leading part, makes it likely that the monk of Peterborough has got hold of a romance glorifying the earl of Chester, attributing to him much of the importance and many of the achievements of the Earl Marshal, and taken it for sober history. Later in the same work Dugdale gives yet another story connected with Randolf:

> In the time of this Roger [de Lacy, Constable of Chester], Ranulph, Earl of Chester, the last of that name, marching with some forces into Wales; for want of more strength, was constrained to betake himself unto a castle in those parts (viz. Rothelan), where being besieged by the Welsh, he sent for this Roger, then at Chester, to come to his relief: Who, forthwith gathering together divers Minstrels and a multitude of loose people, advanced thitherward; which so alarmed the Welsh, supposing them to have been Soldiers, that they soon left their siege. The Earl therefore for this good service, by his Constable, gave him the Patronage of all the Minstrels in those parts; which he and his Heirs have ever after retained, but conferred upon Dutton his Steward, and his Heirs, the execution of that Authority.

Much the same story appears in Holinshed, who ascribes it to 'an old record' which may well have been that used by Dugdale.[1] Whether either or both of these stories supplied the content of the rhymes known to Langland it is, of course, impossible to say. Certainly one would expect the second of them to have been especially popular with medieval minstrels.

On f. 206 of BM. Additional MS. 25459 is a list of the books belonging to Sir Simon Burley which were found at Baynards Castle after his execution. Most of them were in French, and only one, *j. livre de Englys del Forster et del Sengler*, is specifically said to have been in English. No romance is now known which would fit such a title, nor is there any obvious theme for which it would be at all suitable. It could, perhaps, have been a book on venery, but that is unlikely, and the probability is that we have here yet another lost English romance. Incidentally these were not the only books owned by Burley, as is shown by the statement of his servant that he had in his keeping a volume belonging to the knight called the *livre de songes de Panyell*.[2]

[1] W. Dugdale, *The Baronage of England* (London 1675) i, 42ff., 101; R. Holinshed, *Chronicles of England, Scotland and Ireland* (London 1807) ii, 260–1. See also J. H. Round, *Peerage and Pedigree* (London 1910) ii, 302ff.
[2] M. V. Clarke, *Fourteenth Century Studies* (Oxford 1937), p. 120.

In 1474 John Paston writes to Sir John Paston asking, among other things, for his 'book of the Metyng of the Dwke and of the Emperour'. What this may have been it is now impossible to say; perhaps the title would fit one or other of the Charlemagne romances. It does not seem to appear in an inventory of books, written in the hand of Sir John Paston, and drawn up towards the end of the reign of Edward IV. This includes among the romances versions of *Guy of Warwick*, *Richard the Lion Heart*, and *Child Ypotis*. In addition there was also *Guy and Colbronde* – presumably some form of *Guy of Warwick* – and the *Greene Knyght*.[1] The title of the second of these is partly lost, the paper having been torn lengthwise so that only half the original sheet now remains. It might perhaps have been a version of one of the surviving Gawain romances, but there can be no certainty.

It seems not unlikely that Malory's Sir Ironsyde, the Red Knight of the Red Lands, in the self-contained story of Gareth, may come from a lost English romance of which he was the hero. He appears also in *Sir Gawene and the Carle of Carelyle* and in *Sir Lambewell*, the first of which was probably originally composed some fifty years before Malory, whilst the Ironsyde allusion in the second may also conceivably be independent of Malory. It would appear that in Malory's original the knight must have had this obviously English name, and consequently that the language of his source for the Gareth story was in English, whether or not it was an adaptation of a French romance of Gaheret. But if this was the case, only these vague reminiscences of the lost English romance now remain.[2]

The characteristic English traditions of Guy of Warwick and Bevis of Southampton appear in Irish at this period in forms which presuppose English originals. Moreover, in the case of the first of these it seems clear that the Irish version must come from a form of the story which is unrepresented in the surviving manuscripts.[3] The popularity of the romance is shown not only by the number of surviving versions of it, but also by the fact that the fourteenth-century earls of Warwick were convinced that they possessed genuine relics of the hero. So, in 1369, Thomas, earl of Warwick,

[1] J. Gairdner, *The Paston Letters* (London 1904) v, 207; vi, 65.
[2] *Research Studies* (Washington State University) xxxii, 125–33.
[3] R. Flower, *The Irish Tradition* (Oxford 1947), p. 138.

leaves to his son the sword and 'coat of mail sometime belonging to that famous Guy of Warwick', and a similar bequest appears in 1400 in the will of his son.[1]

Finally, some mention should be made of the list of romances in *The Complaynt of Scotlande*.[2] This is a sixteenth-century work consisting of two principal parts – the author's *Discourse* on the affliction and misery of the country, and his *Dream of Dame Scotia* with her complaint against her three sons. These are joined by what the author calls his *Monologue Recreative* in which he relates the circumstances that interrupted his discourse, and takes advantage of the interruption to introduce what he knows of native songs, dances, and tales, under pretence of having had these brought to his notice during his 'recreative ramble'. Included in the list are the titles of many romances still surviving. Of those which cannot be definitely identified, there are from the Matter of Britain:

the tail of Syr Euan, Arthours knycht – possibly a version of the extant *Ywain and Gawain*, or perhaps a lost romance on Ywain.

Arthour knycht he raid on nycht vitht gyltin spur and candil lycht – , no romance is known with which these lines could be connected, and in any case they read more like a ballad than a romance.

The only uncertain title of the Matter of France is,

the tail of the brig of the mantribil – probably a reference to *Ferumbras*, since in that romance Mantribil is a bridge over the river Flagot.

A number of stories on classical themes are listed, but they have nothing to do with the medieval Matter of Antiquity, and it is unlikely that any of them were known in this country before the sixteenth century. The remaining romances are:

Robert le dyabil duc of Normandie – , not extant in Middle English but two versions appear in early printed books.

the tayl of the volfe of the varldis end – , *volfe* is presumably an error for *velle* 'well'. A fairy tale with that title is known, but it is uncertain whether it goes back to medieval times.

---

[1] N. H. Nicolas, *Testamenta Vetusta* (London 1826), pp. 79, 153.
[2] Ed. J. A. H. Murray (EETS. ES. 1872–3), pp. 63ff., and for identifications, pp. lxxiiiff.

Ferrand erl of Flandris that mareit the deuyl – , possibly a story similar to that which Giraldus Cambrensis tells of the origin of the Plantagenets, but none is known with Ferrand as the hero.

the taiyl of the reyde eyttyn vitht the thre heydis – not now extant, but it was evidently known to Sir David Lyndesay since, during the minority of James V, he was accustomed to lull him to sleep with tales 'off the reid Etin, and the gyir carlyng'.[1]

the tayl of the giantis that eit quyk men – presumably a version of either Jack the Giant-killer or Jack and the Beanstalk.

On fut by fortht as I culd found – more like the opening line of a ballad than of a romance. Not now known, but according to the old table of contents to the Asloan manuscript, there formerly appeared, in a part of the manuscript that has since been lost, 'Master Robert Hendersonnis Dreme, On fut by forth'.[2]

the tail of the thre futtit dog of norrouay – not now known.

the tail quhou the kyng of estmure land mareit the kyngis dochtir of vestmure land – probably a version of the *King Estmere* ballad.

Skail Gillenderson the kyngis sone of Skellye – presumably an Old Norse legend that cannot now be identified.

the tail of Floremond of Albanye that sleu the dragon be the see – not now known.

the tail of Syr valtir, the bald Leslye – not now known.

the tail of the pure tynt – said to be a common nursery tale in Scotland.

Claryades and Maliades – a sixteenth-century Scottish version, translated from French, is still extant. In it the translator refers to an earlier version, probably in English, of which no trace now remains.[3]

the tayl of the зong Tamlene, and of the bald Braband – Tamlene seems to have been a fairy character, and the reference here is probably to a ballad.

Syr Egeir and Syr Gryme – referred to elsewhere in fifteenth-century works, but surviving only in the Percy Folio and in early seventeenth-century printed books.

So far as this list is concerned it may be noted that it includes few romances of the three great matters, but quite a number which

---

[1] J. Small, *Lyndesay's Monarche, &c.* (EETS. 1865–6), p. 264.
[2] W. A. Craigie, *The Asloan Manuscript* (STS. 1923), p. xiv.
[3] *Clariodus* (Maitland Club 1830), pp. v–vi, 351.

could be classified as belonging to the Matter of England. This helps to strengthen the assumption that not many of the former have been lost, but that the extant romances based on native traditions represent only a few of those once current.

7

SHORT NARRATIVE

One of the most surprising things about Middle English literature is the almost complete absence of the fabliau as compared with its popularity in French. Apart from those in the *Canterbury Tales* there is, in the earlier period, only one such tale in English, *Dame Siriʒ*. It is difficult to believe with some that this is due to any inherent strain of puritanism in the English character, and there is in fact a certain amount of evidence to suggest that the fabliau was as popular in this country as it was in France. The extant moralized fabliaux perhaps presuppose earlier unmoralized ones, though it is not often that there is anything to indicate the language of these. However, so far as one such collection is concerned, *Les Contes Moralisés* of Nicholas Bozon, there is evidence to suggest that some of them at any rate may be based on earlier stories in English. This is perhaps indicated by the English names of some of the characters, e.g. *Croket, Hoket,* and *Loket* (p. 137), *William Werldeschame* (p. 166), *Sterlyn* and *Galopyn* (p. 180). Since Bozon is writing in French the names would presumably have been in that language had he invented them himself, and the most plausible explanation for their presence in a French work is that they have been taken over from English originals. Moreover, English phrases appear in some of the tales, while English proverbs in prose and verse are not infrequent.[1] The same thing is found in some of the collections of moral Latin stories,[2] again perhaps indicating English originals for some of them. No doubt, too, the *cantilenas sive fabulas de amasiis vel luxuriosis* against which the University statutes in 1292 warned the students of Oxford, were works of the fabliau type.[3] On the whole it is probable that the poverty of Middle

---

[1] P. Meyer and L. T. Smith, *Les Contes Moralisés de Nicole Bozon* (Paris 1889), pp. 12, 20, 23, 44, 78, 110, 117, 145, 151.
[2] T. Wright, *Latin Stories* (Percy Society viii), pp. 24, 50, 52.
[3] *Munimenta Academica Oxon.* (RS. 50) i, 60.

English in this type of literature is more apparent than real. After all the fabliau is essentially a popular type of literature, and in the earlier peiod it would have had little chance of being written down except in a moralized version.

Another type of short narrative in which Middle English literature is surprisingly deficient is the beast tale. The lost collection of English fables turned into French by Marie de France (see p. 68) certainly contained examples of this kind of story, but no English work comparable with the continental Reynard cycle has survived. Before Caxton's translation of it only three isolated episodes are known in English, the *Vox and the Wolf*, Chaucer's *Nuns' Priest's Tale*, and the 26-line rhyme of the *Fox and the Goose*, written in a fifteenth-century hand on a fly-leaf of MS. Royal 19 B. iv, and beginning:

> 'Pax uobis,' quod the ffox,
> 'For I am comyn to toowne.'[1]

However, there is in addition a certain amount of evidence for the former existence of other episodes from the cycle. A catalogue of the library of Dover Priory was compiled by John Whytefeld in 1389, and in item 170, a volume of miscellaneous treatises, there was one which is described as the *Fabula de Wlpe medici in angl.*, with the incipit 'Hit by ful whylem'.[2] A number of episodes in the cycle would fit such a title, and it is impossible to decide which of them might have been represented by this lost poem.

A hint of another lost beast tale in English is perhaps provided by Odo of Cheriton (c. 1180–c. 1246). Odo came of an aristocratic family, studied at Paris, and travelled widely in France and Spain. His works include sermons, books on theology, and a series of fables, the last of which seems to have been composed some time after 1225, and must have been particularly popular if we are to judge from the many surviving manuscripts. According to one of the fables:

Isengrim, penitent and lamenting his past sins, wished to become a monk, and this was allowed. He received the tonsure and the cowl,

---

[1] Another version in C.U.L. MS. Ee. 1. 12, and both in R. H. Robbins, *Secular Lyrics of the XIVth and XVth Centuries* (Oxford 1955), pp. 43–5. See also *Journal of English and Germanic Philology* li, 393–4; *English Studies* xxxiv, 163–4.　　　　　　　　　　　　　　[2] *Canterbury and Dover*, p. 460.

along with the other things pertaining to a monk. He was then placed in the school and taught in the first place to say the Pater Noster, but he repeated, 'A lamb or a ram'. The monks taught that he should ever look to the cross and to the sacrifice, but he always turned his eyes to the lambs and the rams.

Moral. Many monks are like this. They always repeat, 'A lamb or a ram.' That is, they ask for good wine and always have their eyes on a loaded tray or a heaped-up dish. Whence it is often said in English:

> If al that the Wolf unto a preest worthe,
> and be set unto book psalmes to lere,
> yit his eye is evere to the wodeward.[1]

The lines fall into passable alliterative verse, and it is at any rate possible that Odo is quoting from some contemporary English poem on the subject, though since slightly different versions of the English appear in the various manuscripts, it may have been extant only in oral form.

In Barbour's *Bruce* there is mention of the story of the fox and the fisherman, in terms suggesting that it was fairly well known at the time. Douglas is giving advice on the best way of attacking the English:

> Do we with our fayis tharfor   Nota. how the
> That ar heir liand vs befor,   fox playt
> As I herd tell this othir ȝer   wyth the
> How that a fox did vith a fischer.   fischar.[2]

However, nothing is known of any vernacular version of this story, and a reference such as this is hardly proof of its former existence.

In addition, there is a good deal of evidence from pictorial representations of various kinds to suggest that beast tales were as popular in this country as on the continent. It has been possible to collect references to some 250 illustrations in manuscripts, carvings, and stained glass which bear witness to the popularity of the subject, and these can only represent a fraction of those once existing. Representations of several branches of the French *Roman de Renart* are to be found in such illustrations. From

---

[1] L. Hervieux, *Les Fabulistes Latins* (Paris 1884) ii, 610–11. For variants of the English, see T. Wright, *Latin Stories* (Percy Society viii), pp. 55, 229, and *Speculum* ix, 219, n, 2.

[2] W. W. Skeat, *The Bruce* (EETS. ES. 1870–7) xix, 645ff.

Branch I Reynard's trial and some of the incidents leading up to it are well represented, and Reynard the Minstrel also seems to have been a popular subject (Ib). Other episodes evidently well known were those of Reynard and Chantecler (II), Reynard the Physician (X), and Reynard's funeral procession (XVII). There is also considerable such evidence for the alliance between Reynard and the ape which is only rarely referred to in the *Roman de Renart*, as well as for Reynard in his various religious roles.[1] Altogether it seems clear that the lack of extant written works on the subject in Middle English is due more to accident than to lack of contemporary interest.

Eight Breton lays, written at various dates, survive in English, and there is some evidence that there may have been others. Marie de France, in the twelfth century, is usually supposed to have been the first to versify the prose *contes* of the original lyrics, yet in one of her lays she seems to imply that other versions of them were extant – possibly written even before her own translations into Anglo-French. She speaks of an English lay named *Gotelef*, as if she knew of its existence, though if it ever did appear in English it has long since been lost. But it is difficult to be certain that Marie really is referring to an actual English work, since in another of her lays she promises:

> Une aventure vus dirai,
> dunt li Bretun firent un lai.
> Laüstic a nun, ceo m'est vis,
> Si l'apelent en lur païs;
> ceo est *russignol* en Franceis
> e *nihtegale* en dreit Engleis.[2]

Here she appears to be merely giving the English and French equivalents of the Breton word, and the same may be true of the former reference, though the words used would seem rather to favour the existence of an English lay. In addition, it may be worth noting that when, in the *Roman de Renart*, Reynard is pretending to be an English minstrel, he tells Ysengrim that he knows many Breton lays:

> Je fout savoir bon lai breton
> et de Mellin et de Notun,

[1] K. Varty, *Reynard the Fox* (Leicester U.P. 1967).
[2] K. Warnke, *Die Lais der Marie de France* (Halle 1900), pp. 185, 146.

dou roi Lartu et de Tritan,
de Charpel et de saint Brandan.[1]

Reynard, in accordance with his disguise, speaks in a kind of anglicized French; *Charpel* is apparently his version of *Chievrefueil* (*Gotelef*), and this may provide further evidence for the former existence of such a lay. Certainly, it would seem that a minstrel from England was expected to sing about King Arthur, Tristan, Merlin, and St Brendan. Nothing appears to be known of Notun, and there is no extant lay of St Brendan, though he is well enough known in the legendaries. However, it would probably be unwise to attempt to deduce too much from a reference such as this.

Throughout the medieval period the debate was a favourite type of literature, and a fair number of examples in English still exist. The most important of such poems in the earlier period is *The Owl and the Nightingale*, extant in two manuscripts, and with evidence of at least one other. When the catalogue of the library of the Premonstratensian monastery at Titchfield was drawn up in 1400, one of the manuscripts, C II, included amongst its contents an item *De conflictu inter philomenam et bubonem in anglicis*. This must have been a copy of the English poem, and the other contents of the manuscript show that it was not identical with either of the two in which the poem has been preserved. A work on the same subject, though presumably either in French or Latin, appears among the books *in gallicis* in the same library.[2] Further evidence for the popularity of debates between the owl and the nightingale is perhaps to be found in the late thirteenth-century treatise on the French language by Walter de Bibbesworth:

> Aloms ore iuer a boys,
> Ou la russinole, *the nithingale*
> Meuz chaunte ki houswan en sale (*houle*).[3]

However, this may be no more than a testimony to the popularity of the subject. Again, in MS. Rawlinson poet. 34, containing a collection of saints' lives along with *Sir Degare*, there appear eighty-six lines of a debate between a clerk and a nightingale of which the first page is missing, while a poem on the same subject,

---

[1] M. Roques, *Roman de Renart* (Paris 1948–63), lines 2435ff.

[2] *Proceedings of the Leeds Philosophical Society: Literary and Historical Section* v, part iii, pp. 150ff.; part iv, pp. 252ff.

[3] A. Owen, *Le Traité de Walter de Bibbesworth* (Paris 1929), p. 110.

but this time with the end absent, is in C.U.L. MS. Ff. 5. 48. Unfortunately the two poems cannot be used to fill in the missing parts of each other, since the relationship between them seems to be a very general one.[1]

A debate known today only from an Anglo-French version is *La Geste de Blancheflour e de Florence*, the last stanza of which appears to claim that it was translated into French by Brykhulle from the English of a certain Banastre:

> Banastre en englois le fist,
> E Brykhulle cest escrit
> En franceois translata.[2]

The lines, however, could mean that both the English and the Anglo-French writers are using the same source, possibly a Latin one. Certainly, whatever Brykhulle may have been doing, he can hardly have been making a literal translation of an English poem. Although on the face of it the poem is a debate on the familiar question of whether a clerk or a knight is to be preferred as a lover, in fact the Anglo-French poem is an exercise in vocabulary. Many of the stanzas are little more than lists of names of various things, and the poem was evidently intended to teach both French and morality at the same time.[3] Nevertheless, whatever the exact interpretation of the lines may be, they do provide evidence of a lost poem on the subject by Banastre. A man of that name is referred to as an English writer by Tanner, and in the *Scala-chronica* there is mention of a William Banastre, along with Thomas of Erceldoun, in words which suggest that the former, like the latter, had written English poems.[4] The various Banastres may perhaps be identical, though the name is not uncommon, and there is hardly enough evidence to connect the writer of the lost English debate poem with any of the known bearers of the name.

The earliest known reference to the Robin Hood stories is that in the B-text of *Piers Plowman* (c. 1377), when Sloth says:

> I can nouȝte perfitly my pater-noster as þe prest it syngeth,
> But I can rymes of Robyn hood and Randolf erle of Chestre.
> (V, 401–2).

---

[1] Both in R. H. Robbins, *op. cit.*, pp. 172–9.   [2] *Romania* xxxvii, 234.

[3] M. D. Legge, *Anglo-Norman Literature and its Background* (Oxford 1963), p. 335.

[4] J. A. H. Murray, *Thomas of Erceldoune* (EETS. 1875), p. xviii, n. 1.

In the Monkbretton *Chartulary*, in a document of 1422, appears a reference to 'the stone of Robin Hode'. This was in what is now Skelbrooke township in the West Riding, its site corresponding with that of the present-day Robin Hood's Well. This correspondence is enough to associate the older place-name with the Robin Hood of the ballads, and not with some otherwise unknown individual who chanced to bear the famous name.[1] None of the extant Robin Hood ballads can be dated earlier than the end of the fifteenth century, yet these two references provide evidence to show that he was famous well before that time.

Even so, it seems to have taken him a considerable time to attract the notice of writers, and it is not until the sixteenth century that references to Robin Hood become frequent enough to show that he has at last been accepted as a popular hero. But already in the fifteenth he is known to the Scottish historians. He is mentioned by Andrew Wyntoun (d. 1425):

> Litil Iohun and Robert Hude
> Waythmen war commendit gud;
> In Ingilwode and Bernnysdaile
> Þai oyssit al þis tyme þar trawale.[2]

Since none of the extant ballads associates Robin Hood with Inglewood in Cumberland, this may be an indication of lost poems on the subject. In 1438 the *Aberdeen Manuscript Council Register*, records a case concerning a ship called 'Robyne hude' or 'ly Robert hude'.[3] Bower (d. 1449) speaks of

> that most famous robber Robert Hode and Litill-John with their companions, at comedies and tragedies of whom the lazy mob gape, and of whose deeds minstrels and poets love to sing,

and he has a story concerning the hero which is very similar to the extant *Robin Hood and the Monk*, and obviously based on some lost ballad.[4] The English historians of the fifteenth century have nothing to say of him, the few references by English writers of this

---

[1] *MLR.* xxviii, 484. The date of the Monkbretton document is certainly a century later than the 1322 assigned to it by its editor, see A. H. Smith, *The Place-Names of the West Riding of Yorkshire* (Cambridge 1961) ii, 36.

[2] F. J. Amours, *Wyntoun's Original Chronicle* (STS. 1902–14) v, 137.

[3] A. J. Mill, *Mediæval Plays in Scotland* (Edinburgh 1927), p. 23, n. 1.

[4] W. Goodhall, *Johannis Forduni Scotichronicon* (Edinburgh 1759) ii, 104ff.

period coming from elsewhere. Already, by the beginning of the century, he has become proverbial, and is mentioned in *Friar Daw's Reply*, 'And many men speken of Robyn Hood & shotte neuere in his bowe'.[1] Chaucer has a similar proverb in *Troilus and Criseyde* (ii, 859–61), and although he himself makes no mention of Robin Hood, some of the scribes recognize the saying and supply glosses referring to the hero. *Dives and Pauper* (c. 1410) reprimands those who 'gon levir to heryn a tale or a song of Robyn Hode or of sum rubaudry than to heryn masse or matynes'. In a lawsuit in 1428–9 the judge refers in an off-hand way to a ballad beginning 'Robin Hode en Barnesdale stode', which he evidently expected the court to know, though it cannot now be identified and has presumably been lost.[2] There may perhaps be some connexion with the ballad of Robin Hood, now represented only by four lines in English, followed by a Latin translation of them, which an unknown scribe, during the first quarter of the fifteenth century, scribbled in a manuscript in the Lincoln Cathedral Chapter Library:

> Robyn hod in scherewod stod,
> Hodud & hathud, hosut & schod.
> ffour and thuynti arowus he bar
> In hi[s] hondus.[3]

Under the year 1439 the *Rolls of Parliament* tell of a certain Piers Venables who, 'in manere of Insurrection, wente into the wodes in that Contre, like as it hadde be Robyn-hode and his meyne',[4] while Stow noted the appearance in 1417 of a malefactor calling himself Friar Tuck, though whether his source for the information was at all contemporary we do not know.[5] Sir John Paston, in 1473, writes to his brother lamenting the loss of a servant whom he had kept to play Robin Hood, and who, apparently taking his role too seriously, had imitated his exemplar by going off into Barnesdale forest.[6] In the sixteenth century Grafton claims that 'in an olde and auncient Pamphlet I finde this written of the sayd Robert

---

[1] P. L. Heyworth, *Jack Upland, Friar Daw's Reply and Upland's Rejoinder* (Oxford 1968), p. 80.

[2] W. C. Bolland, *A Manual of Year Book Studies* (Cambridge 1925), p. 107, n. 2.   [3] *MLR.* xliii, 507–8.   [4] *Rotuli Parliamentorum* v, 16.

[5] J. Stow, *Annales*, continued by E. Howes (London 1615), p. 352.

[6] J. Gairdner, *The Paston Letters* (London 1904) v, 185.

Hood', and goes on to tell of his alleged noble descent, and his death at the hands of the Prioress of 'Bircklies' nunnery in York-shire.[1] The 'pamphlet' has presumably long since been lost, but by this date references are frequent, and there can be no doubt of the hero's widespread popularity.[2]

A story known only from an incidental reference in Ordericus Vitalis is that of the giant Buamundus. The chronicler is explaining why the name Bohemond was given to the son of Robert Guiscard:

> His own baptismal name was Mark, but his father, having heard the story of the giant Buamundus in the happiness of a feast, jestingly called his son by the giant's name.[3]

What the story of the giant may have been we do not know, nor can we say whether the stories were current only on the continent or whether they had made their way into England as well. Similarly, two other heroes, of whom little is known but the names, are mentioned by Giraldus Cambrensis. In the course of an attack on the sins of the clergy, he likens some priests to

> the singers of fables and romances, who, seeing that the romance of Landericus does not please their audience, immediately begin to sing of Wacherius, if this does not please, of something else.[4]

Giraldus is here borrowing directly from the *Verbum abbreviatum* of Petrus Cantor, except that the latter has *Narcisus* instead of *Wacherius*. It has been suggested that Landericus is to be identified with Landri, count of Nevers, and that there evidently existed a romance telling of his adventures, known today only from a Latin version by Hugh de Poitiers, a twelfth-century monk of Vézelay. He wrote a history of the foundation of his abbey, including as an introduction a short account of the legendary origin of the counts of Nevers.[5] As for Wacherius, he has been identified with Warocher,

[1] *Grafton's Chronicle* (London 1809) i, 221.
[2] On Friday, March 9, 1733, a certain William Alcock was executed at Northampton for the murder of his wife. 'On his way to the Gallows he sung part of an old Song of Robin Hood, with the Chorus, *Derry, derry, down*, etc., and swore, kick'd, and spurn'd at every person that laid hold of the Cart' (*Gentleman's Magazine* iii, 154).
[3] Ordericus iv, 212.   [4] *Gemma Ecclesiastica*, p. 290.
[5] *Patrologia Latina* ccv, 101. See also *Romania* xxxii, 1ff., where F. Lot gathers together the evidence for the existence of a lost French romance on Landri.

the hero of *Reine Sebile*. In any case, stories concerning these two were evidently current in twelfth-century France, though whether they were also known in England must remain doubtful.

A more humble subject of popular tales was a certain Einhard, a lay-brother of the Witham Charterhouse. He had apparently been sent at various times to assist new foundations in different parts of Europe, but on being ordered to Denmark he rebelled and was expelled from the order. After much suffering he was re-admitted and, although by now apparently a centenarian, was sent to the new foundation at Witham, where he became a celebrated character whose fame spread far beyond the walls of the monastery, and of whom stories in the vernacular were widely known throughout the countryside.[1]

In 1402 Sir Edmund Mortimer was taken prisoner by Owen Glyndower. He was treated kindly by his captors, and rumours evidently got about that the captivity was not unwelcome. Consequently the king not only forbade the payment of ransom for him, but also confiscated his plate and jewels. Mortimer then made common cause with Glyndower, married his daughter, and joined the revolt of the Percys. The defeat at Shrewsbury changed the whole position, and gradually reduced Glyndower's revolt to its original character of a native Welsh rising against the English. From this point of view Mortimer's help was much less necessary, and he faded into the background. He was finally besieged in Harlech Castle by the forces of the king and died during the siege. His actions seem to have had no particular result, but all the same he struck the imagination of his contemporaries to such an extent that his adventures are said to have been commemorated in songs:

> ... my lord the said sir Edmund, whose father, the lord of Usk, gave me an exhibition at the schools, was by fortune of war carried away captive ... At last, being by the English host beleaguered in the castle of Harlech, he brought his days of sorrow to an end, his wonderful deeds being to this day told at the feast in song.[2]

Neither Mortimer nor his adventures would appear to have been important or interesting enough for contemporary celebration, but a definite statement such as this can hardly be ignored. Presumably

[1] *Magna Vita Sancti Hugonis* (RS. 37), p. 217.
[2] E. M. Thompson, *Chronicon Adæ de Usk* (London 1904), p. 246.

the songs told of Mortimer's adventures in the Welsh revolt, perhaps in English, perhaps in Welsh, or possibly in both languages.

In one of the stanzas of a thirteenth-century lyric, *Annot and Johon*, the heroine is compared with heroes and heroines famous in legend and romance:

> He is medierne of miht mercie of mede
> Rekene ase *Regnas* resoun to rede,
> Trewe ase *Tegeu* in tour, ase *Wyrwein* in wede,
> Baldore þen *Byrne* þat oft þe bor bede,
> Ase *Wylcadoun* he is wys, dohty of dede,
> Feyrore þen *Floyres* folkes to fede,
> Cud ase *Cradoc* in court carf þe brede,
> Hendore þen *Hilde* þat haueþ me to hede,
> He haueþ me to hede þis hendy anon,
> Gentil ase *Ionas* heo ioyeþ wiþ Ion.[1]

Tentative identifications of most of these are possible. *Regnas* probably refers to an Old Norse legend, since stories of the wise counsels of Ragna appear in the *Orkneyinga saga*. *Tegeu*, according to the Welsh *Triads*, was one of the three faithful wives of the island of Britain. She is said to have been the wife of Caradawc Vreichvras and to have saved him from a serpent which had attached itself to his arm and was draining away his life. Tegeu managed to lure it away so that it fastened on her own breast; in order to save her life the breast was cut off and a gold one substituted.[2] *Wyrwein* may perhaps be for Garwen, daughter of Henin Hen, and one of the three mistresses of Arthur. *Byrne* looks like a form of Bjorn, and may refer to the Bjorn of the *Orkneyinga saga* whose brother Heming, a noted archer, on one occasion shot at a nut on the head of his brother. But even if this is the Byrne intended it throws no light on the exploit referred to here. *Wylcadoun* has not been identified, but was probably some Celtic heroine. *Floyres* is the Floripas of *Sir Ferumbras* who had a magic girdle which freed all who wore it from the effects of hunger or thirst. *Cradoc*, who alone of Arthur's knights succeeded in carving the boar's head, appears in the ballad of *The Boy and the Mantle*. *Hilde* may be a reference to the widespread Hild-Gudrun story,

---

[1] C. Brown, *English Lyrics of the XIIIth Century* (Oxford 1932), pp. 138, 226ff.

[2] R. Bromwich, *Trioedd Ynys Prydein* (Cardiff 1961), pp. 512–13.

though the allusion here is too vague for any certainty. *Jonas* is perhaps the Jonaans who, in the *Queste del Saint Graal*, appears as one of the descendants of Celidoine, the first king of Scotland; he is said to have gone to Wales and there to have married King Moroneu's daughter.

Here, then, we have a number of heroes and heroines, mainly Celtic and Scandinavian, referred to as if the author expected his readers to recognize the references immediately. Few of them appear in the extant Middle English literature, and although isolated references such as this can hardly prove the existence of written works in the vernacular, it seems possible enough that stories of some of them were known in England at this period.

So far as this type of literature is concerned, it is only rarely that the titles of books mentioned in wills are of much interest. John Raventhorp of York (d. 1432) possessed a fair number of the usual kind of religious books, and one which may have been more interesting. He leaves to Agnes de Celayne, along with various household goods, a *librum Angliæ de Fabulis et Narracionibus*.[1] The form *Angliæ* looks suspicious and may well be a mistake for *Anglice*. But if so it is now impossible to say what the work could have been, though had it survived it is likely that our hopes would be disappointed; it would probably turn out to be a bestiary, a lapidary, or a collection of moralized tales such as the *Gesta Romanorum*.

[1] SS. xxx, 29.

8

RELIGIOUS AND DIDACTIC LITERATURE

Much of the extant Middle English literature, more especially from the earlier part of the period, is didactic or religious in tone, as is inevitable from the conditions of survival. Before the fourteenth century writing is in the hands of clerics or of professional scribes, and books copied by them are usually destined for one or the other of the great monastic libraries. It is true that occasionally the extant catalogues reveal the presence of works which, theoretically, should not have been there, but on the whole secular narrative or lyrical poetry are rare, while religious and didactic works are prominent. Because of this the latter types of literature in the vernacular had a much better chance of survival; they were more likely to be written down and to find a safe and inconspicuous home in the monastic library. Yet, although it is probable that a much higher proportion of such literature has survived, even so it is certain that a good deal has been lost.

In the first place, it is clear that a good many of the manuscripts of extant works have disappeared, whether worn out by constant use, or destroyed by accident. Occasionally a single remaining leaf gives evidence of such a loss. So, for example, part of a lost version of *The Gast of Gy* appears in Gonville and Caius MS. 175, and 176 verses in MS. Rawlinson Misc. 1370 is all that remains of a manuscript of Robert Mannyng's *Chronicle*. Similarly, two leaves, formerly used as paste-downs and now in the Bodleian, are the only representatives of a lost text of the *Southern English Legendary*, while a double leaf of vellum, used as a binding for a Latin printed book of 1573, contains 99 lines of an English text of *Mandeville* in a hand of the first half of the fifteenth century.[1] Again, a lost manuscript of the *Ancrene Riwle* is represented by a single leaf, in an early fourteenth-century hand, now in the

[1] *Bodleian Library Record* vi, 663; *English Studies* xxxviii, 262–5.

Bodleian. It was found in the library at Lanhydrock, Bodmin, in the late nineteenth century, and had apparently been used as the wrapper of an octavo-sized book.[1]

However, the survival of these, as of other manuscripts of extant works, would have added little to our knowledge of this type of Middle English literature. Perhaps more important is the disappearance of the writings of a twelfth-century northern monk. Jocelyn of Furness, in his life of St Walthen, tells of a certain Brother Walter who, after the death of the saint, lost his faith through the wiles of the devil. St Walthen appeared to him in a vision and reasoned with him, so that he was greatly strengthened in faith, and immediately began to compose a great number of religious works in English, in such noble verse that his hearers were frequently reduced to tears.[2] Despite this praise of them, it is unlikely that the loss of Brother Walter's works is of much importance from a literary point of view, but linguistically they might have added much to our knowledge of the northern dialect at this date.

At some time between 1140 and 1215 a certain anchorite by the name of Hugh asked a priest called Robert for a rule of life. Robert replied that he had already 'been zealous in translating various passages from English books into Latin'.[3] In the context the wording suggests the existence during the twelfth century of various rules in English, but if so it is difficult to identify Robert's originals with anything now extant. They could hardly have been the surviving English translations of original Latin rules, for example those of St Benedict or St Chrodegang, for the Latin originals of these would be easily available, and there would be no need for re-translation. The only rule of which we know that was composed originally in English, and probably during the second half of the twelfth century, is the *Ancrene Riwle*. None of the extant manuscripts of the Latin version of this work is earlier than the first half of the fourteenth century, and the English original is unlikely to have been written early enough for it to have been translated by Robert. It would appear that there must have been current during the twelfth century various religious writings in English of which no trace now remains.

---

[1] Ed. A. Zettersten (EETS. 1962), pp. 163–71.
[2] *ASS.*, *August* i, 272d; *RES.* NS. v, 113–22.   [3] *Continuity*, p. xciii.

All that we know of one English work is the title of a Latin version of it. This is the *Libertates Ecclesiæ S. Joh. Beverlac.* which a certain Alfred *de Anglico in Latinum transtulit*. The Latin version was apparently contained in MS. Cotton Otho C. xvi, one of the manuscripts destroyed in the Cottonian fire, and only the title now remains. However, if the Alfred in question were the chronicler Alfred of Beverley, we should hardly expect anything of much interest from him.[1]

Fabyan mentions a book which, had it survived, would have been of considerable interest. According to him, the names of the portgreaves of London,

> of olde tyme, with the lawys and customys than vsed within this cytie, were regestryd in a boke called the Domysday, in Saxon tunge than vsed: but in later dayes, when the sayd lawes and customes alteryd and chaunged, & for consideracion also that the sayd boke was of small hande, & sore defaced, it was the lesse set by, so that it was enbesylyd, or loste; so that the remembraunce of suche rulers as were before the dayes of this Rycharde the first, whose storye shall nexte ensue, are loste and forgoten.[2]

Fabyan is hardly a good authority for the existence of a book which had been lost so long before his time, and he gives no source for his statement.

One of the most important of the extant Middle English historical works is John Barbour's *Bruce*. It would seem, however, that Barbour was not the first, as he was certainly not the last, to write on this subject. In 1615 there was printed at Dortmund a poem with the same title by a certain Patrick Gordon who, in his preface, speaks of an old

> tome almost inlegeable in manie places, vanting leaves, yet hade it the beginning, and hade bein sett doune by a monk in the abey of Melros, called Peter Fenton, in the year of God one thousand thrie hundreth sixtie nyne . . . it was in old ryme like to Chaucer, but vanting in manie parts, – and in special from the field of Bannochburne fourth . . . so that it could not be gotten to the press, yet such as I could reid thereof hade many remarkable taillis worthie to be noted.[3]

---

[1] T. Wright, *Biographia Britannica Literaria* (London 1846) ii, 158.
[2] Fabyan, p. 293.
[3] R. L. G. Ritchie, *The Buik of Alexander* (STS. 1925) i, civ.

Since Peter Fenton's work, whether he was the author or merely the scribe, was 'in old ryme like to Chaucer' it must presumably have been in the vernacular. That being so, unless it was merely an early manuscript of Barbour, its loss has deprived us not only of a possibly valuable historical source, but also of the earliest considerable work in the Scottish dialect.

Although the *Bruce* is the only surviving work certainly by John Barbour, various others, now lost, have been attributed to him. Wyntoun several times refers to Barbour's *Brut*, and the various references suggest that it may have been a translation of Geoffrey of Monmouth's *Historia Regum Britanniae*, or at any rate based on it. Wyntoun also mentions on various occasions a work on the genealogy of the Stewarts – the *Stewartis Oryginalle* –[1] and although this has been taken to be merely an alternative title for the *Brut*, on the whole it is unlikely that the two titles represent the same work.

One of the most important of the religious figures of the fourteenth century was Richard Rolle of Hampole. Most of his vernacular writings have probably been preserved, but in MS. Harl. 1706, containing various works ascribed to Rolle, there is mention of a book by him 'cleped Toure of all Toures', all trace of which has long since vanished.[2] Another lost work by the same author may perhaps be referred to in a puzzling entry in the catalogue of the library of Henry Savile of Banke (d. 1617), in which item 206 is said to contain a letter sent by Master Walter Hilton to a Gilbertine nun, and in the letter was expounded the order and rule which Richard of Hampole, at the request of the said lady, had translated from Latin into English.[3] It is barely possible that one of Rolle's charges lived to come under the care of Hilton, but if so nothing is known of this particular work.

John Wyclif played an even more important part than Rolle in the religious life of his period. About the time when his personal influence was at its height, he issued a work on *The Thirty Three Conclusions on the Poverty of Christ*, which is said to have appeared in English as well as in Latin, but of which only the latter version

[1] F. J. Amours, *Wyntoun's Original Chronicle* (STS. 1902–14) ii, 201; iii, 91, 247, 435; iv, 17, 21, 23; ii, 153, 315; v, 257.

[2] G. R. Owst, *Literature and Pulpit in Medieval England* (Cambridge 1933), p. 78, n. 5.   [3] *Trans. Bib. Soc.* ix, 201.

138

is now extant.[1] Again, in the interrogations of suspected Lollards during the fifteenth and early sixteenth centuries, Wyclif's *Wyket* is occasionally mentioned. No manuscript of this work has survived, but it was printed in 1546 as from Nuremberg, though this may have been merely a cover for illegal publication in this country. Similarly, Thomas Abell, one of the Coventry Lollards of 1511–12 confessed to a belief in 'Wycliffe', though there is nothing to show which of the tracts was in his possession.[2]

In 1392 one of Wyclif's followers, a certain William Smith, was in trouble with the authorities because of his unorthodox activities. Owing, it is suggested, to a disappointment in love, he had joined the Lollards of Leicester. On one occasion, when at an inn with a companion, they found themselves hungry, with a supply of cabbages but no fuel with which to cook them. Thereupon they chopped up an old image of St Katherine that they found there, and used this as fuel, an act which proved so offensive to local feeling that they were turned out of the inn. This took place in 1382, and ten years later Smith had to do penance for it. In addition, he was compelled to hand over to the archbishop the religious works which he had written in English on the gospels and the epistles and concerning various bishops, the compilation of which had occupied him for eight years.[3] It is hardly likely that these were original works; they were more probably copies of some of the Lollard treatises in circulation at this time, and other versions of them may still survive. A later Lollard was less fortunate, and the proceedings for heresy against John Claydon of London, currier, tell of the many English books possessed by the accused, but the title of only one of them – the *lanterne of light* – is given. This, together with the others, was ordered to be burned, and Claydon himself is said to have suffered at Smithfield in 1415.[4] Incidentally it came out in his examination that Claydon himself could not read, and so could enjoy his library only with the help of others.

In the later heresy proceedings the books owned by suspects are

[1] H. B. Workman, *John Wyclif* (Oxford 1926) i, 312.
[2] J. A. F. Thomson, *The Later Lollards 1414–1520* (Oxford 1965), pp. 113, 242ff.; H. B. Workman, *op. cit.* ii, 39, n. 1.
[3] *Chronicon Henrici Knighton* (RS. 92) ii, 313.
[4] E. F. Jacob, *The Register of Henry Chichele* (Canterbury and York Society 47) iv, 132–8; J. Foxe, *Acts and Monuments* (London 1837) iii, 531ff.; L. M. Swinburn, *The Lanterne of Light* (EETS. 1917).

not as a rule named, but referred to only by some such phrase as books in English of reproved reading. Most of those of which some description is given were portions of the Bible in the vernacular, usually the New Testament. John Hacker's book of the ten plagues of Egypt, and Thomas Mann's on how Adam and Eve were expelled from Paradise, may have been parts of the Old Testament, or possibly heretical tracts. In addition, a copy of Tobit is mentioned; one of the London Lollards of 1510–11 admitted to the possession of a book containing the coming of Antichrist and the passion of Nicodemus, while another book, that cannot now be identified, was one that said of the Lollards that their sect would be in a manner destroyed, but that it would eventually prevail.[1]

Another reformer who suffered for his unorthodoxy was Reginald Pecock (?1395–1460), bishop of Chichester. Six of his English works survive, but in them are references to others which do not now exist: the *Afore-Crier* or *Bifore-Crier*, *Book of Divine Office*, *Book of Learning*, *Book of Priesthood* or *of Priests' Power* and *Twelve Advantages of Tribulation*. In addition, there are allusions to five lost works in Latin, and to another twenty-five of which the language is uncertain. Consequently, of forty-one works by Pecock only six are now extant, though it is only fair to say that the former existence of all forty-one is far from certain. Some are mentioned as having already been written, some are to be written in the future, while the references to others are ambiguous.[2] It is not impossible that some at any rate of the titles represent works which Pecock intended to write but never did.

Literature of a more orthodox type appears in Archbishop Arundel's reference to the English version of the gospels possessed by Anne of Bohemia:

he seide it was more Joie of hir than of any whoman that evere he knewe; ffor, not withstanding that sche was an alien borne, sche hadde on Engliche al the foure gospeleris with the docturis upon hem, and he seide sche hadde sent hem unto him, and he seide thei weren goode and trewe, and comended hir in that sche was so grete a lady and also an alien, and wolde so lowliche studiee in so vertuous bokis.[3]

[1] J. A. F. Thomson, *op. cit.*, pp. 242ff., 93, 162, 131
[2] V. H. H. Green, *Bishop Reginald Pecock* (Cambridge 1945), pp. 238ff.
[3] M. Aston, *Thomas Arundel* (Oxford 1967), p. 327.

It seems likely that the glosses to the gospels were those of Purvey, and in that case Arundel's authorization could not have been earlier than about 1387. Again, under the year 1447–8, a London chronicle mentions the death of William Lichfeld,

> þat made in his dayes M^{lll} iiij^{xx} and iij sermones, as it was founde in his bokes of his owne hande writing.[1]

Some of these may still survive, but certainly not all of them.

An extant Irish version of the *Harrowing of Hell* is said to derive from a lost Middle English poem on the subject;[2] and Caxton, in his prologue to the *Eneydos*, mentions Skelton's translations of 'the epystlys of Tulle and the boke of dyodorus syculus'.[3] The latter survives in a single manuscript, but Skelton's translation of Cicero has disappeared. The only one of Caxton's own works known to have been lost is his version of the life of Robert, earl of Oxford:

> reduced and translated out of Frenche, . . . with diverse & many great myracles whiche God shewed for him as wel in his lyfe as after his death, as it is shewed all a longe in hys sayde booke.[4]

The earl of Oxford in question may have been the favourite of Richard II, killed in France whilst engaged in a boar hunt, but was more probably Robert, third earl, who took the part of the barons against King John, and was buried in the priory at Hatfield Broadoak. At the end of the fifteenth century Gavin Douglas made a translation of Ovid's *De Remedio Amoris* which has not survived,[5] nor has Henry VIII's treatise on vocal prayer which is said to have been praised by Wolsey.[6] Again, the *Plumpton Letters*, consisting of some 250 letters written to a Yorkshire family between 1460 and 1552, have also disappeared. They were transcribed during the seventeenth century for Sir Edward Plumpton (1581–1654), after which all trace of the originals was lost. The transcripts came into the possession of Christopher Towneley

---

[1] C. L. Kingsford, *English Historical Literature in the Fifteenth Century* (Oxford 1913), p. 296.

[2] R. Flower, *The Irish Tradition* (Oxford 1947), p. 130.

[3] W. J. B. Crotch, *The Prologues and Epilogues of William Caxton* (EETS. 1927), p. 109.

[4] O. Richardson, *The Foure Sonnes of Aymon* (EETS. ES. 1884), p. 3.

[5] J. Small, *The Works of Gavin Douglas* (Edinburgh 1874) i, cxxviii.

[6] H. M. Smith, *Pre-Reformation England* (London 1938), p. 507.

(1606–74), and were published by T. Stapleton in 1839, after which the transcripts too apparently vanished.[1]

It might have been hoped that medieval wills and the extant catalogues of monastic libraries would provide further clues to some of the lost religious and didactic literature. Both, however, are disappointing. A fair number of English books are mentioned in wills, but when they can be identified they are usually those which are still extant in numerous manuscripts. At other times the description is too general for any certainty as to the exact work intended, while occasionally there are merely general bequests of English books with no titles given. Lady Alice West (1395) bequeathes to her daughter Johanna 'alle the bokes that I haue of latyn, englisch, and frensch', and a similar bequest appears in the will of Sir Brian Roucliffe (1494–5).[2] Similarly, the stock of two London grocers who became bankrupt in the 1390's contained two *libros de Englysshe* valued at 8d.[3] The earliest mention of English books in a will occurs in that of Ralph Baldock, bishop of London (d. 1313). He left a number of ornaments and scholastic books to St Paul's, and amongst the latter was an *Exposicio Anglice cum alijs tractatibus*.[4] Apparently he also had several unspecified works of Bede in English, though what these could have been at this date it is difficult to say, and he kept in his study at Stepney an alphabetical *Exposicio* in English which, from the character of the other books in the list, seems to have been some kind of a sermon aid. In 1346 Johanna de Walkyngham left 'a certain book written in English letters' to Walter de Creton, and since the greater number of books appearing in wills are devotional, this was probably the case here.[5] Robert de Walcote, goldsmith, of London, in 1361 leaves to 'John de Garyngton, Peter Hiltoft, and William Lytton respectively . . . three books of colour (*tres libros coloris*)'.[6]

[1] *Notes and Queries* cciii, 140–1.

[2] F. J. Furnivall, *The Fifty Earliest English Wills* (EETS. 1882), p. 5; SS. liii, 106. See also A. Gibbons, *Early Lincoln Wills* (Lincoln 1888), pp. 26, 37, 45, 75, 89, and on bequests of books in wills, *MLR.* xv, 349ff.

[3] S. Thrupp, *The Merchant Class of Medieval London* (Chicago 1948), p. 162, and see also pp. 248, 249.

[4] Not, as *HMC.*, *9th Report*, Appendix, p. 46, *Expositio Anglice infortiati*. R. H. Bartle, *Times Literary Supplement*, 1953, p. 187, has shown that this apparently puzzling title is in fact due to a misreading of the manuscript.

[5] SS. iv, 17.

[6] R. R. Sharpe, *Calendar of Wills . . . Court of Husting, London* (London 1890) ii, 25.

The bequest sounds intriguing, but probably means no more than three illuminated manuscripts, most likely in Latin.

During the fifteenth century English books appear more frequently. Among some twenty books contained in sixteen bequests by London merchants between 1403 and 1483 were three Bibles, three legends of the saints, one bound with the gospels, the book of Job, the *Speculum Ecclesie*, a copy of the Franciscan *Fasciculus morum*, a dictionary, and a group of books on grammar. These were presumably in Latin, but there was also a book entitled *Sydrak* which may have been in English, an English translation of Bonaventure, several volumes vaguely referred to as English books, and one of 'Prikked Songs'. In addition, during the same century, several apothecaries left medical books, both in Latin and English.[1] In 1404 Sir Lewis Clifford, the Lollard, mentions 'my book of tribulation', which, whatever it may have been, was most probably in English,[2] while Eleanor Purdeley (1433), widow, of London, lists in her will 'the Storie of Josep, Patrikek purgatore, and ye sermon of altquyne'.[3] Alianora Roos of York (1438) leaves 'an English book called the first book of Master Walter', and 'a book called Maulde buke'.[4] The first was probably one of Hilton's works, but what the second may have been we have no means of telling, though it was presumably in English. The will of Robert Norwich (1443) includes 'a paper book of the Household of the Duke of York, with other contents; and one little quire of paper, with the Kings of England versified . . . Also . . . one book called Hocclef'.[5] The unusually long will of John Baret of Bury (1463) includes,

> x. marks to the peyntyng rerdoos and table at Seynt Marie avter of the story of Magnificat, that in caas be ye awter be seet aftir my entent, as is wretyn aftyr. And in the enner part of ye lowkys w^t jnne there be wreten the balladys I made therefore, and the pardon wretyn there also . . . to Dame Jone Stoonys . . . myn book of ynglych and latyn with diuerse maters of good exortacions, wretyn in papir & closed with parchemyn . . . to sere John Cleye . . . with my maister Prisote, my boke with the sege of Thebes in englysh.[6]

---

[1] S. Thrupp, *op. cit.*, p. 163.
[2] N. H. Nicolas, *Testamenta Vetusta* (London 1826), p. 164.
[3] F. J. Furnivall, *op. cit.*, p. 2.   [4] SS. xxx, 65.
[5] *Norfolk and Norwich Archaeological Society* iv, 332.
[6] *Bury Wills and Inventories* (CS. 1850), pp. 15ff.

The Siege of Thebes was presumably by Lydgate, but the 'balladys' have long since been lost, and it is impossible to identify the work in 'ynglych and latyn', though it was probably devotional. In 1467 Arthur Ormesby made his will before setting out for the Holy Land. Only one of his books is said to contain anything in English, and this is

> my boke called boneaventure de vita christi and in the same boke a wark called speculum christianorum and in the end of the same an holy trete in English of contemplacon.[1]

Peter Arderne, a lawyer, seems to have possessed a fairly large number of books when his will was drawn up in 1467, and these included,

> my boke of Legenda Sanctorum in Englissh; & my boke of Englissh called Bonnaventure de Vita & Passione Christi . . . my booke of English of Boys de Consolatione Philosophiæ, with the booke of Huntyng therin . . . a grete booke of Gramer, with the Sege of Troy, borded . . . my booke of ye Lyfe of Saint Thomas of Canterbury.[2]

The only work of much interest here might have been that on hunting. In 1472 John Hamundson of York leaves to William Ledes 'a book of Chronicles in English, written on paper', and to Nicholas Benyngton 'a book called Horsehede'.[3] The first was probably some version of the *Brut*, and it is likely that the title of the second merely refers to a design stamped on the cover. An unnamed 'grete English boke' occurs in the will of Sir Thomas Lyttleton (1481), and in the same year that of Margaret Purdans includes three English books, 'Le doctrine of the herte', an English book of St Bridget, and a book called 'Hylton'.[4] An unnamed book, which we know to have been in English only because of its incipit, 'for as much', occurs in the will of John Lese of Pontefract (1486), and similarly the incipit of the second folio 'karecteres', of a manuscript left by Thomas Symson of York (1491) is all there is to show that it too was in English.[5] In 1493 a testator leaves 'To my cousin Joane ffitzlowes my litill englissh

---

[1] *Trans. Bib. Soc.* vii, 116.

[2] SS. liii, 102, n.   [3] SS. xlv, 198ff.

[4] N. H. Nicolas, *Testamenta Vetusta* (London 1826), p. 367; *Norfolk and Norwich Archaeological Society* iv, 335.

[5] SS. xlv, 220, n., 160, n.

booke like a prymer', though whether the likeness was in content or merely in size is not clear.[1]

So far most of the references have been to works which there is reason to believe are now lost, though these may sometimes have included copies of others still in existence. Naturally enough, a far greater number of wills show bequests of works which were popular then and are still preserved in numerous copies, though it is usually impossible to determine whether the particular manuscript referred to still survives. The author most frequently mentioned is Richard Rolle, and his writings, both Latin and English, seem to have been popular and widespread. In 1391 Sir William de Thorp leaves an unnamed work of 'Richard Heremit',[2] and works by the same author appear in a volume containing treatises by John of Hoveden, Richard the Hermit, Walter Hilton, William Rymyngton, and Hugh of St Victor, mentioned in the will of John Newton, treasurer of York Minster (d. 1414).[3] Lord Scrope of Masham (1415) possessed a copy of Rolle's *Incendium Amoris*, the autograph of his *Judica me Deus*, a manuscript of the *Pricke of Conscience*, and a 'Primer containing the Matins of the Blessed Virgin Mary in English'.[4] In the same year Edward Cheyne bequeathed a copy of Rolle's *Psalter*, while in 1428 John Newton leaves to Nicholas Hulme the *Duodecim Capitula*, and thirty-one years later Hulme leaves the same book to Nicholas Blakwell.[5] In 1431 William Gate, chaplain, bequeathes to Richard Drax the *Lectiones Mortuorum*, while in 1432 Robert Semer, sub-treasurer of the church of York, possessed a work on the *Placebo* and *Dirige* which he ascribed to Rolle. Robert Alne (1440) leaves to the library of York Minster a copy of Rolle's *Melum contemplativorum*, as well as a number of other books; in 1446 Thomas Beelby of York leaves to William Duffield a copy of Rolle's *Psalter*, and an inventory of the goods of the same William Duffield, made in 1452, includes this book and the *Lectiones Mortuorum*.[6] An unnamed book by Rolle, along with an English version of Boethius, were in the possession of John Seggefyld, fellow of Lincoln College,

---

[1] H. Littlehales, *The Prymer* (EETS. 1895), p. xlii.
[2] A. Gibbons, *Early Lincoln Wills* (Lincoln 1888), p. 80.
[3] SS. iv, 364ff.
[4] T. Rymer, *Foedera* (London 1729) ix, 276–7.
[5] E. F. Jacob and H. C. Johnson, *op. cit.* ii, 49; SS. ii, 77; xxx, 219.
[6] SS. xlv, 58, n., 91, n.; xxx, 78ff.; xlv, 133.

Oxford, in 1457,[1] while in 1468 an inventory of the goods of Elizabeth, widow of William Siwardby, includes Rolle's *De Meditatione Passionis Domini*, English versions of the *Revelations* of St Bridget, the *Life of Christ*, and *De Misterio Passionis Domini*. Robert Est of York (1474-5) claimed to possess the autograph of Rolle's *Psalter*, which he left to the nuns of Hampole, and in 1479 Thomas Pynchebek leaves to William Flawter Rolle's work on the *Dirige*.[2]

The *Pricke of Conscience*, often ascribed to Rolle, is also frequently mentioned in wills. In 1399 Thomas Roos of Ingmanthorp leaves to William de Helagh 'a book called Maundevyl, and a book [called] the Pricke of Conscience'.[3] The same work appears among the forfeited goods of Lord Scrope of Masham in 1415;[4] Thomas Harlyng possessed it in 1422,[5] and in 1434 Robert Cupper of Yarmouth leaves a copy to his son.[6] Other manuscripts of the work appear in the wills of William Revetour of York (1446), and of Agnes Stapilton (1448), the latter of whom also possessed at least two other English books, the *Chastising of God's Children* and the *Vices and Virtues*, whilst in 1474 Stephen Preston of Sylton, Dorset, also possessed a copy of the *Pricke of Conscience*.[7]

Copies of Langland's *Piers Plowman* occur in at least three wills, the earliest being that of Walter de Bruge of York (1396). John Wyndhill, rector of Arncliffe (1431) leaves to John Kendale 'an English book of Pers Plughman', and to Robert Forest 'an English

---

[1] *Munimenta Academica Oxon.* (RS. 50) ii, 666.

[2] SS. xlv, 163, 160, 199, n.

[3] SS. iv, 252. The first mention of the work is in 1396-7 when the Prior of Newstead brought an action against John Ravensfield for the detention *unius libri vocati Stymylus Conscientiae* (H. E. Allen, *Writings ascribed to Richard Rolle* (London 1927), p. 384).

[4] *Archaeologia* lxx, 82.

[5] E. F. Jacob and H. C. Johnson, *op. cit.* ii, 246.

[6] *Norfolk and Norwich Archaeological Society* iv, 326.

[7] SS. cxvi, 48ff.; *Collectanea Franciscana* ii, 107. It was one of the books, along with a Bible in English, copies of the Gospels and of the Ten Commandments, which the unfortunate Richard Hunne ordered his servant to bring to him when in prison at St Paul's (J. A. F. Thomson, *op. cit.*, p. 168). According to Foxe (iv, 235), Richard Colins of Ginge (c. 1521) was accused before the bishop of Lincoln of having in his possession certain English books, one of which was the *Pricke of Conscience*. Further evidence for the popularity of the work is provided by the window of All Saints' Church, York, which illustrates the Fifteen Signs before Judgment by pictures 'bearing as legends couplets from the *Prick of Conscience*' (H. E. Allen, *op. cit.*, p. 386).

book concerning the exposition of the Gospels',[1] and there is the bequest of a 'book called piers plowman' in the will of Thomas Roos (1433).[2] In addition, on the fly-leaf of a manuscript of Raymond de Pennaforte's *Summa de Penitentia* is an inventory of the books of Thomas Stotevyle, drawn up in 1459–60. The list, comprises forty books, amongst them the *Narraciones Cantuariensis* and *Petrus Plowman*, as well as various romances, *Alisaundir*, *Befuitz de Hamton*, *Le Sege de Ierusalem*, *Le Sege de Troye*, whose titles suggest that they were in French.[3]

The works of Chaucer and Gower appear fairly frequently in fifteenth-century wills. The earliest occurrence of the former seems to be in that of Richard Sotheworth (1419), who leaves to John Stopyndon 'my book of Canterbury Tales'.[4] In 1420 John Brynchele, citizen and tailor of London, leaves to David Fyvyan 'a book in English called Boecius de Consolacione Philosophie', perhaps Chaucer's translation, and to William Holgrave 'my book called Talys of Caunterbury'.[5] Another copy occurs in the will of Sir Thomas Cumberworth (1450), whose books also included 'my boke of actif life', 'my boke of uesseden Passion', 'my boke de vita christi', as well as an English translation of William Deguilleville's *Pelerinage de l'Ame*.[6] Another of Chaucer's works is noted in the will of William Banks of York (1458), who leaves to Elena Marshall 'an English book called Trolias',[7] while a copy of the *Canterbury Tales* was also in the possession of Thomas Stotevyle (1459–60). In 1471 Lady Elizabeth Bruiyn of S. Ockenden, Essex, includes among other bequests one of 'the boke called canterbury tales';[8] John Parmenter, commissary of the archbishop of Canterbury, also leaves to Walter Nonne 'a book called Canterbury Tales' (1479), and in an inventory of the goods of Sir Thomas Ursewyk (d. 1479) there is a short list of books in his chapel, among which were 'an Englysch boke called Maundevyle', and 'an Englysche

---

[1] SS. iv, 209; xxx, 32ff.   [2] F. J. Furnivall, *op. cit.*, p. 2.
[3] J. M. Manly and E. Rickert, *The Text of the Canterbury Tales* (Chicago 1940) i, 610ff.
[4] J. M. Manly and E. Rickert, *op. cit.* i, 606.
[5] F. J. Furnivall, *op. cit.*, p. 136.
[6] A. Clark, *Lincoln Diocese Documents* (EETS. 1914), pp. 45ff. For the book by Deguilleville, see *HMC.*, *6th Report*, Appendix, p. 288.
[7] SS. xxx, 217ff.
[8] *Trans. of the Essex Archaeological Society* (NS) ii, 56–7.

boke of Canterbury Talys'.[1] Among the household goods forfeited by Sir Thomas Charlton were three English books, a *Canterbury Tales*, a 'troyles', and a version of *De regimine principum*.[2] In 1495 Richard Dodyngton bequeathes a 'Book of Canterbury Taylles'; and on the fly-leaf of MS. Royal 15 D. ii, in a fifteenth-century hand, a list of books probably belonging to John, Lord Welles (d. 1499), or to his wife Cecilia (d. 1507), includes,

> A boke of caunturbere tlase.
> A boke of Charlman.
> A boke cald ye sheys of Jerusalem.
> A boke cald mort arthre.[3]

According to the will of William Knoyell (1501):

> As for a book called Bocas I wol that my son have him during his life and to leave him in the place for his heirs for evermore and the book of Canterbury talys I will he be delivered to my cousyn William Carraunt for I had him of his grauntfader.[4]

The grandfather referred to was probably William Carraunt, a squire in the royal household, who died in 1476. In 1501 Thomas Horde leaves to a certain Rowland 'An English boke of Caunturbury tallys',[5] and John Goodyere of Monken Hadley in 1504 possessed 'a boke of regimine principum' in parchment, 'a boke of dives et pauper in printe', a book of 'the Knyght of the Tower' in print, the 'Canterbury Tales' in parchment, 'an old boke of the cronycles of yngeland', 'an olde boke of bonaventur', and a 'queyr of phisick of the secrets of women'.[6] Finally, Margaret Beaufort, countess of Richmond (d. 1509), leaves 'a booke of velom of Canterbury tales in Englische'.[7] Some of the manuscripts mentioned here have certainly been lost, and although others are possibly identical with one of the extant manuscripts, it is seldom that any confirmation is available.

In 1431 John Morton of York leaves to the countess of Westmorland 'an English book, called Gower', which was presumably

[1] J. M. Manly and E. Rickert, *op. cit.* i, 615, 616.
[2] S. Thrupp, *op. cit.*, p. 248.
[3] J. M. Manly and E. Rickert, *op. cit.* i, 618.
[4] *Somerset Record Society* xvi, 19–21.
[5] J. M. Manly and E. Rickert, *op. cit.* i, 620.
[6] *Trans. Bib. Soc.* vii, 111.
[7] J. M. Manly and E. Rickert, *op. cit.* i, 621.

the *Confessio Amantis,* while two unnamed books by the same author appear in the will of Sir Edmund Rede (1487).[1]

English versions of the whole or part of the Bible are occasionally noted, as in the will of Robert de Felstede of London (1349) which mentions 'le Byble' and a psalter written in Latin and English.[2] The first was probably in French; the psalter seems too early to be that of Rolle and may have been a copy of the *West Midland Psalter.* In 1392 Robert de Roos leaves to his daughter Alianora a 'Bibyll' of which the language is not specified, but since most of the other books mentioned in the will were in French, it is likely that this was also in that language. John Hopton possessed an English version of the Gospels in 1394; and the English psalter in the possession of Isabella Persay of York in 1401 was probably that ascribed to Rolle.[3] Another English copy of the Gospels appears in the will of John Bount of Bristol (1404);[4] the books of John Clifford, mason, of Southwark, included in 1411 a copy of the Gospels for Sundays in English,[5] and another appears in the will of William Revetour (1446). Works derived from the Bible are sometimes to be met with. The *Vita Christi* occurs in the wills of Thomas Horneby (1485) and William Ward (1496),[6] whilst the 'boke of Bonaventure and Hilton in the same in Englishe' in the will of Cecily, duchess of York (1495), may have been the same work.[7] Finally, in 1502 Robert Battresby, clerk, leaves a book called 'The Life of Jesu' to the common library of the University of Cambridge,[8] and a similar book is listed in the inventory of the goods of Elizabeth Siwardby (1468).

English versions of the *Legenda Sanctorum* are mentioned in the wills of Thomas Berkley (1415), William Revetour (1446), William Bruyn (1477), and Ann, duchess of Buckingham (1480).[9] *Grace*

[1] SS. xxx, 13ff.; *Trans. Bib. Soc.* vii, 117ff.
[2] R. R. Sharpe, *Calendar of Wills . . . Court of Husting, London* (London 1889) i, 636.
[3] SS. iv, 179, 196, 271. See also A. Gibbons, *op. cit.,* p. 118.
[4] T. P. Wadley, *Notes on Wills in the Great Orphan Book and Book of Wills* (Bristol 1886), p. 73.
[5] C. L. Kingsford, *Prejudice and Promise in XVth Century England* (Oxford 1925), p. 40.
[6] SS. xlv, 165, n.; liii, 114.
[7] *Wills from Doctor's Commons* (CS. 1862), pp. 1ff.
[8] N. H. Nicolas, *Testamenta Vetusta* (London 1826), p. 444.
[9] E. F. Jacob and H. C. Johnson, *op. cit.* ii, 124; *Norfolk and Norwich Archaeological Society* iv, 335; N. H. Nicolas, *op. cit.,* p. 356.

Dieu, the usual title of the English translation of William Deguil-leville's *Pelerinage de l'Ame*, appears in the wills of Sir Thomas Cumberworth (1450), John Clerk (1451), and Thomas Chaworth (1458), while devotional books on the Pater Noster are bequeathed by Sir John Scrope (1455), and John Burn of York (1479–80).[1]

Agnes Stapilton (1448) leaves her book called *Chastisyng of goddes childern* to the Cistercian nuns of Esholt, near Leeds, while Mercy Ormesby in 1451 bequeathes a copy of the same work to the Benedictine nuns of Easebourne Priory in Sussex,[2] and Lady Peryne Clanbowe (1422) leaves to Elizabeth Ioye 'a boke of Englyssh, cleped "pore caytife" '.[3] The works of Hilton are not infrequent. They have appeared in some of those already mentioned, and in the will of Robert Wolveden (1432), treasurer of the church of York, there is a reference to 'a devout work written by Walter Hilton'.[4] Gilemota Carreeke of York (1408) leaves to Alice, daughter of William Bows, 'an English book de Spiritu Guidonis', presumably a copy of the extant *Gast of Gy*,[5] and Sir Thomas Chaworth (1458) bequeathes to Richard Byng-ham 'an Englissh booke called Orilogium Sapienciæ'.[6] The *De consolatione philosophiæ*, perhaps in the translation by Chaucer, appears in the wills of John Brynchele (1420), John Seggefyld (1457), and Peter Arderne (1467). In 1493 Roger Drury of Hawstead leaves 'ij Inglyshe bocks, called Bochas, of Lydgat's makyng',[7] and copies of *Mandeville* appear in the wills of George Darell (1432),[8] and Thomas Roos (1399), and in the inventory of the goods of Sir Thomas Ursewyk (1474). In 1467 Robert Skrayn-gham bequeathes to another merchant a 'great English book called Polycronicon';[9] the will of John Fell of York (1506) includes a book of chronicles,[10] probably some version of the *Brut*, and similar

---

[1] SS. xxx, 151, 190; xlv, 199, n.

[2] *Trans. Bib. Soc.* vii, 116. 'It is not without irony that these records should have survived of the presentation of a work which presupposes in the women religious for whom it is written the highest standards of personal conduct to what must surely have been two of the worst-conducted nunneries in fifteenth-century England.' J. Bazire and E. Colledge, *The Chastising of God's Children* (Oxford 1957), p. 38.

[3] F. J. Furnival, *The Fifty Earliest English Wills* (EETS. 1882), p. 50.

[4] SS. xlv, 91ff.   [5] SS. iv, 352.   [6] SS. xxx, 228.

[7] *Bury Wills and Inventories* (CS. 1850), p. 246.   [8] SS. xxx 28.

[9] C. L. Kingsford, *op. cit.*, p. 41.

[10] SS. liii, 244.

works appear in the wills of Thomas Chaworth (1458) and John Hamundson (1472).

Perhaps the most disappointing sources for our knowledge of the lost literature are the extant catalogues of monastic and other libraries. They vary considerably in the care with which they are compiled, and so in the amount of detailed information that is given. If a manuscript was mainly or entirely in French or English this is usually indicated; but often enough the different contents are not noted, and it may be listed only under the first or the most important treatise which it contains. In such cases it could have included less important works in English of which no hint is given. Moreover, when an English item is specifically mentioned, the description may be so vague that it is difficult to say whether it was merely a copy of a still extant work or the only evidence of one that has otherwise entirely disappeared. From the twelfth century eight catalogues, fragmentary or complete, of important monastic libraries have been preserved,[1] but they give no information about any Middle English works. This is hardly surprising; books in English during the first half of the century would have been written in the traditional West Saxon literary language, while as for the books written later in the century, only very occasional ones could have found their way into a monastic library early enough to be entered in a catalogue of the same century.

During the thirteenth century, and especially towards the end of it, the extant catalogues tend to become more elaborate and detailed, but vernacular works are still usually in Old not in Middle English. A fragmentary catalogue of Bury shows only two English works, of which one is certainly and the other probably Old English. That of Rochester, drawn up in 1202, includes two of the Old English manuscripts listed in the earlier catalogue, together with a *Medicinale anglicum*, probably also in Old English. Similarly, St Paul's has only two Old English Bibles. The catalogue of Glastonbury (1247) shows eight manuscripts in English, but the only one that can be identified is in Old English, and since most of the others are marked 'old but legible' or 'old and illegible', it is likely that they too were in Old English. The thirteenth-

[1] Burton; Christ Church, Canterbury; Durham; Peterborough; Reading; Rochester; Welbeck; Whitby.

century catalogue of Leominster, apart from a work on St Guthlac (see p. 90), has only:

> Medicinalis unus anglicis litteris scriptus . . .
> Liber qui appellatur landboc.[1]

The former was presumably a version of one of the late Old English medical treatises, and the latter a cartulary. The catalogue of Flaxley shows the following English works:

> 69–70. Duo libri anglici . . .
> 73. Phisicus liber anglice.[2]

Again, the second of these was probably a version of one or the other of the extant Old English medical works; as for the others, all that can be said is that they are not to be found among the extant manuscripts known to be from Flaxley. A similarly indefinite entry, *Libri de littera Anglica duo*, lists the only English books in the library of Rievaulx.[3] The late thirteenth-century catalogue of the abbey of St Radegund at Bradsole shows no English works, nor does the fragmentary one of the same date from Ramsey.[4]

During the fourteenth century the catalogue of the Exeter Cathedral Library (1327) notes only three manuscripts in English or containing English works. Of these, one is certainly Old English and the others were probably so. An indenture (1343) to secure the return of books lent by the prior and convent of the Hinton Charterhouse to another religious house lists about a score of books, but there is nothing to show that any of them contained English writings.[5] The catalogue of the Austin friars at York (1372) certainly shows no important works in English, though there may have been English items in some of the manuscripts, as for example in no. 366 which contained a *geometria wlgaris*, and no. 452 which had a *tractatus parvus de wlgari Judicio sermonis*, but both have been lost.[6] Amongst the chained books in the chapel of St George at Windsor, when the catalogue was drawn up in 1384–5, there were two French books, the *Romance of the Rose* and

---

[1] *EHR.* iii, 117ff. [2] *Centralblatt für Bibliothekswesen* ix, 205–7.
[3] E. Edwards, *Memoirs of Libraries* (London 1859) i, 337.
[4] *EHR.* liii, 88ff.; *Chronicon Abbatiæ Rameseiensis* (RS. 83), pp. lxxxv–xci.
[5] E. M. Thompson, *The Carthusian Order in England* (London 1930), p. 323.
[6] *Fasciculus J. W. Clark dicatus* (Cambridge 1909), pp. 2–96.

another that was probably *Percival and Gawain*, but none in English.[1] The catalogue of Dover Priory (1389) shows English items in one manuscript only, a lost episode from the Reynard cycle (see p. 124), and a copy of the *Proverbs of Hending*. The 1391 catalogue of Durham notes only two English works, both in Old English, while the library of Christ Church, Canterbury, possessed in the early fourteenth century a number of Old English works, but the only one in Middle English was a version of the *Poema Morale*, listed as *Rithmus Anglice*, in what is now MS. Bodl. Digby 4.[2] A fragmentary early fourteenth-century catalogue, possibly from the Cluniac priory of Bermondsey, contains no English works specifically mentioned as such. However, the compiler does not appear to have been particularly conscientious, since he notes that, in addition to the books catalogued, the monastery possessed some eighty manuscripts or parts of manuscripts whose contents he does not trouble to describe.[3] The catalogue of Lanthony mentions nothing in English, but in any case gives only the main item of each volume with no details,[4] while a fragmentary one from Ramsey shows a single work in English, probably a copy of the *Old English Chronicle*. Apart from an English life of St Thomas Becket (see p. 93), the late fourteenth-century list from Peterborough had only some English poverbs in one of the manuscripts. But the cataloguer also notes that there were in the library 'a few books which had not been examined'.[5]

The earliest of the extant fifteenth-century catalogues is that of Titchfield, drawn up in 1400. In addition to a lost version of *The Owl and the Nightingale* and an English collection of saints' legends, the library contained in Q XI the *De die iudicii in anglicis*, presumably a copy of one of the Middle English poems which treat of the Fifteen Signs before Judgment.[6] The 1416 catalogue of Durham had only a single book in English, and that in Old English, while a list of books in the Cambridge University Library (c. 1424) shows a *Fasciculus Morum* which, judging from the incipit to the second folio, 'Lest ye ofte', contained at any rate

---

[1] *Trans. Bib. Soc.* xiii, 55.   [2] *Canterbury and Dover*, p. 92.
[3] *EHR.* xlviii, 431ff.
[4] *Centralblatt für Bibliothekswesen* ix, 207ff.
[5] *Trans. Bib. Soc., Supplement* v.
[6] *Proceedings of the Leeds Philosophical Society: Literary and Historical Section* v, part iii, 150ff.; part iv, 252ff.

some English.[1] The imperfect catalogue of Hulne Priory (1443) lists no English books, nor do any appear in that of Elsyngspital (1448).[2] An inventory of the goods of Sir John Fastolf (c. 1450) shows a number of books said to be in French, but some were almost certainly in Latin, and others may perhaps have been in English. In 1466–7 Ewelme Almshouse possessed four French books, but the only English one was a copy of Lydgate's version of Deguilleville's *Pelerinage de l'Ame*.[3] No English books appear in the 1499 list from the Collegiate Church of St Andrew at Bishop Auckland, or in the early fifteenth-century catalogue of Meaux Abbey.[4] That of the College of St Mary at Winchester, drawn up sometime during the reign of Henry VI, lists among the grammatical books:

> liber continens quandam compilationem de informatione puerorum, cum aliis parvis tractatibus, 2° folio, *Ablatyf cas*, in Anglice.[5]

No complete catalogue of the library of Witham Charterhouse now exists, but MS. Bodl. Laud 154 contains three lists of books to be found there in the fifteenth century. Two of the lists give, more or less in duplicate, the contents of twenty-four books presented to the Charterhouse by John Blacman, and English works appear in two of them, a *devota meditacio in anglicis* in no. 15 and a *tractatus de armis in anglicis* in no. 23. The second might have been interesting, but was probably merely an English version of Vegetius. The third list includes another forty-four volumes, also probably given by Blacman, but the contents of the different manuscripts are not detailed and no English works are specifically mentioned.[6] The fifteenth-century catalogue of an unidentified English religious house has no works described as being in English, although one of them, 'Milk et breed', certainly was so, since this is a not unusual title for Chaucer's *Astrolabe*.[7] So far as we can tell, the late fifteenth-century catalogue of St Augustine's, Canterbury, had only four works in English. Two of them were certainly in Old English, and

[1] *Cambridge Antiquarian Society, Communications* ii, 239ff.
[2] SS. vii, 128ff.; J. P. Malcolm, *Londinium Redivivum* (London 1803) i, 27ff.
[3] *HMC., 8th Report*, Appendix, pp. 268, 629.
[4] SS. ii, 101; *Chronica Monasterii de Melsa* (RS. 43) iii, lxxxiii.
[5] *Archaeological Journal* xv, 59ff.
[6] E. M. Thompson, *The Carthusian Order in England* (London 1930), pp. 316ff., 320ff.   [7] *MLN.* liv, 246ff.

the others were the *Gesta Guydonis* (see p. 111) and the extant BM. MS. Arundel 57 containing Michael of Northgate's *Aȝenbite of Inwyt*.[1] An inventory of the library of Clare College, Cambridge, drawn up in 1496, has as one of its items:

> cronica in Anglicis in rotula que incipit *Her was*.[2]

Naturally enough there are comparatively few catalogues from the sixteenth century. The library of the Augustinian Abbey at Leicester contained over a thousand volumes when the catalogue was drawn up, but of these only a single unnamed tract in a volume of medical works is given as being in English.[3] No complete catalogue of the library of the London Charterhouse has survived, but there are various lists of books which were sent at different times from there to other houses. The most interesting is a certificate for twenty-four books taken from the House of the Salutation, sometime during the sixteenth century, by John Spalding on his return to Hull. The list contains several works which the title or the incipit to the second folio show to have been in English. These included *The Chastising of God's Children, The Pilgrimage of the Soul, Speculum vite Christi, The Book of Good Manners*, Hampole's *Meditacio passionis Christi, Meditacio Sancti Augustini*, as well as English versions of Acts and of the Epistles, together with a Psalter glossed in English, 'parte of the statutis in yngleshe', and an unnamed treatise by Rolle.[4] Three other lists of books sent from the same monastery also survive, but in none of them is there any mention of works in English. An inventory of the goods of Exeter Cathedral, drawn up in 1506, includes also the library of some six hundred volumes, but the only one of these said to have been in English is *Bocas in Sermone Anglico*, presumably Lydgate's *Fall of Princes*. In addition *30 libri antiqui* were kept *in antiquo scaccario*, and these perhaps included some of the English books which appear in the catalogue of 1327.[5]

The most elaborate of the sixteenth-century catalogues is that of the Bridgettine monastery of Syon. The order was a double one, and men and women appear to have had separate libraries, the

---

[1] *Canterbury and Dover*, p. 374. [2] *Trans. Camb. Bib. Soc.* i, 105ff.
[3] *Trans. of the Leicestershire Arch. Soc.* xix, 2ff., 378ff.
[4] E. M. Thompson, *op. cit.*, pp. 324–30.
[5] G. Oliver, *Lives of the Bishops of Exeter* (Exeter 1861), pp. 366–75.

extant catalogue being that of the men's library. It was a large but comparatively uninteresting collection of about fifteen hundred volumes, more than a quarter of which were printed books. The following English works appear in manuscripts or printed books which have apparently not survived: various grammatical (A 4, A 34) and medical works (B 5, 6, 29, 31, 40, 43); a glossed Psalter (F 48) and Bible (R 2); treatises on the Seven Deadly Sins (L 43, N 28), the Seven Penitential Psalms (M 15), and the Ten Commandments (N 28). Hilton's works are in M 24, 97, one of Rolle's in M 118, the *Revelations of St Matilda* in M 98, and collections of sermons in N 35, S 57, 58, while in addition there were various saints' lives. The original index gives a few English works not in the catalogue proper, notably the sermons of Brother Roger of Syon and an English version of one of the treatises of Aquinas.[1] Many of the works are probably extant in other manuscripts, and none of them sounds particularly interesting. In fact the whole library, though no doubt adequate enough, seems rather dull. Also from the sixteenth century is an anonymous inventory which shows two English books, both in print, a *Speculum Vitae Christi*, and one with the probably miswritten title *Barth' et An^{ts} in Anglicis Ethimolog'*.[2]

It is unfortunate that complete catalogues of the monastic libraries were not made at the time of the dissolution. We are probably too apt to assume that this event dealt an irreparable blow to our knowledge of medieval literature. There is certainly evidence enough for the wanton destruction of immense numbers of manuscripts at this time, but the extant catalogues do not indicate that the monastic libraries had much to lose that was of any great interest. In fact it might even be possible that what little in the vernacular has survived owes its preservation to the fact that at the dissolution it passed into the hands of laymen, since the later monastic catalogues almost invariably include fewer English works than the earlier ones. In the sixteenth century vernacular writings began to appear gain, but they are usually more or less contemporary ones. On the whole it seems very probable that much of the lost Old and Middle English literature had already disappeared long before the dissolution, though there

---

[1] M. Bateson, *Catalogue of the Library of Syon Monastery, Isleworth* (Cambridge 1898).   [2] SS. liii, 280.

is, of course, far too little evidence for any certainty on the point to be possible. We have no means of telling whether the catalogues that happen to have been preserved are at all representative, nor can we be certain that even the complete ones listed all the books in the possession of the monastery. As at Exeter, the older books may still have been preserved but, since they were now almost unintelligible, have been withdrawn from circulation and not entered in the catalogue. Whatever the reason, an examination of the extant catalogues does give the impression that the later the catalogue the fewer the English books that will be found in it. This is especially noticeable when we have catalogues of different dates for one and the same library. The early twelfth-century catalogue of Durham shows some ten English books, none of which can be identified with the two appearing in those for 1391 and 1416. In the twelfth century Peterborough possessed at least two Old English books, neither of which is in the late fourteenth-century catalogue. Exeter, in 1327, had three manuscripts with English works in them, but none of them is to be found in the inventory of 1506. The question might have been answered had Henry's commissioners been as interested in the books as they were in the other goods of the monasteries. Leland usually noted down some of the more interesting of the manuscripts he saw, but he never appears to have made any exhaustive lists. The only monasteries for whose libraries we have any information at the time of the dissolution are those of Monkbretton and Kilburn. In the case of the former the greater part of the library seems to have been acquired by the prior and sub-prior, and in 1558 an inventory was drawn up which shows the whereabouts of some of the books. William Brown, formerly prior, possessed thirty-seven volumes, of which four were probably in English, *Legenda Anglicana*, *Legenda Aurea in englysche*, *Flowr of Comawndments*, and *Ye pylgramage of perfeccyon*. Thomas Wylkynson and Richard Hinchclyf had acquired over a hundred volumes, apparently from Thomas Frobyscer, formerly sub-prior, but only two of them seem to have been in English, *Scala perfectionis* and *Schepard Kalendare*.[1] Consequently, out of nearly a hundred and fifty volumes only six were possibly in English, and none of these was

---

[1] J. W. Walker, *Chartularies of Monkbretton Priory* (Yorks. Arch. Soc.: Record Series lxvi), pp. 5ff.

of any age. Similarly, in the inventory of Kilburn Nunnery the only books mentioned, apart from service books are 'two bookes of Legenda Aurea, the one in prynt, and the other wryten, both Englyshe'.[1] Such evidence as this is practically valueless. We cannot be certain that we have a complete list of the books possessed by either monastery, and two such small and comparatively unimportant houses can hardly be regarded as representative. In all probability the question is one that can never be answered with any certainty, but on the whole it may be suspected that the loss of much medieval literature in the vernacular is one of the disasters for which Henry VIII was not directly responsible.

[1] *Monasticon* iii, 424.

9

LYRICAL POETRY

The earliest English lyrics that have survived come from the thirteenth century, and most of these are religious. Nevertheless there is some evidence for lyrical poetry, both religious and secular, from an earlier period than this. If the twelfth-century chronicler of Ely could be trusted Cnut would be the first known composer of such verse in English. The king, while on a journey by water to Ely, is said to have heard from a distance the chanting of the monks, and to have composed verses on the subject:

> Merie sungen ðe muneches binnen Ely
> ða Cnut ching reu ðer by.
> Roweþ cnites noer the lant
> and here we þes muneches sæng.

and other verses which follow, which even to the present time are still sung publicly in dances and remembered in proverbs.[1]

While the anecdote may leave us sceptical about Cnut's claim to be the first lyrical poet in English, it yet provides proof for the existence of such verse at least as early as the twelfth century. At an even earlier date Thomas of Bayeux, archbishop of York (d. 1100), is said to have composed many hymns, thus providing pious sentiments for the tunes of the minstrels.[2] The archbishop's hymns were presumably in Latin, but the songs of the minstrels, whose tunes he borrowed, are likely to have been in one of the vernaculars.

St Godric of Finchal is perhaps the man with the best claim to be considered the earliest lyrical poet in English whose name is known. In his early days he had travelled widely as a merchant and pilgrim, but eventually settled down as a hermit at Finchal. After his death his biography was written by Reginald, a monk of Durham, and in it examples are given of the saint's lyrical poetry, the

---

[1] *Liber Eliensis*, pp. 153-4.   [2] *Gesta Pontificum*, p. 258.

gift of which had come to him through divine inspiration. According to Reginald, the Virgin, accompanied by St Mary Magdalene, appeared in a vision to Godric in the chapel at Finchal which he had dedicated to her, and taught him the words and melody of an English hymn:

> Sainte Marie virgine,
> Moder Jesu Christes Nazarene,
> on-fo, scild, help þin Godric;
> on-fang, bring eȝhtlech wið þe in Godes riche.

Roger of Wendover gives a slightly different version of this, and adds a second stanza:

> Seinte Marie, Christes bour,
> Meidenes clenhed, moderes flour,
> Delivere mine sennen, regne in min mod,
> Bringe me to blisse wit thi selfe God.

Reginald also tells how, on the death of Godric's sister Burgwen, the saint saw in a vision the Virgin followed by two angels who bore the soul of his sister. They were singing a hymn in English, of which the following two lines are given:

> Crist and Seinte Marie, sio on scamel me iledde,
> þæt ic on this hi-herthe ne sculde uuit mine barefot itreide.

A later biographer, Geoffrey of Durham, gives a single stanza of a hymn to St Nicholas:

> Sainte Nicholaes, godes druð,
> tymbre us faire scone hus.
> At þi burth, at þi bare,
> Sainte nicholaes bring vs wel þare.[1]

This is all that remains of the verse of St Godric, and it happens to have been preserved only because the biographers were interested in the circumstances of its composition.

The poetry of Thomas of Bayeux and of St Godric was religious, but other lyrics current in the twelfth century were certainly

---

[1] SS. xx, 119, 144; RS. 84, i, 72ff.; J. Hall, *Selections from Early Middle English 1130–1250* (Oxford 1920) i, 5; ii, 241ff. The first has also been added on the last leaf of a late twelfth-century manuscript of the *Vitas Patrum* from Biddlesden Priory, Bucks., now C.U.L. Mm. 4. 28 (Ker, p. 40).

secular. The songs which welcomed Richard I on his arrival at Acre were presumably so, but probably in French.[1] Also secular, and almost certainly in English, were those of the youths who preceded Thomas Becket, while Chancellor, on his splendid progress to the French court.[2]

Often enough, as here, the references to the lost lyrical poetry are quite general, but sometimes odd lines or even stanzas have been preserved. Such lyrics would presumably be in rhyme, after the French models, though it is clear enough that alliterative poetry continued to be composed in this country. Evidence for this comes from Giraldus Cambrensis, according to whom the Welsh

> make use of alliteration in preference to all other ornaments of rhetoric, and that particular kind which joins by consonancy the first letters or syllables of words. So much do the English and Welsh nations employ this ornament of words in all exquisite composition, that no sentence is esteemed to be elegantly spoken . . . unless it be fully polished with the file of this figure,

and he goes on to give examples of regular alliterative lines in English.[3] The same author, in the *Gemma Ecclesiastica*, has a chapter condemning the dancing or singing of songs in churches or churchyards; and one of his anecdotes shows that such songs might be in English. On one occasion a certain Worcestershire priest was kept awake the whole night by revellers dancing in the churchyard. The result was that when he began the service next morning, instead of the correct *Dominus vobiscum*, he repeated the refrain that had been ringing in his ears all night, 'Swete lamman dhin are'. The event caused such a scandal that the then bishop of Worcester pronounced an anathema upon anyone who should ever again sing that song within the limits of the diocese. Elsewhere Giraldus gives a rhyming toast, which he says was common amongst the English Cistercians. The proposer, instead of the usual *wesseil*, says:

> Loke nu frere,
> Hu strong ordre is here.

---

[1] T. Gale, *Historiæ Anglicanæ Scriptores* (Oxford 1687) ii, 331–2.
[2] William FitzStephen, *Vita Sancti Thomæ* (RS. 67) iii, 31.
[3] *Descriptio Kambriæ* (RS. 21) vi, 187ff.

In place of the usual *drincheil*, the response is:

> Ihe, la ful iwis,
> Swide strong ordre is dhis.[1]

The author of the *Ancrene Riwle* quotes two lines which have been taken to be proverbial, but which sound much more like the refrain of a contemporary love lyric:

> euer is þe eie to þe wude leie,
> þerinne is þet ich luuie.

It may be significant that another of the manuscripts gives a different version:

> ach eauer is þe echȝe to þe wodeleȝe;
> & þe halte bucke climbeð þeruppe.
> Twa & þreo, hu feole beoð þeo?
> þreo halpenes makeð a peni.

It looks as if the scribe of this manuscript knew the song and was quoting from a different stanza.[2]

We should hardly expect to find lines from a love lyric in a work of religious edification, and it is even more surprising to discover that the text of a twelfth-century sermon apparently consisted of two lines from a similar song:

> Atte wrastlinge mi lemman i ches,
> and atte ston-kasting i him for-les.

. . . Mi leue frend, wild wimmen & goliue i mi contreie, wan he gon o þe ring, among manie oþere songis, þat litil ben wort þat tei singin, so sein þei þus: 'Atte wrastlinge mi lemman &c.'

A slightly different version, with two additional lines, appears in C.U.L. MS. Ii. 3. 8:

> Atte ston castinges my lemman i ches,
> and atte wrastlinges sone i hym les;
> allas, þat he so sone fel;
> wy nadde he stonde better, vile gorel?

But the many other songs known to the preacher have all been lost, and only these lines survive.[3]

---

[1] *Gemma Ecclesiastica*, pp. 119ff.; *Speculum Ecclesiæ*, p. 209.

[2] J. Morton, *The Ancren Riwle* (CS. 1853), p. 96. For arguments in favour of taking the lines as a proverb, see *English Studies* xxxv, 11–15.

[3] *Anglia* xlii, 152; R. H. Robbins, *Secular Lyrics of the XIVth and XVth Centuries* (Oxford 1955), p. xxxix.

It is clear enough that there must have been a flourishing lyrical literature in English during the twelfth century, though almost nothing now remains of it. It is equally certain that the later extant lyrical poetry represents a mere fraction of that actually composed. Much of our knowledge of it comes from the chance preservation of a few manuscripts containing collections of these lyrics, but such anthologies were probably rare enough in Middle English times. Many of the poems that were composed were probably never written down, and many that are still extant have been preserved only by the merest chance. Odd snatches of song have been jotted down on the margins or fly-leaves of manuscripts, just as they happen to have caught the fancy of some hearer, and a glance through the standard editions will show something of the unexpected places in which lines from medieval lyrics have been found.

In consequence it is not surprising that during the later period numerous references appear to lyrics which are probably no longer extant. When the references are quite general, there are no means of knowing whether the particular poems have survived, or even the language in which they were written. So, for example, in a law-suit recorded in the Hundred Rolls:

a lady claims a missal worth twenty shillings, a manual worth 6s. 8d. and two rolls of songs worth sixpence and twopence respectively which were snatched from her on the king's highway between Boughton and her home at Wereham on Easter Day 1282.[1]

Moreover, 'to the ears of John Bromyard, the love-ditties of the dancers sound no better than pig-squealing'.[2] In 1303–4 Edward I on his progress through Scotland was entertained on the way between Gask and 'Uggelville' by seven maidens who sang various songs to him 'as was the custom in the days of Alexander the king', and his accounts record the gift of 3s. to them.[3] In the register of William of Wykeham, under the year 1384, it is forbidden 'to sing lascivious songs, to perform plays, or to frequent

---

[1] H. M. Cam, *The Hundred and the Hundred Rolls* (London 1930), p. 182.
[2] G. R. Owst, *Literature and Pulpit in Medieval England* (Cambridge 1933), p. 383.
[3] J. Bain, *Calendar of Documents relating to Scotland* (Edinburgh 1888) iv, 475.

dances or other foolish games', and in 1387 the same bishop thunders against

> these secular women [who] often keep up their chattering, carolling [*cantalenas*] and other light behaviour, until the middle of the night, and disturb the aforesaid nuns, so that they cannot properly perform the regular services.[1]

John of Trevisa, in his translation of Bartholomew's *De proprietatibus rerum*, tells how 'Nouryces vse lullynges and other cradyl songs to pleyse the wyttes of the chylde', but none of these lullabies has survived.[2] In 1438 James Bagule, rector of All Saints' Church, York, leaves to William Hanke *unum librum de canticis cum glaspys argenti et unum librum rubium de Balads*, though with no indication of the language in which these *Balads* were written.[3] The catalogue of Thomas Markaunt's library, drawn up in 1439, includes a

> Liber canticorum musicalium et aliorum
> 20 fo.   Tenor so fayr
> Pen. fo.   and as I wente.[4]

Whilst at Calais in 1473-5 George Cely apparently took up the study of music, and the *Cely Papers* include a list of his expenses in connexion with this. In addition to dances and practice on the harp and lute, he also learned seven songs, four of which cannot now be identified and would appear to have been lost:

> O ffresches Flour.
> tosJuirs.
> Off seche cvm playn.
> My dely wo.[5]

Similarly, the accounts for 1498-9 of the precentor of Tattershall Church and College refer to a song called 'Maydens of London'.[6]

However, general references such as these are of comparatively little interest. More tantalizing are those which quote a line or a

[1] Warton ii, 221, n. 2; E. Power, *Medieval English Nunneries* (Cambridge 1922), p. 157.
[2] I. and P. Opie, *The Oxford Dictionary of Nursery Rhymes* (Oxford 1951), pp. 18-19.   [3] SS. xxx, 80.
[4] M. R. James, *The Sources of Archbishop Parker's Collection of Manuscripts* (Cambridge Antiquarian Society 1899), p. 82.
[5] *RES. NS.* viii, 270-4.
[6] *HMC. Manuscripts of Lord De L'Isle and Dudley* i, 194.

stanza of a lyric which has otherwise disappeared. Such snatches are to be found in Latin chronicles, in works of edification, whether Latin or English, and even in sermons. Indeed, one of the most famous of all medieval sermons, once ascribed to Stephen Langton, was preached on the text *Bel Aliz matin leva*, a line from a French love lyric. It seems to have been not uncommon for medieval preachers to quote from the vernacular in the Latin sermons, and fragments of a good many lost lyrics are found embedded in them.[1] These are usually religious, but lines from secular lyrics also occur. For example, a Latin sermon in a late thirteenth-century volume of miscellaneous theological pieces, Balliol College, Oxford, MS. 230, compares 'those Christians who at one moment make haste to heaven and at another relapse' with 'boys who play'

'Quot leucas habeo ad Beverleyham?' Alius dicit 'viij'. Primus dicit 'Possum venire per lucem?' Alius dicit iuramento 'Ita potes', et ille incipit bonum cursum ac si festinanter ire vellet, et tunc retro saltat et est in pristino statu et dicit 'Ha ha petipas ȝuot ich am þer ich was'.

According to Langbaine, this early version of 'How many miles to Babylon?' was still current in the early seventeenth century. A treatise on the Seven Deadly Sins and the Ten Commandments in a fourteenth-century volume of Anselm and Augustine in the same library, contains a reference to fallen virgins in childbirth who change their tune to,

> Vaylaway whi dedy so,
> Now ich am in alle wo.[2]

A Latin sermon in MS. Cotton Faustina A. v refers to

iste mulieres . . . þat lulle þe child wyth þair fote & sinnges an hauld song, sic dicens:

> Wake wel, Annot,
>   þi mayden boure;
> & get þe fra Walterot,
>   for he es lichure.[3]

---

[1] See G. R. Owst, *Preaching in Medieval England* (Cambridge 1926), pp. 231, n. 1, 272, etc.; *Literature and Pulpit in Medieval England* (Cambridge 1933), *passim*.

[2] R. A. B. Mynors, *Catalogue of the Manuscripts of Balliol College, Oxford* (Oxford 1963), pp. 242, 216.

[3] R. H. Robbins, *Secular Lyrics of the XIVth and XVth Centuries* (Oxford 1955), p. xxxix.

Similarly, two secular scraps appear in some sermons of the thirteenth and fourteenth century in the Berlin Preussische Staatsbibliothek, Lat. theol., f. 249:

i   So longe ic haue lauedi
                   yhoued at þi gate,
               Þat mi fot is ifrore faire lauedi,
                   for þi luue faste to þe stake.

ii   Weilawei þat ich ne span,
                 þo ich into wude ran.[1]

In a fourteenth-century sermon in C.U.L. MS. Ii. 3. 8 is an English verse of secular origin which, in its context, has been transformed into a complaint of Christ:

Cokewold, relictus ab uxore sua propria iam uti poterit post pascha illa amorosa cantilena:

               Ich ave a love untrewe
                   þat myn herte wo,
               Þat makes me of reufol hewe,
                   late to bedde go.
               Sore me may rewe
                   þat evere hi lovede hire so.

Moreover, a sermon of the same date on the text *Quia amore langueo*, in Balliol College, Oxford, MS. 149, has ingeniously applied to Christ a secular verse enumerating the signs of love-longing:

               He Iesus is myth and waxit wan,
               He syket as a sorful man.
               Alone he drawes fro compenye,
               And ever he herkenes one ys drurie.
               Loneliche he spekis to his herte,
               For hym he suffrus peynis smert.[2]

Any blank piece of vellum seems to have been regarded as a suitable place on which to record a verse or a stanza which has struck the hearer. So, for example, a thirteenth-century manuscript in the Worcester Cathedral Library has eight leaves of

[1] *Anglia* lxxxiii, 35–47.
[2] R. Woolf, *The English Religious Lyric in the Middle Ages* (Oxford 1968), pp. 47, 192.

miscellaneous matter at the beginning, on the last of which appear the following English verses:

> He may cume to mi lef bute by þe watere.
> wanne me lust slepen þanne moti wakie,
> Wnder is þat hi liuie.

On the blank page of another manuscript in the same library are lines, subscribed *dixit Robertus seynte Mary Clericus*, which the latest editor takes to be parts of three different poems:

i   Ne saltou neuer, leuedi,
    Tuynklen wyt þin eyen.

ii   Hic abbe ydon al myn youth,
    Ofte, ofte, ant ofte,
Longe yloued ant yerne ybeden:
    Ful dere it his a-bout.

iii   Dore, go þou stille,
    Go þou stille, -e,
Þat hic abbe in þe boure
Ydon al myn uylle, -e.

The first two lines are perhaps from a love song addressed to a lady; lines 3-6 are by an old man who looks back with regret at the many love affairs of his youth; and 7–10 express a lover's anxiety at the creaking of the bower door.[1] On f. 28a of MS. F. 126 in the same library are some fragmentary lines beginning 'Gay, gay, þou art yhent'.[2] Again, MS. Harl. 7322 is a collection of theological and moral pieces, interspersed with which are a number of English couplets and quatrains, mostly religious, but including the following which may originally have been secular:

> Me þingkit þou art so loueli,
>   so fair & so swete,
> Þat sikerli it were mi det
>   þi companie to lete.

---

[1] *Leeds Studies in English* iv, 44ff.; *Notes and Queries* ccx, 245–6.
[2] C. Brown and R. H. Robbins, *The Index of Middle English Verse* (New York 1943), No. 900.

A stanza from a drinking song appears on the fly-leaf of Trinity College, Dublin, MS. 214:

> Her I was and her I drank;
> far-wyll dam, and mykyll thank.
> Her I was and had gud cher,
> And her I drank wyll gud ber.[1]

In a manuscript in the National Library of Wales, in the middle of a series of prophecies and astrological pieces in Latin, English, and Welsh, are two lines of a lover's complaint:

> Alas, howe schale my hert be lyght,
> Wyth dart of loue when hyt ys slayn.[2]

At the end of a fifteenth-century manuscript in the Lincoln Cathedral Chapter Library are the following verses:

> I haue grete marvell off a bryd,
> That w^t my luff ys went a way.
> Sho byldis hyr a noþer sted,
> Ther ffore I morne both nyght & day.
> I cothe neuer serffe þ^t bryd to pay,
> Ne frenchypp w^t hyr con I none ffynd,
> Bott ffast ffro me sho fflys a way.
> A las þ^t euer sho was unkynd,
> A las qui is she w^t me wroth,
> & to þ^t bryd I trespast noght,
> ʒe gyff sho be neuer so lothe,
> Sho shall come owte off my thoght.
> Now off me sho gyffis ryght noght,
> Bot byldis hus fer under a lynd.
> In bytter balns sho has nu boght.
> A las þ^t euer sho was unkynd,
> A las qui is þis brydis . . .
> I wen . . . . luff . . . .[3]

On f. 14b of Pembroke College, Cambridge, MS. 258 are the following lines headed *Cantus occidentalis*, and in a thirteenth-century hand:

---

[1] R. H. Robbins, *op. cit.*, nos. 142, 12.
[2] *Essays and Studies*, NS. xxi, 1–28.
[3] R. M. Woolley, *Catalogue of the Manuscripts of Lincoln Cathedral Chapter Library* (London 1927), p. 95.

> Murie a tyme I telle in May,
>   Wan bricte blosmen brekeþ on tre,
> Þeise foules singe nyt ant day;
>   In ilche grene is gamen an gle.[1]

Various fragments of verse are scribbled on the fly-leaf of MS. Bodl. Rawlinson D 913, and may perhaps have formed part of the repertoire of a fourteenth-century minstrel. On the recto are:

i
> Of euerykune tre,
> Of euerykune tre,
> þe hawe-þorn blowet suotes,
> Of euerykune tre.
> My lemmon sse ssal boe,
> My lemmon sse ssal boe,
> þe fairest of euer[y k]inne,
> My lemmon sse ssal boe.

ii
> þe godemon on is weie . . .

iii
> ichaue a mantel i-maket of cloth . . .

iv
> Ne sey neruer such a man,
> A Iordan was, and wente he
> to gogeshale panyles.

On the verso are *The Irish Dancer*, *The Maiden on the Moor*, lines from two French songs, and also:

i
> Wer þer ouþer in þis toun
>   Ale or wy[n],
> Isch hit wolde bugge
>   To lemmon myn.
> Welle, wo was so hardy
>   Forte make my lef al blody?
> Þaut he were þe kinges sone
>   Of Normaundy,
> ʒet icholde a-wreke boe
>   For lemman myn.
>
> Welle wo was me tho,
>   Wo was me tho.
> Þe man that leset þat he leuet,
>   Hym is al so.

[1] *Anglia* xlii, 147, n.

So sse me lerde,
Ne no more i n[e] can,
But crist ich hire biteche,
Þat was my lemman.

ii   Al nist by þ[e] rose, rose,
Al nist bi þe rose i lay,
Darst ich noust þ[e] rose stele,
Ant ȝet i bar þe flour awey.

Al gold Ionet is þin her,
[A]l gold Ionet is þin he[r],
Saue þin Iank[y]n l[emman dere],
[Sa]ue Iankyn lemman [de]re,
[Sa]ue þin onlie d[ere].

iv   Ye sir [þat is] idronken,
dronken, dronken, ydronken,
. . . . atta dronken,
As tabart atte wyne.
Hay . . . . malkin,
Suster walter peter.

v   Þe dronke al depe,
Ant ichulle eke.

vi   Stondet alle stille,
Stille, stille, stille,
Standet alle stille,
Stille as any ston.
Trippe a littel wit þi fot,
Ant let þi body go.[1]

Four lines of a poem in MS. Bodl. 692 are now the only ones completely legible:

Joly cheperte of Aschell downe,
Can more on love than al this towne.
Lord, wy, wy, &c. Lord where he goȝth.
A . . . . . ester þou schoperte for al thy fray
. . . . my . . ke away
For ryȝt here of getest þou notȝ.[2]

[1] *Anglia* xxx, 173ff.; *Notes and Queries* ccvi, 245ff.
[2] R. H. Robbins, *op. cit.*, p. xl.

Comparatively little of the remaining eight lines can now be read. In BM. MS. Additional 5666, along with the music, is the burden and three lines from the first stanza of a love song of the late fourteenth or early fifteenth century:

> I have loued so many a day,
> Ligthly spedde, but better I may.
>
> This ender day wen me was wo,
> Naghtgale to meue me to,
> Vnder a bugh ther I lay.[1]

The fifteenth-century Gonville and Caius College, Cambridge, MS. 383 contains a number of lyrics in carole form. Prefixed to one are the words:

> Bryd on brere y telle yt to,
> Non oþer y ne dare.

This is apparently not the refrain, since after the first stanza the words are begun again, crossed out, and a different refrain written. They may represent an alternative burden, but more probably they indicate the tune to which the lyric is to be sung. In MS. 465 in the same library are the lines:

> Wyt a . . . . so wondyrleche grete.
> þe comb yt ys of red coral,
> þe bec yt ys of yete.[2]

On the margin of MS. 221 appears a thirteenth-century scrap which may perhaps be religious:

> Waylowy so dere boht,
> þat it sal þus ben.[3]

Lines of other lyrics are to be found in some of the manuscripts in the library of Trinity College, Cambridge. On f. 27b of MS. 323 are various scribbles, including the following in a thirteenth-century hand:

> Ic chule bere to wasscen doun
> I þe toun
> Þat was blac ant þat was broun.

[1] J. Stevens, *Mediæval Carols* (London 1952), p. 110.
[2] M. R. James, *Gonville and Caius College: Catalogue of Manuscripts* (Cambridge 1908) ii, 437, 540.   [3] *Anglia* lxxxiii, 35–47.

On f. 1a of MS. 1434, in a fifteenth-century hand:

> God grant me gras to gehte a gayn
> Ye luffe y^t I haue loste.

In a hand of the same date in MS. 1157:

> My loue she mornt ffor me, for me,
> My loue she mornes for me.[1]

On the last leaf of a Psalter appears 'I am not unkynd to love as I ffynd', which reads like a line from a lost love lyric,[2] as also do some words in a fifteenth-century hand on the top margin of a leaf of MS. Bodl. 34, 'ly þow me ner lemmon in þy narms'.

Two quatrains, perhaps a complete lyric, are found in the manuscript of the Old English *Blickling Homilies*:

> Trust in my luf, hy schall be trw
> Hertly to hold þat I haf heght.
> Yowr reght reuwyd for to reuw,
> And you to menske with mayn & meght.

> Sen tym me luf wasse on yow leght,
> It last lelly all way.
> And thus hy murn both day & neght,
> The more I luf þe more I may.[3]

MS. HM. 503 in the Huntington Library contains a Wycliffite tract in a hand of the fifteenth century. On the fly-leaf is what appears to be the first stanza of a lyric of which the remainder has been lost:

> Sche þat Y loue alleþermoost & loþist to begile,
> Sche dwelliþ out in a wildirnes, so fer out in an yle.
> & it were betwix us but an hundir myle,
> Sche miзt not be out of my þouзt a paternoster while.
> Wiþ an Y & an O, Crist Y hur biteche;
> And Y lay louesik in my bed Y bed non oþer leche.[4]

Elsewhere two lines appear in MS. Sloane 3160:

> All wyth a throwe and a lowe and lully,
> I haue Ioly a pryn for þe mastry. (f. 24v)

[1] M. R. James, *Trinity College, Cambridge: Catalogue of the Western Manuscripts* (Cambridge 1900–2) i, 441; iii, 461.

[2] C. Wordsworth and H. Littlehales, *The Old Service-Books of the English Church* (London 1910), p. 60.

[3] *Anglia* lxxxiii, 35–47.   [4] *Medium Ævum* xxx, 170–5.

In Royal 19 B. iv, in a hand of the second half of the fifteenth century:

> Sin it is lo
> That I muste goo,
> & pass yow ffro
>   My lady dere. (f. 98r).

In MS. Peniarth 356 in the National Library of Wales:

> Þe ny3tyngale synges
> Þat all þe wod rynges,
> Scho singyth in hire song
> Þat þe ny3t is to long. (p. 196).[1]

Naturally such snatches of verse are not always secular, and lines from religious lyrics are even more frequent. In the four-teenth-century MS. Bodl. 26, in a series of sermon outlines by a Franciscan there appears, along with other English pieces, a fragmentary carol with a burden several times repeated in the text:

> My do3ter, my darlynnge
> Herkne my lore, y-se my thechyng.[2]

This might originally have been part of a secular poem, as is also the case with a single stanza in the *Maister of the Game*:

> My loue so swyte
> Iesu kype
>   Where soo euer that yow be;
> All for yowere sake
> My harte doth schake,
>   And sore hyt gryvys me.[3]

and with two lines in C.U.L. MS. Additional 2585 (2):

> [I] wote a boure so bricht,
> Es kidde with kaiser and knicht.[4]

On the other hand, various fragments in Gonville and Caius

---

[1] *Anglia* lxxxiii, 35–47.
[2] *Modern Language Notes* liii, 239–45.
[3] *Essays and Studies*, NS. xxi, 28.
[4] *Anglia* lxxxiii, 35–47.

College, Cambridge, MS. 383 are certainly religious, and so is the following in MS. 512 in the same library:

> Lytel wotyt onyman hu derne loue was fu[n]de,
> But he þat was on Rode don, and bouth vs wyth his wonde.
> For loue of man he made hymself vnsunde;
> He haueth ykast a grysli gast to grunde.
> He bouth vs wyth hys suete blod,
> Hu myth he don vs more [god].[1]

At the end of a sermon on f. 120b of MS. 15 in the library of St John's College, Cambridge, is written:

> Hwyt was his nakede brist,
>   And his blodi side.
> Wan was his fayre neb,
>   Hys wu[n]den depe and wyde.
> On fif stedes of hys bodi
>   L'e stremes renne of blode.[2]

Arras Bibliothèque de la Ville, MS. 184, apparently written c. 1400, had formerly belonged to the Augustinian house of Mont-Saint-Eloi, near Arras. The early folios contain sermons and notes for sermons in both Latin and English, and in one of them is the following:

> Hoc ergo libro in cruce expanse canta cantica amoris, uidelicet:
>   Nede mot y loue wher men loue me,
>   Els wer to blame; God schulde þat y lie.
> Et hoc canta cantica doloris:
>   Wan y þenke on þe hie tre at Crist was yhangyng,
>   Carful may myn harte be, my hondus y may wryng.
> Hec etiam canta cantica leticie, uidelicet:
>   Of all flours et c.

The third of these is the beginning of a still extant poem, and it is possible that the other two similarly represent opening lines of poems which in these cases have not survived.[3] The well-known 'Nou goth sonne vnder wod' comes from the meditation on the passion for Sext in the *Speculum Ecclesie*, and it therefore remains

---

[1] M. R. James, *Gonville and Caius College* ii, 436, 583.

[2] M. R. James, *A Descriptive Catalogue of the Manuscripts in the Library of St John's College, Cambridge* (Cambridge 1913), p. 20.

[3] *PMLA.* lxix, 984. The third is in C. Brown, *Religious Lyrics of the XIVth Century* (Oxford 1924), pp. 178ff.

a possibility that it may originally have been part of a longer poem on the Hours of the Cross, or perhaps of one on the Passion.[1] Two fragmentary stanzas of a song to the Virgin in BM. MS. Additional 5666 begin:

> Now has Mary born a floure,
> All þis world to gret honour. (f. 3r)[2]

On f. 419 of Trinity College, Cambridge, MS. 1109, in a fourteenth-century hand, appears:

> Simenel hornes
> Ber none þornes,
>   alleluya,[3]

while on f. 122 of the early fifteenth-century MS. Royal 20 A. i, among other scribbles, are the lines:

> Amonge al merthes manny,
> We chol senge of o lady,
> In al this wordil nis svch a siht.[4]

Written in a hand of the fifteenth century on f. i3 of Pierpont Library MS. M 898 is a single stanza:

> Bewty is subiect vnto age,
>   Sicknes the same will stayne,
> And whoso wythered is with yeares,
>   Cannot be younge agayne.[5]

Two fifteenth-century poems have been found on a strip of vellum amongst the Ormond manuscripts in Kilkenny Castle. The first is a love poem:

> Gracius & gay,
> On hyr lyytt all my tho3th.
> Butt sche rew on me to day,
> To deth sche hatt me broth.
> Hyr feyngerys bytt long and small,
> Hyr harmus byth rown & toth,
> Hyr mowth as sweth as lycory,
> [I]n hyr lyyt all my toth.

---

[1] See R. Woolf, *The English Religious Lyric in the Middle Ages* (Oxford 1968), p. 242. [2] *Anglia* lxxxiii, 35–47.
[3] M. R. James, *Trinity College, Cambridge* iii, 91.
[4] G. F. Warner and J. P. Gilson, *Catalogue of Western Manuscripts in the Old Royal and King's Collections* (London 1921) ii, 350.
[5] *PMLA.* lxxvi, 22.

175

> Hyr Iyne bytt feyr and gray,
> Hyr bruys bytt wel y benth,
> Ass rode as rede as rosse yn may,
> Hyr medyll ys small and gent.
> Sche ys swett vnder schett,
> I low hyr [and] no mo,
> Sche hatt myne harth to kepe,
> In londes wher sche go.
> Sodenly tell y pray,
> To [þe] my low ys lend,
> Kysse me yn my way,
> Onys ar y wen[d].

The second is a macaronic religious poem:

> Pryd, p[ryd] wo thow be, *mater uisyorum.*
> Lucifer, alas for the, *gaudia polorum.*
> Lucifer was angyll bryȝth, *in arce polorum* . . .

and so on for another nine lines. Also from Ireland is a late thirteenth or early fourteenth-century poem on f. 1 of the *Liber Primus
Kilkenniensis.* 'The page in question had originally contained
what appeared to be a list of burgesses, but this had become
illegible from long exposure, and after the names had faded out'
some verses, which appear to be an extract from a poem on the
Old and New Dispensations, were written across them.[1]

One type of verse of which little has survived is that which was
occasionally found on wall-paintings in some of the great houses.
The duke of Northumberland's houses at Leconfield and Wressel
were enriched by various proverbial sayings. 'In the rooffe of the
hyest chawmbre in the gardynge' at Leconfield, the theme was
Hope, from the Percy motto:

> Esperaunce in the worlde nay.
> The worlde variethe every day.
>
> Esperaunce en dieu in hym is all,
> For he is above fortunes fall.

Other moral verses, contrasting sensual and intellectual pleasures,
decorated the garret over the 'bayne':

---

[1] *Proceedings of the Royal Irish Academy, Section C,* xli, 205ff.; *Notes and
Queries* xxvii, 47.

Riche apparell, costly and precius,
Makithe a man lusty, cumly and gloryus;
Vestueris of estate wrought preciusly,
Causithe man to be honowrede and muche sett by . . .

I floure in youthe delyght and pleasure,
To fede all my fantasys I want no treasure,
I synge and daunce, I revell and play,
I am so lovede of ladyes I nede not to pray.

All wordely pleasures vanysshethe away,
To day a man in golde, to morrow closyde in clay.[1]

The scribe of MS. Bodl. 315 has copied into it five inscriptions
from the refectory of the Austin Priory at Launceston, Cornwall,
the second of them also appearing in a Glastonbury miscellany
of the fifteenth century:

Hoo that comy3t to an howse,
Loke he be noo thyng dongerowse,
　　To take seche as he fyndy3t;
And yf he woll not do soo,
Reson agree3t thertoo,
　　To take suche as he bryngy3t.[2]

Similarly, in Horley church, Oxfordshire, a large wall-painting of
St Christopher and the Christ-child, has two scrolls bearing
English couplets, and at Stratford-upon-Avon there was formerly
a set of Middle English mortality verses.[3]

As an indication of the strange places in which lyrics are sometimes found, mention may be made of one which has been written
on the back of a papal bull. The bull was apparently issued in 1199
to the priory of St James by Exeter, confirming the monks in the
privileges of the Cluniac order. A contemporary copy was made,
perhaps at Paris, and sent to the priory. On the back of it, in
what is probably a fourteenth-century hand, are the words and
music of an English lyric:

Bryd one brere, brid, brid one brere,
Kynd is come of loue loue to craue.

[1] J. G. Russell, *The Field of Cloth of Gold* (London 1969), pp. 54, 185.
[2] A. G. Rigg, *A Glastonbury Miscellany of the Fifteenth Century* (Oxford 1968),
p. 71; *Archiv* cc, 338–43.　　　　[3] *Notes and Queries* clxxvi, 387; ccxii, 131.

> Bliðful biryd, on me þu rewe,
> Or greyð, lef, greið þu me my graue.
>
> Hic am so bliþe, so bryȝit brid on brere,
> Quan I se þat hende in halle.
> Yhe is quit of lime, loueli, trewe,
> Yhe is fayr and flur of alle.
>
> Mikte hic hire at wille hauen,
> Stedefast of loue, loueli, trewe,
> Of mi sorwe yhe may me sauen;
> Ioye and blisse were eere me newe.[1]

The clerk of the Tolsey Court Book, now in the Bristol archives, sometime between 1487 and 1497 relieved his feelings by scribbling down, in the middle of a monotonous list of debts, a few lines from a contemporary sea shanty:

> Hale and howe Rumbylowe
> Stire well the gode ship and lete the wynde blowe.
> Here comethe the Pryor of Prikkingham and his Convent,
> But ye kepe þe ordoure well, ye shull be shent,
> With hale & howe &c.[2]

A single stanza from a secular song appears, along with some moral Latin verses, on the bottom half of f. 13a of the *Acta Capitularia, 1410–29* in the York Minster Library:

> Vnder a law as I me lay,
> I herd a may makand hyr mone,
> And euer scho sayd wela [w]ay,
> For faute of loue I stand alone.

Both English and Latin are in the same hand as the probate of a will immediately above, and it would seem that the chapter clerk was in this way beguiling the tedium of his clerical duties.[3] A late thirteenth-century court roll of Hawkesbury, Gloucestershire, has on the recto of the first page, in a hand of about the middle of the fourteenth century:

---

[1] *Antiquaries Journal* xv, 1ff.
[2] E. M. Carus-Wilson, *Medieval Merchant Venturers* (London 1954), p. 12.
[3] *Speculum* xxvi, 142.

> In sory tyme my lyf is y-spent,
>   & euer so lengur more & more,
>   & ȝut wel more but hyt amend;
>   Y may not liue, y nam but lore
> Hure loue to lenun & y ne may;
>   For sykurlyche y wot hyt wel.[1]

A more surprising discovery is that of a stanza of Middle English secular verse scribbled on one of the pillars of the now half-ruined church at Duxford, Cambridgeshire:

> With wiel my herte is wa,
>   & closyd ys w^t care.
> L & S sekurly
> [Ca]use me to syth ful sar.
> I & . . . .
> . . . . for to smarte.
> V & . . . . Y withall,
> . . . . . joy come to thin herte.

Another, rather more suitable to the surroundings, was scratched on the wall of Barrington Church in the same county:

> Lo fol, how the day goth,
> Cast foly now to the cok.
> Ryth sone tydyth the wroth,
> It ys almast xii of the clok.[2]

Two lines of verse also appear on one of the pillars of Landwade St Nicholas, a private chapel belonging to the Cotton family:

> Fare well all clene Melawdy,
> Fare well all ladyes and . . .

Similarly, on the pillars of St Mary's, Lydgate, Suffolk, there are three fragments of music. Two of them have 'well' followed by four musical notes, fa, re, mi, la, after which appears 'dy', and then a square divided equally into four sections with a dot in each, followed by 'yne'. The square apparently represents the four at dice, *cater*, and the whole seems to be a rebus reading 'Well fare mi lady Cateryne', perhaps a line from a contemporary song.[3]

---

[1] *Neuphilologische Mitteilungen* lx, 287–8.

[2] *Cambridge Antiquarian Society: Communications* xix, 57.

[3] V. Pritchard, *English Medieval Graffiti* (Cambridge 1967), pp. 54, 144.

Passages of vernacular religious verse are sometimes quoted in Latin moral stories, and in one of them we even find two lines of secular verse:

A certain man was greedy and ate in the early morning when others went to church, and this he did habitually. One day he ate in this way, and afterwards went off to the woods, singing this song:

> Jolyfte, jolyfte,
> Maket me to the wode the.

He advanced for a short distance, and then fell over backwards. He arose and again fell in the same way. Seeing this from a distance, a certain knight went to him and found him to be dead, with his tongue hanging out of his mouth like that of a dog, his whole face as if it were on fire, and the eyes glaring like those of a madman.[1]

A Latin poem on the battle of Neville's Cross contains English words which could perhaps have been taken from a contemporary lyric:

> Clamabant 'In a day go we to the tyrie wyth hay',
> Ipsis sit Waleway, meschef, tristissima, woday.[2]

It is less surprising to find verses in a love-letter, though in this case the letter is in French with the verses in English:

> Haue gooday nou Mergerete,
> Wiþ grete loue y þe grete.
> Y wolde we miȝten us ofte mete,
> In halle, in chaumbre, and in the strete,
> Withoute blame of the contre.
> God ȝeue that so miȝte hit be.[3]

The report of a lawsuit is perhaps the last place in which we should look for an example of medieval lyrical poetry. Yet in a case brought by Lord Neville of Raby against the prior and convent of Durham, a stanza from an English poem was quoted as part of the evidence. To be sure, this was no ordinary lawsuit. As rent for his lands at Raby Lord Neville was supposed to bring a stag to the monastery at Durham on September 4, the feast of the Translation of St Cuthbert. The stag was to be offered at the

---

[1] T. Wright, *Latin Stories* (Percy Society viii), p. 81.
[2] T. Wright, *Political Poems and Songs* (RS. 14) i, 48.
[3] *MLR.* xxxvii, 420.

shrine of the saint, and afterwards removed to the kitchen of the prior. But a dispute arose concerning the exact procedure. According to the prior, Lord Neville should come with a few servants, hand over the stag, and leave, whereas Lord Neville claimed that the stag should be brought into the cathedral to the sound of the horns of his followers, that he and his servants should then take possession of the prior's house, and feast there for the following day and night. In 1290 when the offering was duly made, there was a pitched battle between Lord Neville's men and the monks, in which the latter, armed with the great candlesticks used in the services, succeeded in driving Lord Neville's men out of the cathedral and retaining possession of the stag. Afterwards, during the lifetime of this Lord Neville, the offering was given up. In 1331, when his son proposed to revive it, the prior objected, and thereupon Lord Neville brought a writ of novel disseizin against him. This curious case, in which a tenant insisted in paying rent to a reluctant landlord, was lost by Neville; unjustly so, perhaps, since the prior was unable to deny that such a custom had existed, though he quibbled over some of the details. During the course of the lawsuit an interesting piece of evidence was produced to show that the offering had formerly been made on September 14, Holy Rood Day. This consisted of four lines of a lament which, so the prior said, had been sung on the death of Lord Neville's great-grandfather, Robert de Neville, who had died round about 1280:

> Wel, qwa sal thir hornes blau,
>   Haly Rod thi day?
> Nou is he dede and lies law,
>   Was wont to blaw thaim ay.[1]

Consequently, in the middle of the account of a lawsuit, we come across this single stanza of a lost Middle English ballad.

The objection to the devil's monopoly of all the best tunes is to be found during the medieval period. The habit of Thomas of Bayeux of providing pious words for the profane songs of the minstrels has already been mentioned, and the well-known 'Sumer is icumen in' was perhaps only written down as an indication of the tune to which some pious Latin verses were to be sung. But

---

[1] SS. ix, 112; *Archaeologia Aeliana, 4th Series*, i, 133.

the best example of this tendency comes from the *Red Book of Ossory*, in which is preserved a collection of Latin hymns in a fourteenth-century hand. Prefixed to these, and in the same hand, are tags of English and Anglo-French secular songs. A note in the manuscript claims that the Latin hymns were composed by the then bishop of Ossory, perhaps Richard de Lesdrede (1318–1360), in order to displace certain 'popular and secular songs'. Presumably the tags come from these, and indicate the tunes to which the Latin hymns are to be sung. It is to this pious motive that we owe all that remains of half a dozen English lyrics:

i   Alas, hou shold y syng,
Yloren is my playnge.
Hou sholdy wiȝ ȝat olde man
To leuen and let my leman,
    Swettist of al ȝinge.

ii   Haue mercie on me frere;
    Barfote ȝat ygo.

iii   Do. Do. nightyngale syng full myrie;
Shal y neure for ȝyn loue lengre karie.

iv   Haue god day my leman.

v   Gaueth me no garlond of grene,
Bot hit ben of Wythones yuroght.

vi   Hey how ȝe cheualdoures woke al nyght.

The third is repeated in a slightly different form, and there are also two fragments in Anglo-French.[1] In a religious lyric in the Library of Trinity College, Cambridge, MS. 1157, the secular 'Come over the borne, Besse' serves as a framework for a traditional complaint, while in MS. Royal 17 B. xliii, the element of secular love song is confined to the no doubt borrowed refrain:

Com home agayne,
Com home agayne,
Min owine swet hart, com home agayne.

[1] St John D. Seymour, *Anglo-Irish Literature 1200–1582* (Cambridge 1929), p. 97; *MLN.* liii, 241; *Speculum* xxvii, 504.

Similarly, in *The Gude and Godlie Ballatis* is an excellent lyric, the secular original of which is not known, but it is clearly echoed in the second, fourth, and eighth lines of the stanza, with their pattern of repetition:

> All my lufe, leif me not,
> Leif me not, leif me not,
> All my lufe, leif me not,
>   This myne allone:
> With ane burding on my bak,
> I may not beir it, I am so waik;
> Lufe, this burding fra me tak,
>   Or ellis I am gone.[1]

Some of the Middle English poets occasionally quote from contemporary lyrics. It will be remembered that in the *Nuns' Priest's Tale* Chauntecleer and Pertelote sing 'in sweete accord, "My lief is faren in londe!" '. In this instance, the stanza of a song, of which this is the first line, appears in a manuscript in the library of Trinity College, Cambridge, and is no doubt that of which Chaucer was thinking. No such discovery has thrown any light on the Pardoner's song 'Com hider, love, to me' (*Prologue* 672), or on the songs beginning 'Now, loue, þou do me riȝte', and 'Doubil me this bourdon' in the spurious 'adventure of the pardonere and tapstere'.[2] In the *Miller's Tale* Nicholas sings 'the kynges noote' (3217), tentatively identified with 'king villȝamis note' in *The Complaynt of Scotlande*; and no doubt 'many a song and many a leccherous lay' of Chaucer's has also perished, along with the 'book of the Leoun'.[3] Again, in one of the stanzas of a fifteenth-century poem on the *Timor Mortis* theme, the opening words are given of two lyrics, one in English and one in French:

> Whe schold neuer lust, hop, ne dawnce,
> Noþer syng no song of þis new ordenance,
>   As, 'Herte myne, well may þou be, glad and lusty to be',
> Or ellys, 'Ma bel amour, ma ioy en esperance',
>   But sey, 'Timor mortis conturbat me'.[4]

[1] R. Woolf, *The English Religious Lyric in the Middle Ages* (Oxford 1968), pp. 195, 408.
[2] F. J. Furnivall and W. G. Stone, *The Tale of Beryn* (EETS. ES. 1909), pp. 3, 14.
[3] F. N. Robinson, *The Complete Works of Geoffrey Chaucer* (Cambridge, Mass. 1961), pp. 265, 773.   [4] *MLR.* xxviii, 235.

In a poem on how the Apostles made the Creed by a certain 'Farnelay', scorn is directed at those who do not sing holy songs, but instead the

> songe of Hey Derry Danne,
> Howe þe grome gate gyrse by þe rede syde.[1]

References to contemporary songs appear also in Skelton. In *The Bowge of Courte* it is said of Harvey Hafter that 'euer he sange, "Sythe I am no thynge playne" ' (235), no doubt the first line of some popular song. Later, the same character says that he can sing by rote the two songs beginning 'Prynces of yougthe' and 'Shall I sayle wyth you' (253–4), while in the same poem Ryote is represented as a musical genius, 'And ay he sange, "In fayth, decon thou crewe" ' (360).[2] If the list given in the *Garlande of Laurell* is to be trusted, many of Skelton's own works have disappeared. Some of these we should be glad to have, among them the 'Tratyse of Triumphis of the Rede Rose', 'The Balade of the Mustarde Tarte', 'The Murnyng of the mapely rote', and the 'Epitomis of the myller and his ioly make'.

In the prologue to some of the books of his translation of the *Aeneid* Gavin Douglas, too, mentions various popular songs. In that to Book XII are references to three of them:

> The schip salis our the salt fame,
> Will bring thir merchandis and my lemman hame (197–8).

> I will be blyth and lycht,
> Myne hart is lent apon sa gudly wycht (199–200).

> I come hidder to wow (298).

Another appears in the prologue to Book XIII:

> The joly day now dawis (182),

a song also referred to by Dunbar in his *Address to the Merchantis of Edinburgh*:

> Your commone menstrallis hes no tone
> Bot 'Now the day dawis', and 'Into Joun' (29–30).

[1] R. H. Robbins, *Secular Lyrics of the XIVth and XVth Centuries* (Oxford 1955), p. xl.
[2] Mentioned also in *A deuote trentale for old Ion Clarke* 44, and in *Why come ye nat to Courte* 63. For 'Prynces of yougthe' see also p. 185.

One of the hens in Henryson's *The Cock and the Fox* promises to sing

this sang, 'wes never wedow sa gay' (515).

In *The Fox, the Wolf and the Cadger,* the last of them sings 'Huntis up, up, upon hie' (2083), whilst the Town Mouse and the Country Mouse, seated at their feast, are singing 'Haill yule, haill' (289) when they are interrupted.

Song-books, whether of the fifteenth-century or later, often given some indication of lost lyrics which may go back to a much earlier period. On ff. 114–116v of an Escorial manuscript containing a collection of fifteenth-century music with French, Italian, and Flemish songs, are two lines in English:

> Princesse of youth and flowre of godlihede,
> The perfight meror of all gentilnesse.[1]

In the binding of a set of seventeenth-century part-books in the New York Public Library, Drexel MSS. 4180–5, are several fragments of early Tudor songs. Fifteen pieces in all are represented, of which the following do not appear to be otherwise known:

3. . . . [c]rowne of thorne so scharpe & kene throw my heyd.
4. . . . for þi sake man to whom yf þu call at a[ny?].
6. . . . [lo]kyng for her trew love long or that yt was day.
7. . . . love shuld com. On euery syde þe way she pryde.
8. . . . red rosse fayre and sote off sent trew off [c]olowre.
11. . . . thus hath mayd my payne.
13. . . . to þe nale tryll Card lye down and whele stond styll.[2]

A single quatrain from a sixteenth-century Tudor song-book, MS. Royal, Appendix 58, is often cited as a good example of popular song, though in fact it seems to be quite a sophisticated piece:

> Westron wynde, when wyll thow blow?
> The small rayne downe can rayne.
> Cryst, yf my loue wer in my armys,
> And I yn my bed Agayne.[3]

---

[1] *Music and Letters* xix, 119ff.
[2] J. Stevens, *Music and Poetry in the Early Tudor Court* (London 1961), pp. 426–8.   [3] R. H. Robbins, *op. cit.*, p. xxxviii.

Written below three lines of music on f. 2v in MS. Egerton 3002 is a stanza in English:

> In willdernys
> þer fond I pes,
>   secret, a-lone,
> In gret distresse,
> remediles,
>   makyng her mone.[1]

On f. 230a of MS. Selden B. 24 is a poem of ten or eleven stanzas, much of which cannot now be made out, but beginning:

> [Go fro my] vindow, go, go fro my window
> . . . . [win]dow si[r qu]ho ys at ȝour vndow?
>   go fro my vindow, go.

This is evidently an early version of a popular sixteenth-century song, 'Go from my window', mentioned in Beaumont and Fletcher's *Knight of the Burning Pestle*.[2]

Finally reference should be made to the list of thirty-eight songs and thirty dances in *The Complaynt of Scotlande*.[3] A good many can be identified, and some are certainly from the sixteenth century, as for example the first of them, 'Pastance vitht gude companye', which is by Henry VIII, but it is not unlikely that some of those of which we know nothing may go back to Middle English times.[4]

---

[1] *Essays and Studies*, NS. xxi, 7.   [2] *Anglia* lxxiii, 299–304.

[3] Ed. J. A. H. Murray (EETS. ES. 1872–3), pp. lxxxiiff., 64.

[4] 'Of late yeeres an English Gentleman travelling in Palestine, not farr from Jerusalem, as he passed thorow a Country Towne, he heard by chance a woman sitting at her doore dandling her childe, to sing; *Bothwel bank thow blumest fayre*'. R. Verstegan, *A Restitution of Decayed Intelligence* (London 1634), p. 296.

IO

POLITICAL AND
SATIRICAL POETRY

A considerable amount of poetry dealing with contemporary political and social conditions has survived from the Middle English
period. Examples are extant in all three of the languages then in
use, but we are not here concerned with the Latin or Anglo-
French contributions. The extant works in Middle English date
mostly from the fourteenth and fifteenth centuries, and vary in
length from the pregnant couplet on the fourteenth year of
Richard II:

> The ax was sharpe, the stokke was harde,
> In the xiiii yere of Kyng Richarde,[1]

to important works such as *Piers Plowman, Piers the Ploughman's
Creed,*[2] *Richard the Redeless,* etc. The earliest surviving poem is
one on the battle of Lewes, written by a partisan of Montfort,
which celebrates the defeat of Henry III, and more especially
the discomfiture of Richard of Cornwall. But in addition there are
references to similar poetry from an earlier date, while later
allusions indicate that the extant political poetry represents only
part of what was formerly a much more extensive literature. This
is not surprising, since such verse is essentially ephemeral, and
tends to disappear along with the conditions that gave rise to it.
Only the more important poems had much chance of achieving a
written existence, and any others would owe their survival to
accident.

When only bare allusions are found it is not always possible to

[1] St John's College, Oxford, MS. 209, f. 57a. A variant of this has been
added on a blank leaf towards the end of C.U.L. MS. Dd. 14. 2.
[2] In addition to the extant manuscripts of this work, lines 172–207 also appear
in a late fifteenth-century hand, on f. 3r of BM. MS. Harley 78, and these lines
apparently represent a lost copy of the poem. See *Speculum* xxxiv, 428–36.

be definite about the language in which the poems were written. Most of the references to such poetry during the twelfth century are probably to French works, though possible exceptions are the songs said to have been current concerning St Wulfstan. On one occasion the saint is reported to have repulsed the advances of a wealthy woman who had fallen in love with him, and to have rebuked her severely, whereupon 'the story of this incident spread through the city, and for long it was the theme of songs at all the cross-roads'.[1] On the other hand, the poems against Henry I by a certain Luc de la Barre were certainly in French. Not satisfied with a literary warfare, the poet took up arms against the king, and in 1124 was taken prisoner on the surrender of the castle of Pontaudemer. Henry ordered him to 'be deprived of his sight for having ridiculed him in his songs, and engaged in rash enterprises against him'. Charles of Flanders endeavoured to procure some mitigation of the punishment, but the poet's verses had evidently touched the king to the quick: 'This humorous poet made scurrilous songs about me, and sang them aloud to bring me into contempt, thus often making me the laughing-stock of malicious enemies'. Pardon was refused, and the poet, preferring death to blindness, killed himself by dashing his head against the walls of his prison.[2] Equally certainly in French were the verses composed against each other by Henry of Burgundy and Richard I during the course of the Third Crusade.[3] Richard himself was well known as a poet and troubadour who exchanged insulting verses with other troubadours of the period. Some of his love-poems and *sirventes* seem to be extant, but most of them have long since disappeared.

At other times it must remain uncertain whether the particular songs were in English or in French. When Normandy was invaded by Philip of France, the castle of Vaudreuil, under the command of Robert FitzWalter and Sigar de Quincy, surrendered after a suspiciously weak defence. As a result satirical poems are said to have been composed in both kingdoms, attributing the disaster to treachery.[4] One of the charges brought against William

[1] R. R. Darlington, *Vita Wulfstani* (Royal Historical Society 1928), p. 12.
[2] Ordericus iv, 46off.
[3] T. Gale, *Historiæ Anglicanæ Scriptores* (Oxford 1687) ii, 409.
[4] Ralph de Coggeshall, *Chronicon Anglicanum* (RS. 66), p. 144.

de Longchamp, bishop of Ely, the unpopular chancellor of Richard I, was that

> in order to increase his fame and to glorify his name, he was in the habit of tricking out verses and adulatory jingles that he had picked up by begging, and of enticing jesters and singers from the kingdom of France by his presents, that they might sing about him in the streets; and but lately it was everywhere said that there was not such a person in all the world.[1]

Elsewhere Longchamp is said to have been ignorant of English, and it was this that led to his capture when fleeing the country disguised as a woman. Since the minstrels are specifically said to have been imported from France, it would seem reasonable to suppose that their songs must have been in French, though if so it is difficult to believe that their propaganda could have been particularly effective in this country.

References from a later date are almost certainly to English songs, even if the fact is not specifically mentioned, as occasionally it is. According to Fabyan, a certain 'metrician' made various ballads concerning King John, the Emperor Otto, and Philip of France, and he gives an example of them:

> O quem mirabilia, good Lord thy werkys been
> In punysshement of synners, by thy myght, wondersly;
> As, by olde storyes, it is playnly seen
> One synner the other hath correcte vtterly.
> As Aalizaunder, with Iulius, Pompey, and Tholomy,
> And many other, which as thy scourgys were,
> To punysshe synners, and themselfe also dere,

and so on for another two stanzas. Fabyan is not, of course, a particularly good authority for the reign of John, nor does this read at all like a contemporary popular song; it is much more likely to have been a later purely literary effort. The same author tells also of a certain 'panflete', which he claims to have seen, and which explained the reason for the enmity between Edward I and the city of London:

> in an olde panflete it apperyth that ye sayd Gregory Rokkisley, toke certayne brybes of the bakers, and sufferyd them to sell brede lackynge .vi. oz. or .vii. vnces in a peny lofe.[2]

[1] Roger de Hoveden, *Chronica* (RS. 51) iii, 143.   [2] Fabyan, pp. 322, 389.

Again, Fabyan's authority is slight, but the 'panflete', if it ever existed and was at all contemporary, would at that date almost certainly have been in verse. In 1323 Edward II travelled through the north of England. On his way he spent some days at Whorlton Castle, where he is recorded to have presented 3*s.* to Alianore le Rede and Alice de Whorlton for 'chanting of songs of Simon de Montfort before the king, and other songs'.[1] The only extant English poem which would fit such a description is *The Song of Lewes*, but the sentiments there expressed make it most unlikely that it could have been sung before Edward II.

No doubt many of the more important statutes of the Middle English period were ridiculed in verse by the people affected by them. One such Anglo-French poem on the Statute of Trailbaston happens to have survived. It professes to have been written by an outlaw in the woods, and then dropped on the highroad so that it might fall into the hands of travellers.[2] A stanza in French and English against the writ *De Quo Warranto* of Edward I appears in some of the manuscripts of Walter of Guisborough's chronicle:

> On a certain occasion when the king was holding a parliament, and the sons of the magnates were standing about him in the evening, he said to them, 'What do you talk about between yourselves when I am in council with your fathers?' One of them replied, 'You will not be angry if I speak truly?' The king, 'Certainly not'. 'My lord king we speak in this way, –
>
> > Le roy cuuayte nos deneres
> > e la rayne nos beau maners
> > e le Quo voranco
> > sale mak wus al at do'.[3]

Whether there was any more to it we can hardly say – it seems complete enough as it stands. But this stanza happens to have been preserved only because the Latin chronicler, who has just given the famous if probably apocryphal reply of the earl of Warenne to the royal justices, wished to emphasize the dislike of the magnates for this measure.

---

[1] *Yorkshire Archaeological Journal* xxxvi, 30.

[2] T. Wright, *Political Songs* (CS. 1839), p. 231. Compare also the verses written on handbills and thrown 'be the wey', when the Emperor Sigismund thanked 'Blessid Inglond, ful of melody', after his visit in 1416 (John Capgrave, *The Chronicle of England* (RS. 1), p. 314).

[3] E. Rothwell, *The Chronicle of Walter of Guisborough* (CS. 1957), p. 216.

Nearly all the extant political poetry is anonymous. The earliest writer of such verse in English whose name is known, and some of whose works still remain, is Laurence Minot, a northerner who celebrated in verse the chief events of the reign of Edward III. It may be, however, that Minot had a predecessor in the preceding reign. A certain Robert Baston, a Carmelite monk and prior of the convent at Scarborough, was in the retinue of Edward II during the expedition to relieve Stirling which ended at Bannockburn. His task apparently was to celebrate the deeds of the army, and Scottish chroniclers make merry over the fact that the poet was captured by Bruce, and compelled to compose a poem on the defeat of the English as the price of his freedom. Some of his Latin poems may be extant, and he is said by Bale to have written *Poemata et Rhythmi, Tragoediæ et Comoediæ vulgares*, some of which were presumably in English.[1] However, the later bibliographers are not particularly good authorities for fourteenth-century vernacular writings, and are apt to attribute extant anonymous works in English to known Latin writers.

Mention has already been made of the poems celebrating the triumphs of Edward III, but there were events earlier in his reign concerning which songs are also said to have been composed, though not by his unofficial laureate. While he was king only in name, there was a good deal of desultory fighting against the Scots. This did not end until 1328, when a peace was signed by which the independence of Scotland was recognized, and Joanna, sister to the young king, was married to David Bruce. The peace was unpopular in England, and the songs were composed by the Scots who saw in the treaty another victory over the English. According to Fabyan:

it was not longe after or the Scottis in despyte of ye Englysh men, callyd hir Iane make peace, and also to theyr more derysyon made dyuerse truffys, roundys, & songys, of the which one is specially remembryd as folowyth.

> Longe beerdys hartles,
> Paynted hoodys wytles,
> Gay cotis graceles
> Makyth Englande thryfteles.

[1] Warton ii, 213.

A somewhat different account appears in the *Brut*, an earlier authority than Fabyan. Here the rhyme is connected, not with the marriage of Joanna to David Bruce, but with one of the periodical raids into England, during which 'þe Scotes made a bille þat was fastenede oppon þe cherche dores of Seint Peres toward Stangate' in York, with these same verses on it.[1]

Such a use of the church doors for the dissemination of political propaganda is not uncommon in medieval times. Towards the end of the fifteenth century a Coventry church was apparently used in this way. A certain Laurence Saunders appears to have been at that time an active member of the Dyers' guild, and a thorn in the side of the corporation. In 1494 he was imprisoned for causing a riot in the town, but was evidently not without supporters for

within viij dayes after Lammasse ther was a bill sett vppon þe north Chirch durre in seynt Mighels Chirch be some evell disposed person vnknowen the tenour wherof hereaftur ensueth:—

> Be it knowen & vnderstand
> This Cite shuld be free & nowe is bonde.
>
> Dame goode Eve made it free;
> & nowe þe custome for woll & þe draperie.
>
> Also hit is made þat no prentes shalbe
> but xiij penyes pay shuld he.
>
> þat act did Robert Grene,
> þerfore he had many a Curse, I wene.
>
> And nowe a noþer rule ye do make
> þat non shall ryde at Lammas but they þat ȝe take.
>
> When our ale is Tunned
> ȝe shall haue drynk to your Cake.
>
> Ye haue put on man like a Scot to raunsome,
> þat wolbe remembred when ȝe haue al forgoten.
> Caviat'.

[1] Fabyan, p. 439; F. W. D. Brie, *The Brut* (EETS. 1906–8), p. 249.

Saunders was again imprisoned in 1496:

> Wheruppon ij seducious billes were founde i-sette vppon þe Mynster durre in þe feste of seynt Anne, & a noþer was cast &c. Wherof the tenour here-after ensuen.

Then follow eight three-line stanzas and twelve couplets in support of Laurence Saunders as the champion of the common people.[1]

Earlier, in 1450, the publishing of libels in this way had apparently become so common that it was necessary for the king to issue a proclamation forbidding the posting of bills and lampoons in public places.[2] In 1448, according to John Pigot,

> billes were set on the gates of powles writen to this effecte . . .
> But Suthfolke, Salesbery and Say
> Be don to deathe by May
> England may synge well away.[3]

Similarly, in 1456:

> Item the xix day of September in the nyght tyme wer sett upon the Standard in ffletestrete a fore the duk of york being þer than lodged in the Bisshop of Salisbury place certain dogges hedes w^t Scriptures in their mouthes balade wise which dogges wer slayn vengeably the same nyght.[4]

In the same year the fate of John Holton demonstrated what happened to those who offended the great; for his attacks *per scripturam billarum* on the king's person, he was drawn, hanged, and quartered.[5] Another chronicle tells of the posting up, in 1460, of a 'balat' containing eighty-six lines in English, with a Latin refrain, on the city walls of Canterbury, welcoming the impending

---

[1] M. D. Harris, *The Coventry Leet Book* (EETS. 1907–8), pp. 566, 577–8. The couplets are in R. H. Robbins, *Historical Poems of the XIVth and XVth Centuries* (New York 1959), p. 63.

[2] T. Rymer, *Foedera* (London 1727) xi, 268.

[3] C. L. Kingsford, *English Historical Literature in the Fifteenth Century* (Oxford 1913), p. 370.

[4] R. Flenley, *Six Town Chronicles of England* (Oxford 1911), p. 144. The verses are printed by R. H. Robbins, *op. cit.*, pp. 189–90.

[5] *Registrum Abbatiæ Johannis Whethamstede* (RS. 28) i, 247–8.

invasion of the earls of Warwick and Salisbury.[1] The well-known couplet,

> The Cat, the Rat, and Lovel our dog
> Rule all England under a hog,

was posted on the doors of St Paul's by William Collyngbourne, and for this he was, in 1484,

> put to the moost cruell deth at the Tower Hylle, where for hym were made a newe payer of galowes. Vpon the whiche, after he hadde hangyd a shorte season, he was cutte downe, beynge alyue, & his bowellys rypped out of his bely, and cast into the fyre there by hym, and lyued tyll the bowcher put his hande into the bulke of his body; insomuch that he sayd in the same instant, 'O Lorde Ihesu, yet more trowble,' & so dyed to the great compassion of moche people.[2]

In 1418 the Mayor, Bailiffs, and Commonalty of Cambridge complained to the King's Council that many of the scholars had caused great terror to the Mayor by lying in wait to kill him and his officers. When they were unable to do this,

> they affixed on the mayor's gate a certain schedule, to his great scandal, and so that the mayor and burgesses dared not to preserve the peace.

> Billa posita super hostium Majoris. Citatio Peremptoria.
> Looke out here Maire with thie pilled pate,
>   And see wich a scrowe, is set on thie gate;
> Warning thee of hard happes,
>   For and it lukke thou shalt have swappes:
> Therefor I rede keepe the at home;
>   For thou shalt abey for that is done;
> Or els kest on a coate of mayle;
>   Truste well thereto withouten faile.
> And great Golias, Joh. Essex,
>   Shalt have a clowte with my karille axe
>   Wherever I may him have.
> And the hosteler Bambour, with his goat's beard,
>   Once and it hap shal be made afeard,
>   So God mote me save.

[1] J. S. Davies, *English Chronicle from 1377 to 1461* (CS. 1856), pp. 91ff.; also in R. H. Robbins, *op. cit.*, pp. 207ff.
[2] Fabyan, p. 672.

And ȝit with thie catche poles hope I to meete,
 With a fellowe or twayne in the playne streete,
 And her gownes brake.
And that harlot Hierman, with his calves snowte,
 Of buffets ful sekerly shall bern a rowte,
 For his werkes sake.
And yet shall hankyn Attilbrigge,
 Full ȝerne for swappes his tayle wrigge,
 And it hap arith.
And other knaves all on heape,
 Shall take knockes full good cheape,
 Come once winter nith.
But nowe I praye to God Almyth,
 That whatsoever ȝowe spare,
That metche sorowe to him bedith,
 And evill mote he fare.
Amen, quoth he, that beshrewed the Mair's very visage.[1]

Again, in 1424, William Paston laid information against a certain
Walter Azlak, who

> to the seyd William Paston swiche and so many manaces of deth and
> dismembryng maden and puttyn by certeyns Englische billes rymed
> in partye, and up on the yates of the Priorie of the Trinite chirche
> of Norwiche, and on the yates of the chyrche of the Freres Menures
> of Norwiche, and the yates of the same Cite called Nedeham yates
> and Westewyk yates, and in othre places wyth inne the seyd Cite by
> the seyd Walter and Richard sette, makyng mension and beryng this
> undyrstondyng that the seyd William, and hese clerkes, and servauntes
> schuld be slayn and mordered in lyke forme as the seyd John Grys
> in the seyd forme was slayne and mordered: conteyning also these
> too words in Latyn, _et cetera_, by which wordes communely it was
> undyrstandyn that the forgeers and makers of the seyd billes imagyned
> to the seyd William, hese clerkes and servauntes, more malice and
> harm than in the seyd billes was expressed.[2]

In 1465, on the occasion of a quarrel between the priests and
friars of London, the latter were preached against by Doctor
Edwarde Story, and in reply the friars

---

[1] C. H. Cooper, _Annals of Cambridge_ (Cambridge 1842) i, 161. Also in G. G
Coulton, _Social Life in Britain_ (Cambridge 1918), p. 66.
[2] J. Gairdner, _The Paston Letters_ (London 1904) ii, 13.

set uppe byllys at every chyrche dore that the docter sayde nott trought, but the trought shulde be schewyd ande sayd by Docter Mayster John Mylverton.[1]

Towards the end of the fourteenth century some of the more important political figures of the time became the subject of songs, composed by either their friends or their opponents. One of the first of these was Peter de la Mare, Speaker to the Parliament of 1376. He apparently touched the imagination of his contemporaries to such an extent that 'numerous songs were composed about his deeds'. Similarly, in 1377, lampoons on John of Gaunt were found posted in different places about the city of London, and for this the unknown authors were excommunicated by the bishop of Bangor.[2] There is no information about the language of any of these poems, but at that date they were presumably in English. This was certainly the case in 1378, when a member of the king's household came to Oxford, and was serenaded by some of the students with a song in English 'containing words against the honour of the king', the affair ending with a general discharge of arrows through the window of his room. Complaint was made, and the Chancellor and Vice-Chancellor of the University were summoned before the Council. When it appeared that no punishment had been inflicted on the culprits, the Chancellor was made to resign and the Vice-Chancellor imprisoned.[3]

John Ball, one of the most prominent of the leaders of the Peasants' Revolt, appears to have encouraged his followers by the circulation of letters 'full of riddles or dark sentences', which usually included verses. Some of these are given by Stow; the first, 'found in the budget of one that should be hanged', being the famous epistle of 'John Shepe, sometime Saint-Mary priest of York'. Stow claims to have seen several other epistles of John Ball, and quotes some of them:

John Ball Saint Mary priest, greeteth well all manner of men, and biddeth them in name of the Trinitie, Father, Sonne, & holy Ghost, stand manlike together in truth, & helpe truth, and truth shall helpe you:

[1] *Collections of a London Citizen* (CS. 1876), pp. 228ff.
[2] *Chronicon Angliæ 1328–1388* (RS. 64), pp. 392, 129.
[3] *Eulogium Historiarum* (RS. 9) iii, 348.

> now raygneth pride in price,
> couetise is holden wise,
> lechery without shame,
> gluttonie without blame,
> enuie raygneth with reason,
> and sloath is taken in great season,
>
> God doe boote for nowe is time. Amen.

Similar letters purport to come from Jacke Miller and Jacke Trewman, and Stow says that he has omitted 'Ion Carters Epistle, a libel, so named, &c.', which was no doubt very similar to the others.[1] During the fifteenth century references to this kind of verse persist. In a Latin sermon by Friar Nicholas Phillipps, dated round about 1434, are three English stanzas, separated by short commentaries, the second of which reads like the genuine fragment of a workers' song that has come to be used for religious purposes:

> Þin ffadere was a bond man,
> Þin moder curtesye non can.
> Euery beste þat leuyth now
> Is of more fredam þan þow![2]

Magdalen College, Oxford, Charter Misc. 306, contains a manifesto in English by the Kentish rebels under Jack Cade in 1450, ending with some lines of verse:

> God be oure gyde,
> And then schull we spede,
>   Who so euur say nay.
> False for ther money reuleth,
> Trewth for his tales spelleth.
>   God seende us a ffayre day!
> Awey, traytours, awey![3]

Similarly, *Gregory's Chronicle* gives a couplet said to have been repeated by the citizens of London in 1461 on the approach of the earl of March to the city:

> He that had Londyn for sake
> Wolde no more to hem take.[4]

---

[1] J. Stow, *Annales*, continued by E. Howes (London 1615), p. 294.

[2] R. H. Robbins, *op. cit.*, p. 62; H. G. Pfander, *The Popular Sermon of the Medieval Friar in England* (New York 1937), p. 49.

[3] *HMC., 8th Report*, Appendix, p. 267; R. H. Robbins, *op. cit.*, p. 63.

[4] *Collections of a London Citizen* (CS. 1876), p. 215.

At the beginning of the fifteenth century Henry Percy appears to have touched the imagination of his contemporaries, as is shown by his nickname Hotspur. Several of the chroniclers give Latin verses commemorating the battle of Shrewsbury, but these are literary rather than popular productions. However, at the end of the Castle Howard manuscript of the metrical life of St Cuthbert appears a rather obscure stanza which may indicate the former existence of popular songs about Hotspur:

> Henry haitspours haith a halt,
>   and he is falleng lame;
> Francis phesite but for that falt
>   Sweares he was not to blame.[1]

The outbreak of war with France in the following reign inevitably led to the appearance of a good deal of verse on the subject. A contemporary poem on the battle of Agincourt is partly preserved in one of the London chronicles. The writer paraphrased a popular ballad until, tiring of this, he contented himself with simply copying it. The lines of the earlier part, with the rhymes and alliteration, are easily to be traced in the prose.[2] Similarly, much of the narrative in the *Brut* concerning the siege of Harfleur and the battle of Agincourt is apparently based on 'some current ballads of the time, whether those which have survived or others that have perished'. Since some of the phrases have no parallels in the remaining poems, the *Brut* would appear to preserve traces of one or more that have been lost.[3] At the very end of the century the accounts of Tattershall College, for the years 1495-6, give the titles of two songs, 'The Cry of Caleys' and 'Flos Florum', of which the former at any rate would seem to have been in English.[4]

An innovation introduced in 1453-4 by John Norman, Lord Mayor of London, apparently led to the composition of a popular song:

And this yere, vpon the morne after Symond and Jude, John Norman befornamed, beyng chosyn Mair for that present yere, was rowed by water to Westmynster w^t the Aldermen; and alle the chief of the

[1] SS. lxxxvii, 245.

[2] C. L. Kingsford, *Chronicles of London* (Oxford 1905), pp. 120ff. Also in R. H. Robbins, *op. cit.*, pp. 74ff.

[3] C. L. Kingsford, *English Historical Literature in the Fifteenth Century* (Oxford 1913), p. 116, cf. p. 239.

[4] HMC., *Manuscripts of Lord de L'Isle & Dudley* i, 197.

Comoners of the Cite went also thedir by barges; which of tymes owte of mynd was vsed before season by the Mairs to ride allwey by land to take their charge. Wherfore the watermen of Themmys made a song of this John Norman, wherof the begynnyng was, 'Rowe thy bote Norman'; which newe custume was welle allowed, and hathe contynued from his daies to this season.

A similar account by Fabyan adds a few more words to the song:

Rowe the bote Norman, rowe to thy lemman,
And so forth, w^t a longe processe.[1]

Some satirical and political poetry was produced by the English settlers in Ireland, though little of it has survived. In 1372 Arnold le Poer is said to have used 'monstrous language' about Maurice FitzThomas, calling him a *Rymour* or mischief-making poet,[2] and in addition two poems of this type are represented by a few remaining lines. MS. Lansdowne 418 contains a single stanza which the scribe says was the beginning of a long ballad, and he has copied these nine lines of it out of a 'smale olde booke in parchment called the booke of Ross or of Waterford'. The writer's original was certainly the present MS. Harley 913, but that part of it which contained the poem has disappeared, and the stanza copied into MS. Lansdowne 418 is all that is left of it. The poem appears to have been a warning to the young men of Waterford to beware of the le Poer family:

There is in this book a long discourse in meter putting the youth of Waterford in mind of harme taken by the Powers, and wishing them to beware for ye time to come. I have written out the first staffe only,

Young men of Waterford learne now to play,
For youre mare is plowis i lai beth awey.
Secure ʒe ʒure hanfelis y^t lang habith ilei,
And fend ʒou of the powers that walkith bi the wey,
　　　I rede.
　　For if hi takith ʒou on and on,
　　From ham scapith ther never one;
　　I swer bi Christ and St Jon
　　　　That of goth ʒur hede.
Now hi wlkith &c.[3]

[1] C. L. Kingsford, *Chronicles of London* (Oxford 1905), p. 164; Fabyan, p. 628. Mentioned also in Skelton's *The Bowge of Courte*, line 252.

[2] M. V. Clarke, *Fourteenth Century Studies* (Oxford 1937), p. 29.

[3] See also St John D. Seymour, *Anglo-Irish Literature 1200–1582* (Cambridge 1929), p. 88.

In the primatial register of John Swayne, archbishop of Armagh 1418–39, appear a dozen lines of verse which were evidently part of a bitter attack on the dress of the time:

> Fleshly lustys & festys
> And furres of divers manner of bestys
>> The Devyll of Hell hath first fonde.
> Hole clothes ywrent in shredes
> And the pryde of women's hedes
>> Hath destroyed this londe.
> God that berreth the crowne of thornes
> Destroy the pryde of women's hornes
>> For His dere Passione.
> And let never har long taylys
> That beth the Devyll of Hell his flaylys
>> Be cause of our confucione.[1]

From Scotland comes only a single isolated reference, and that is the well-known stanza from the lament on the death of Alexander III, which is quoted by Wyntoun:

> This sang wes maid of him forthy:
>> 'Sen Alexander our king wes deid,
>>> That Scotland left in luf and le,
>> Away wes sons of aill and breid,
>>> Off wyne and walx, of gamyn and gle.
>> The gold wes changeit all in leid,
>>> The frute falȝeit on euerilk tre.
>> Ihesu, succour and send remeid,
>>> That stad is in perplexite.'[2]

There are variations in the manuscripts of Wyntoun, and it is possible that early lines in Barbour's *Bruce* are a reminiscence of this song. No doubt other political poems were composed, but apart from those to be mentioned later, no hint of them has survived.

Soldiers' songs may be included here as a sub-division of the political poetry. Such literature must have existed throughout the period, though it is not surprising that it has left little trace of its former existence. Since it is essentially oral and popular, it could only seldom or by accident have achieved a written form.

[1] *Proceedings of the Royal Irish Academy, Section C*, xli, 209.
[2] F. J. Amours, *Wyntoun's Original Chronicle* (STS. 1903–14) v, 144.

Consequently, such poetry is known today only from occasional lines quoted by some of the chroniclers. When the Norman minstrel Taillefer led the attack at Hastings he is said to have encouraged his companions by chanting some version of the *Song of Roland*, but the earliest example in English consists of two lines said to have been sung by the followers of Geoffrey de Mandeville during their ravages in the Fen District. In one of the manuscripts of the *Historia Anglorum* Matthew Paris preserves the tradition that the earl and his followers sang mockingly of their wild doings,

> I ne mai a-live,
> For Benoit ne for Ive,

with reference presumably to the sacking of the monasteries at Ramsey and St Ives. It is interesting to note that, on the evidence of this fragment, some of his followers must have been English, or else that English had already become the usual language of the Normans. A close analogy is the line or two of a song, said to have been sung in 1173 by the Flemish mercenaries of the earl of Leicester, while halted on the heath near Bury, just before their defeat by the king's army:

> Hoppe, hoppe, Wilekin, hoppe, Wilekin,
> Engelond is min ant tin.[1]

But the greater number of such songs deal with the Scottish wars, and parts of a good many of these have been preserved, more especially by Peter of Langtoft and by his translator Robert Mannyng of Brunne. Although Langtoft writes in Anglo-French, there can be little doubt that the songs from which he quotes were in English. He gives occasional stanzas in English; and although, when making use of longer poems, he usually starts with a French version he nearly always ends with English, as if he had tired of the task of translation. Moreover, the different manuscripts have other versions of the English, as if the scribes had felt it better to give the one known to them rather than to copy their originals exactly. Similarly, Mannyng's versions often differ a good deal from those in Langtoft, and he occasionally adds stanzas not found in any of the manuscripts of his original. On the whole, it seems not unreasonable to suppose that both chroniclers are making use of actual songs current at this period, though how far their versions

[1] Matthew Paris, *Historia Anglorum* (RS. 44) i, 271, 381.

represent the originals is a different matter. The earliest of them was occasioned by the withdrawal of homage in 1296 and by the rising of the Scots in that year. It is found in only two manuscripts of Langtoft and is not given by Mannyng:

> Tprut Scot riueling,
> Wiþ mikel mistiming
> Crop þu ut of kage.

Then comes one said to have been sung by the Scots in derision of Edward I when he besieged Berwick:

> Pikit him,
> & dikit him,
>   On scorne said he,
> He pikes & dikes
> 5 in length, as him likes,
>   How best it may be,
> & þou has for þi pikyng,
> mykille ille likyng,
> Þe soþe is to se,

> 10 Without any lesyng,
> alle is þi heþing,
>   Fallen opon þe.
> For scatred er þi Scottis,
> & hodred in þer hottes,
> 15 Neuer þei ne the.
> Right als I rede,
> þei tombled in Tuede,
> Þat woned bi þe se.[1]

Here lines 7–12 in Mannyng do not appear in any of the manuscripts of Langtoft, and the ending may perhaps be Mannyng's own addition. A further reminiscence of the song appears in William Rishanger's chronicle, according to whom, during the siege one of the Scots recited in his own language various opprobrious words against the king, 'Kyng Edward, wanne þu hauest Berwic, pike þe, wanne þu hauest geten dike þe'.[2] A somewhat different version is given in the *Brut* and in Fabyan, which have substantially the same account:

> Kyng Edward went him toward Berwik, and bisegede þe toun; and þo þat were wiþin manliche ham defendede, and sette afire and brent ij of Kyng Edwardes shippis, and saide, in despite and in reprofe of him:

> > Wenes Kyng Edward, wiþ his longe shankes,
> > forto wyn Berwik, al our vnþankes?
> >   gas pikes him!
> >   and when he haþ hit,
> >   gas diche him![3]

The particular reference is apparently to the fact that King Edward

---

[1] Hearne ii, 273.   [2] W. Rishanger, *Annales Angliæ et Scotiæ* (RS. 28), p. 373.
[3] F. W. D. Brie, *op. cit.*, p. 189; Fabyan, p. 398.

is said to have speeded the digging operations by himself wheeling away barrows of earth. The next two quotations in Mannyng appear to be taken from some poem on the battle of Dunbar and on the events leading up to it. Only the last six lines of this are given in English by Langtoft:

Whan ȝe haf þe pris
of ȝour enmys,
    non salle ȝe saue,
Smyte with suerd in hand,
5 alle Northumberland
    with right salle ȝe haue,
& Inglond ȝit alle,
for werre salle
    be tint for þis drede.

10 Scotte neuer bigan
vnto Inglis man
    to do so douhty dede.
Þer on þat grene,
þat kynrede kene,
15   gadred als þe gayte,
Right, als I wene,
on som was it sene,
    þer þe bit bayte.

Then comes an account of the battle, followed by:

Þe Scottis had no grace,
to spede in þer space,
    for to mend þer nisse,
Þei filed þer face,
5 þat died in þat place,
    þe Inglis rymed þis.
'Oure fote folk
put þam in þe polk
    & nakned þer nages,

10 Bi no way
herd I neuer say
    of prester pages,
Purses to pike,
robis to rike,
15   & in dike þam schonne,
Þou wissin
Scotte of Abrethin,
    kotte is þi honne.

The last four lines are completely different in some of the manuscripts of Langtoft:

That in the felde felle.
Thay token any tulke;
The roghe raggy sculke
Rug ham in helle.[1]

The six lines at the beginning of Mannyng have no parallel in Langtoft, and their matter suggests that they were not part of the original song, but simply an introduction to it in the same metre, presumably composed by Mannyng himself. The next quotation comes at the end of the description of the surrender of Dunbar:

Þe Scottis
I telle for sottis,
    & wrecchis vnwar,

Unsele
5 dyntis to dele
    þam drouh to Dunbar.

[1] Hearne ii, 276, 277; Langtoft ii, 248.

Similar lines are found in the *Brut* and in Fabyan, although there they are applied to the discovery of the attempted treachery of Sir Richard Siward, with slight changes in phrasing to make them more appropriate. The next poem celebrates the capture of Baliol and the apparent completion of the conquest of Scotland:

Þe Walsh & þe Irish,
tille our men Inglysh,
  halp douhtily,
Þat we þe Scottis had,
5 & to prison lad,
  & com tille our crie.
Now es alle ent,
& home ere þei went,
  þe Iris & Wals,
10 God gyue at þe parlement,
þe Scottis be alle schent,
  & hanged bi þe hals.
Edward now þenk,
þei did þe a blenk,
15   brent Hexham.
Þe croice & þe rode,
brent þer it stode,
  or þei þien nam.
Now has þou myght,
20 gyf þi dome right,
  þer dede is wele sene,

Els wille þei eft,
on þo þat er left,
  bigynne newe tene.
25 Men may merci haue,
traytour not to saue,
  for luf ne for awe,
Atteynt of traytorie,
suld haf no mercie,
30   wiþ no maner lawe.
Jon þe Baliol,
no witte was in þi pol,
  whan þou folie þouhtis,
To leue þe right scole,
35 þou did als a fole,
  & after wrong wrouhtis.
For boule bred in his [boke],
whan he tynt þat he toke,
  alle his kyngdome,
40 For he has ouerhipped,
his tippet is tipped,
  his tabard is tome.

Langtoft gives only the last six lines in English, and these show significant differences from the versions in Mannyng. In addition, one of the manuscripts of Langtoft, C.U.L. Gg. 1. 1, adds a further six lines that do not appear elsewhere:

He loghe wil him liked,
His packe es thurck piked,
  He wende e were hale.
Begkot an bride,
Rede him at ride,
  In þe dismale.

Later on comes a general description of the state of Scotland, and again Mannyng often differs a good deal from Langtoft, who has only the last dozen lines in English:

Cambinhoy
beres him coy,
þat fendes whelp,
Þer with craft
5 he has þam raft,
it may not help.
Þe trulle þe drenge
on se, þei lenge
þe fendes tueye,
10 Þe hold þam fer,
& dar no ner,
þan Orkeneye.
Andrew is wroth,
þe wax him loth,
15 for þer pride.
He is þam fro,
now salle þei go,
schame to betide.

20 Þou scabbed Scotte,
þi nek þi hotte,
þe deuelle it breke,
It salle be hard
to here Edward,
ageyn þe speke.
25 He salle þe ken,
our lond to bren,
& werre bigynne,
Þou getes no þing,
bot þi riuelyng,
30 to hang þer inne.
Þe sete of þe Scone
is driuen ouer Done,
to London led,
I hard wele telle,
35 þat bagelle & belle
be filchid & fled.

Some lines follow on the execution of Wallace:

At London is his heued,
his quarters ere leued,
in Scotland spred,
To wirschip þer iles,
5 & lere of his wiles,
how wele þat he sped.
It is not to drede,
traytour salle spede
als he is worþi,

10 His lif salle he tyne,
& die þorgh pyne,
withouten merci.
Þus may men here,
a ladde forto lere,
15 to biggen in pays;
It fallis in his iȝe,
þat hewes ouer hie,
wiþ þe Walays.[1]

Finally, the closing passages of one of the manuscripts of Langtoft,
C.U.L. Gg. 1. 1, contains the following, apparently taken from a
satirical poem gloating over the defeat of the Scots. They do not
appear in other manuscripts of Langtoft, and are omitted by
Mannyng:

For þare were þai bal brend,
he kanged ham þidre kend,
and dreued to dote.
For Scottes at Dunbar,
haued at þayre gan char,
schame of þar note.

[1] Hearne ii, 278, 279, 281, 330.

205

Wer neuer dogges þere,
hurled out of herre,
fro coylthe ne cote.

It seems likely enough that the originals of these poems were in
English, though whether they actually were contemporary songs is
a different matter. Some of them read like popular verse, others
have a more literary tinge. The fact that all of them are in the
same metre, whether songs by the Scots against the English or by
the English against the Scots, is perhaps rather suspicious,
especially in view of the fact that quotations from the songs by
other chroniclers indicate different stanza forms. In all probability,
parts of them really were current poems of the period, but these
have been worked over, either by Langtoft or by some other poet.
The differences in Mannyng suggest that he also had access to
the English originals; and although he seems to have been quite
capable of interpolations in the same metre, most of his additions
appear to give the authentic flavour of the original poems. For all
that, it may be that comparatively little of the popular songs
remains in either chronicler; possibly they had been used by other
writers as the basis for longer poems, and translated by Langtoft
into a different language and metre.

Several of these songs on the Scottish wars are found elsewhere.
Some of those in Langtoft and Mannyng appear in slightly different forms in the *Brut* and Fabyan, who also give the first stanza of a
song said to have been sung by the Scots in mockery of the English
after Bannockburn:

þerefore þe Scottes saide, in reprofe and despite of Kyng Edward,
foralsemiche as he louede forto go by watere, and also for he was
descomfitede at Bannokesbourne, þerfore maidenes made a songe
þerof, in that contre, of Kyng Edward of Engeland and in þis maner
þai songe:—

Maydenes of Engelande, sare may ʒe morne,
For tynt ʒe haue ʒoure lemmans at Bannokesborn,
    wiþ hevalogh.
What wende þe Kyng of Engeland haue ygete Scotlande
    wiþ Rombylogh.

Fabyan gives the same stanza, and adds,

This songe was after many dayes sungyn, in daunces, in carolis of ye maydens & mynstrellys of Scotlande, to the reproofe and dysdayne of Englysshe men, w^t dyuerse other whiche I ouer passe.[1]

The reference in the *Brut* to Edward's preference for travelling by water helps to explain the words of the refrain, since in the romance of *Richard Coeur de Lion* the mariners

> roweden harde, and layde to,
> And songe: Heuelow, rummeloo.

Similarly, in *The Squire of Low Degree,*

> Your maryners shall synge arowe
> 'Hey, how, and rumbylawe'.[2]

Evidently the words were distinctive of the refrain of sailors' songs of the period, and hence their use here.

The Scottish chroniclers are for the most part too late to give much information on this subject. Presumably the popular songs of the earlier period had been forgotten by the time they came to write, and they had few written sources on which to draw. Yet Wyntoun gives four lines said to have been sung by the English against Black Agnes of Dunbar:

> Off þis ilk sege in [hething]
> The Inglismen maid oft carping:
> 'I wow to God, scho beris hir weill,
> The Scottis wenche with hir ploddeil;
> For cum I airly, cum I lait,
> I fynd ay Annes at þe ȝait'.

Earlier on the chronicler had referred in general terms to the 'gestis and sangis' concerning Wallace, and similarly Barbour tells of songs still current dealing with a fight between Sir John de Soulis and Sir Andrew Harcla.[3] Elsewhere we hear how, on the night before the battle of Dupplin in 1332, the Scottish troops

---

[1] F. W. D. Brie, *op. cit.*, p. 208; Fabyan, p. 420.

[2] K. Brunner, *Der mittelenglische Versroman über Richard Löwenherz* (Vienna 1913), 2535–36; W. H. French and C. B. Hale, *Middle English Metrical Romances* (New York 1930), p. 746, lines 823–4.

[3] F. J. Amours, *op. cit.* vi, 90; v, 318; W. W. Skeat, *The Bruce* (EETS. ES. 1870–89) xvi, 519ff.

went to bed singing songs about the tailed Englishmen. Inspired, according to Bower, more by wine than by warlike energy, they sang how they would on the morrow turn their tails into ropes to bind them with; or, according to another version and with a reference to the preliminary degradation before capital punishment for treason, of how they would draw the English to the gallows by their tails.[1]

Such songs were not, of course, confined to the Scottish wars. Similar ones against the Flemings also appear. So, on the failure of an attempted siege of Calais:

> amonges Englisshmen were made many rymes of þe Flemmynges; among the which, one is here sette for a remembraunce, that saith on this wise:—
> (66 lines of verse against the Flemings).
> Such & many oþir rymes were made amonge Englisshmen, aftir the Flemmynges were thus shamfully fled frome Caleis.

Another example is given later, but both read much more like literary productions than popular songs.[2]

---

[1] Bower ii, 304–5; *Liber Pluscardensis* i, 265. On the development of the legend of the tailed English, see G. Neilson, *Caudatus Anglicus* (Edinburgh 1896).

[2] F. W. D. Brie, *op. cit.*, pp. 582ff., 600ff.

II

DRAMA

Little is known of the drama in England before 1300, though presumably this country shared in the general development. Few texts have survived, but the religious drama was essentially international and occasional allusions indicate that, as we should expect, it was being staged in England as in the rest of Western Europe. The earliest reference to it comes from the beginning of the twelfth century, when a certain Geoffrey, a Norman clerk and prospective schoolmaster of St Albans, prepared a *ludus de sancta Katerina* at Dunstable. For it he borrowed some copies from the monastery, and these were accidentally burned. Because of this he became a monk and by 1119 had become abbot of St Albans.[1] Nothing more is heard of plays in this country until the end of the century when, according to a description of London prefixed by William FitzStephen to his life of Becket,

> London, in place of shows in the theatre and stage plays, has holier plays, wherein are shown forth the miracles wrought by holy Confessors or the sufferings which glorified the constancy of Martyrs.[2]

In addition, the cathedral statutes of Bishop Hugh of Lichfield (1188–98) provide for the *Pastores* at Christmas and the *Quem Quaeritis* and *Peregrini* at Easter.[3] This is all that we hear of the drama in England during the twelfth century, but there is no reason to believe that our information is at all complete, or that plays had not previously been acted in these and other towns.

This twelfth-century drama was presumably the liturgical Latin drama of the Church, and why extant examples of it should be so rare in England is not an easy question to answer. Perhaps the losses at the dissolution of the monasteries had something to do with it. More probably it disappeared because there was simply

[1] *Gesta Abbatum Monasterii S. Albani* (RS. 28) i, 73.

[2] William FitzStephen, *Vita Sancti Thomae* (RS. 67) iii, 9.

[3] C. Wordsworth, *Statutes of Lincoln Cathedral* (Cambridge 1892–7) ii, 15, 23. In 1179 Giraldus Cambrensis, while dining with the monks of Canterbury,

no reason for preserving it when, by the middle of the fourteenth century, drama had largely passed into the hands of the laity, and this later secular and vernacular drama had displaced the liturgical drama of the Church. In the first place, however, the liturgical drama seems to have been superseded by a transitional type of play in which one of the vernaculars was beginning to be prominent, although characteristics inherited from the Latin plays were still conspicuous.

Some of the thirteenth-century references to plays are probably to this transitional type, though it is rare for any clue to be given from which we can be certain of this. One of the earliest comes from Beverley. A continuator of the life of St John of Beverley tells of a recent (c. 1220) miracle in the Minster. An Easter play was being acted in the churchyard, and so great a crowd had gathered that some boys entered the church, found an open door leading to the roof, and went there to watch the play. The watchmen, fearing for the safety of the glass, gave chase and beat them, with the result that one of the boys fell from the roof and lay as if dead, but was miraculously restored to life by the merits of the saint.[1] Since the play took place in the churchyard, not in the church, it had at any rate one of the characteristics of the transitional drama. An inventory of the goods of Salisbury Cathedral (1222) includes a crown of silver and two of lead, and may be an indication that plays were being acted there.[2] In an award made between 1220 and 1228, concerning the rights of collation to Shipton-under-Wychwood and Brickelsworth, both of which were prebends of Salisbury, there is a reference to *actiones* at various of the villages. The word may perhaps mean 'plays', and if so they must have been more frequent in these parts during the thirteenth century than might have been expected.[3] Some time round about 1244 Bishop Grosseteste of Lincoln mentions *clerici ludos quos*

---

noted the excessive use of signs by the monks and the prior, who expressed themselves in this way far more easily and freely than was fitting, almost as it seemed to Giraldus *ut quasi ad ludos scenicos aut inter histriones et joculatores* (RS. 21, i, 51; cf. 21, iv, 41). Similarly Ailred of Rievaulx regrets that histrionic gestures more suitable for the theatre than the oratory have entered the liturgy (*Patrologia Latina* cxcv, 571, 572).

[1] *Historians of the Church of York* (RS. 71) i, 328.
[2] *Register of St Osmund* (RS. 78) ii, 129.
[3] *Sarum Charters and Documents* (RS. 97), p. 104.

vocant miracula amongst the things which the archdeacons are, as far as possible, to expel from the diocese,[1] while a verse sermon of c. 1250 from an unspecified and unknown locality mentions a 'pleye' which was to follow the sermon:

> Þat he bad he dede him sone
> ant þorou senicholas bone.
> Yf ye wollet stille ben
> in þis pleye ye mowen isen.

The reference is presumably to a dramatic performance of one of the miracles of St Nicholas, and since the sermon is in English, it is probable that the play too was in that language.[2] At York the traditional statutes, which in their present form are supposed to date from c. 1255, provide for the *Pastores* and *Stella*.[3]

To what extent English was used in these thirteenth-century plays is difficult to say. Some sound like the usual liturgical plays, while others, as for example that at Beverley, have at any rate some of the characteristics of the transitional type. In fact, it is represented in England by three, or possibly four, fragments, of which only one dates from the thirteenth century. This last, written on a palimpsest fly-leaf of C.U.L. MS. Mm. 1. 18, in a hand probably to be dated towards the end of the century, contains twenty-two lines in French and the same number in English. Neither appears to be a translation of the other, though the general tenor is the same – an appeal to the audience by the officers of a pagan 'Emperor' to keep quiet and not interrupt the 'game' on pain of dire punishment. The dialect appears to be southern, but there is no other indication of provenance.[4] Another fragment, in a fourteenth-century hand, has been discovered on the back of a manorial roll from Rickinghall in Suffolk. It contains a single stanza in French, a free translation of this into English, and two lines only of a following French stanza, the stage directions being as usual in Latin:

> Lordinges wytouten lesinge
> Ye weten wel that I am kinge

---

[1] *Roberti Grosseteste Epistolae* (RS. 25), pp. 317–18.
[2] *Studies in Philology* xxviii, 594–601.
[3] C. Wordsworth, *op. cit.* ii, 98.
[4] *MLN.* lxv, 30–5.

Her of al this lond.
Therfore i wile that mine barnage,
Ye that ben of gret parage,
That he comin to mi wil.
For al that arn in burw or toun,
I wile he witen mi resoun,
And that is richt and schil.[1]

The leaf appears to have been a waste scrap, discarded because of mistakes by the copyist, and afterwards economically used for manorial accounts. Again, there is no indication of its original provenance, though since the manor formerly belonged to the abbey of Bury, that seems a likely enough guess.

A further text of this type, written during the fifteenth century, comes from Shrewsbury. It includes the parts, with cues, of a single actor in three plays, the *Pastores*, *Quem Quaeritis*, and *Peregrini*, and shows that the Latin text was first sung by a group of performers, and then expanded separately in the vernacular.[2] Also from the fifteenth century are what may be some passages from a passion play performed at Worcester. MS. F. 10 in the Cathedral Library contains a collection of sermons, and in the middle of one of them, otherwise entirely in Latin, are a number of English verses which, it has been suggested, are perhaps taken from some passion play of the transitional type. They certainly read not unlike it, but at the same time similar verses are found often enough in other Latin sermons.[3]

During the fourteenth century there are various references to occasional plays at different places. Probably most of them, if not entirely in English, were mainly so, since many of the places were so small that it is difficult to believe that enough Latin-speaking people could have been available to produce the play. At Cambridge, c. 1350, William de Lenne and Isabella his wife, on their entrance into a guild, give half a mark towards the expenses of a play on the 'Children of Israel',[4] and in 1384 William of Wykeham, bishop of Winchester, forbids the performance of plays in the

[1] *Times Literary Supplement*, 1921, p. 340.
[2] O. Waterhouse, *The Non-Cycle Mystery Plays* (EETS. ES. 1909), pp. 1–7.
[3] J. K. Floyer and S. G. Hamilton, *Worcester Cathedral Library Manuscripts* (Oxford 1906), pp. 5ff.
[4] *Cambridge Antiquarian Society: Octavo Series* xxxix, 51ff.

cemetery of the cathedral.[1] The accounts for 1385 of the chamberlain of King's Lynn include gifts of money for an interlude on
Corpus Christi day and for one of St Thomas the Martyr. Similar
references to plays at the same town continue into the fifteenth
century. In 1449 an ordinance by the Mayor and Council, for the
better government of the craft of Tailors, enacts that various fines
'shal go to the sustentacioun of the procession upon Corpus
Christi day', and in 1462 the accounts include expenses by 'the
Mayor and the most of his brethren' while watching 'a certain
play at the Feast of Corpus Christi'.[2] From Bury comes a return,
drawn up in 1389, describing the foundation and customs of the
guild of Corpus Christi. These include the maintenance of an
interludium de Corpore Christi, but no further information is
given.[3] Also from the fourteenth century is a brief mention of
mystery plays acted in the parish church at Hedon in the East
Riding.[4]

During the fifteenth century references to these occasional plays
are much more frequent. It is possible that many of them had been
given regularly for some time, though gaps in the records do not
allow of any certainty. The accounts of Maxstoke Priory for 1430
include a note that on the Feast of the Purification the *pueri
eleemosynarii* of the monastery had acted a play in the neighbouring
castle belonging to Lord Clinton.[5] The churchwardens' accounts
of Tintinhull, Somerset, include the receipt in 1451-2 of money
from 'a play called Christmasse play',[6] while in 1452 the wardens
of Harling, Norfolk, paid for the 'original of an Interlude played
at the Church gate'.[7] The town accounts of Lydd show a 'play of
Seint George' in 1456, and in 1490 the chaplain of the guild of
St George at New Romney went to see a play at Lydd, probably
the same one, with a view to reproducing it.[8] At New Romney
itself, John Craye and Thomas a Nasshe, wardens of the play of
the Resurrection, brought an action for debt and damages against

---

[1] Warton ii, 221, n. 2.
[2] *HMC., Southampton and King's Lynn*, pp. 223, 165ff., 224.
[3] *MLN.* xlviii, 84.
[4] J. R. Boyle, *The Early History of Hedon* (Hull 1895), p. 140.
[5] Warton iii, 312.
[6] W. Hobhouse, *Church-wardens' Accounts* (Somerset Record Society), p. 184.
[7] *Norfolk Archaeology* xi, 338; J. C. Cox, *Churchwardens' Accounts* (London
1913), p. 268.
[8] *HMC., 5th Report*, Appendix, pp. 521, 548.

John Lylye in 1456. In 1463–4 6s. 8d. was paid to Agnes Forde for the play of the interlude of Our Lord's passion. The 'Pleybook' is mentioned in 1516, and included in an Elizabethan inventory, while in 1517–18 a serjeant of the Lord Warden brings a 'mandate to the Barons of New Romene here, that they ought not to play the play of the Passion of Christ until they had had the King's leave'.[1] The churchwardens' accounts for 1461 of St Edmond's, Salisbury, include an item 'For all apparel and furniture of players at the Corpus Christi';[2] those of St Nicholas, Yarmouth, mention plays on Corpus Christi day in 1473 and 1486, and a play at Bartholomew-tide in 1489;[3] and those of St Margaret, Southwark, include payments for plays on the feasts of St Margaret and St Lucy from 1453 onwards.[4] At Bury in 1477 the by-laws of the Weavers mention 'amongge other pagents' that of 'the Assencion of our Lord God and of the giftys of the Holy Gost', though it must remain uncertain whether this was a true play.[5] The accounts of the guild of the Holy Trinity, Sleaford, note a payment in 1480 'for the Ryginall of ye play for ye Ascencon & the wrytyng of spechys & payntyng of a garmet for god',[6] and items in the accounts for 1482 of St Michael's, Bath, suggest the production of a *Quem Quaeritis*.[7] At Hull the Trinity House accounts between 1461 and 1536 show numerous expenses in connexion with a play of *Noah*. In 1487–8 they record a payment for the writing of the play, while an item in 1484 for 'playng þe spech of God' shows that it was not a dumb-show but an actual play.[8] At Winchester in 1487 Henry VII was entertained at dinner by a performance of the *Christi Descensus ad Inferos* by the *pueri eleemosynarii* of St Swithin's and Hyde Abbey.[9] Entries concerning plays are frequent in the accounts of St Lawrence, Reading, from 1498 onwards, with direct mention of the *Kings of Cologne*, *Adam and Eve*, the play of *Kayme*, and a *Resurrection* play.[10]

---

[1] *HMC.*, *6th Report*, Appendix, p. 541; *5th Report*, Appendix, pp. 544ff.

[2] *Calendar of State Papers – Domestic, Addenda* (1580–1625), p. 101.

[3] *Norfolk Archaeology* xi, 334.   [4] J. C. Cox, *op. cit.*, p. 268.

[5] *Memorials of St Edmund's Abbey* (RS. 96) iii, 361.

[6] E. K. Chambers, *The Mediæval Stage* (Oxford 1903) ii, 395.

[7] *Transactions of the Royal Historical Society* vii, 315.

[8] *MLR.* xxxiii, 489.

[9] Warton iii, 163.

[10] J. C. Cox, *op. cit.*, p. 269; C. Kerry, *History of St Lawrence, Reading* (Reading 1883), p. 233.

Similar references to plays continue during the sixteenth century. The accounts for a play of St George at Bassingbourne in 1511 list some of the properties and also the 'playe book'.[1] At Louth an inventory (1516) of the documents in the rood-loft includes the 'hole regenall of Corpus Christi play', but the only other notice of plays there is of one paid for by the corporation 'in the markitstede on corpus christi day' in 1558.[2] In a commonplace book compiled by a certain Robert Reynys of Acle, Norfolk, there is an epilogue for a mystery play, apparently copied down c. 1555 and beginning:

> Now wursheppful souereyns þat syttyn here in syth,
> Lordys and ladyes and frankelens in fay,
> With alle maner of Abesyans we recomaunde vs ryght
> Plesantly to 30ure persones that present ben in play,
> And for 30ur soferyng sylens that 3e han kept þis day,
> In pleyng of oure play withowte ony resystens,
> Derely we thank 30w with myght as we may . . .[3]

An actor's part in a sixteenth-century play, to which the title *Processus Satanae* has been given, was discovered in the library of Welbeck Abbey. On the back of the strip of paper is written in a later hand, 'old verses/From limebrook'. The only place of this name appears to be a village in Herefordshire, and this may be all that remains of a play once given there.[4] Again, early in the reign of Henry VII William Lucas and Richard Tailor, churchwardens of St James's Church, Pulloxhill, Beds., allege that John Russell and others 'toke vpon them to make a play' in aid of church repairs, but having raised £4 Russell then refused to part with the money.[5] Other references in churchwardens' accounts of the period are not infrequent; those of Ashburton (Devon) include various payments to players between 1492 and 1559; Dunmow (Essex) has a payment for 'a playe boke of Corpus Christi pagaunts' (1553); from Thame (Oxfordshire) comes an item for writing the parts of the Three

[1] *The Antiquary* vii, 24ff.
[2] R. C. Dudding, *The First Churchwardens' Book of Louth* (Oxford 1941), p. 182; R. W. Goulding, *Louth Records* (Louth 1891), p. 55.
[3] *English Studies* xxx, 134–6.
[4] *Malone Society Collections* ii, 3, pp. 239–50.
[5] *Notes and Queries* ccvii, 162.

Kings and Herod (1523); while the accounts of St John's, Glastonbury, refer to a play 'in le belhay'; and there were apparently plays
also at Kendal, Braintree (Essex), and Chelmsford.[1]

In most of these places there is no evidence for the production
of more than one or two plays during the year, but in some of the
more important towns it is clear that a series of scenes was performed by the various guilds in the manner of the extant cycles,
though the evidence sometimes leaves it doubtful as to whether
these were regular plays or merely pantomimes. However, if any
of the following towns did present a series of plays, they have long
since been lost, unless perhaps some of them survive amongst the
extant unlocalized ones.

At Beverley the earliest record of the Corpus Christi plays
occurs in 1377 in the *Ordinacio cissorum de expensis pagine et ludi
Corporis Christi*. In 1390 a list is given of the thirty-six guilds
taking part, and already by that time the plays are 'an ancient
custom', while in 1411 there appears to have been some complaint
that the wealthier citizens were taking no part in the plays, and
regulations were drawn up to compel their participation. Occasionally the title of one of the plays appears in the records, as for
example in 1391 when the 'hayrers' undertake to 'produce in a
satisfactory manner the play called *Paradise*', and in 1392 when the
Smiths are fined 40s. for not giving their play *The Ascension of the
Lord*. In 1414 the ordinances of the *Barbitonsores*, 'ordained and
used from of old', provide that 'they play or cause to be played a
pageant of the aforesaid St John baptizing Christ in the Jordan,
yearly', and in 1493 the Mercers and the Drapers separated, leading to some re-arrangement of the plays, the former taking *Black
Herod*, the latter *Demyng Pylate*. During the sixteenth century
references to the plays continue. In 1520–1 a fine of 2s. was
received from Richard Trollopp, alderman of the 'paynetors',
'because their play of *The Three Kings of Colleyn* was badly and
confusedly played, in contempt of the whole community, before
many strangers'; 1s. was received from Richard Gaynstang, alderman of the 'talours', 'because his play of *Slepyng Pilate* was badly
played contrary to the order thereof made'; and 2s. from William
Patson, alderman of the drapers 'for his play being badly played'.

[1] *MLN.* lv, 83–95; H. C. Gardiner, *Mysteries' End* (New Haven 1946),
pp. 62, 87, 88.

From about 1520 we have a complete list of the guilds with the plays for which they were responsible:

Tylers: the fallinge of Lucifer.
Saddelers: the makinge of the World.
Walkers: makinge of Adam and eve.
Ropers: the brekinge of the Comaundments of God.
Crelers: gravinge and Spynnynge.
Glovers: Cayn.
Shermen: Adam and Seth.
Wattermen: Noe Shipp.
Bowers and Fletshers: Abraham and Isaak.
Musterdmakers and Chanlers: Salutation of Our Lady.
Husbandmen: Bedleem.
Vynteners: Sheipherds.
Goldsmyths: Kyngs of Colan.
Fyshers: Symeon.
Cowpers: fleynge to Egippe.
Shomakers: Children of Ysraell.
Scryveners: Disputacion in the Temple.

Barbours: Sent John Baptyste.
Laborers: the Pynnacle.
The Mylners: rasynge of Lazar.
Skynners: ierusalem.
Bakers: the Mawndy.
Litsters: prainge at the Mownte.
Tailyours: Slepinge Pilate.
Marchaunts: Blak Herod.
Drapers: Demynge Pylate.
Bocheours: Scorgynge.
Cutlers & Potters: the Stedynynge.
Wevers: the Stanginge.
Barkers: the Takinge of the Crose.
Cooks: Haryinge of hell.
Wrights: the Resurrection.
Gentylmen: Castle of Emaut.
Smyths: Ascencion.
Prestes: Coronacion of Our Lady.
Marchaunts: Domesday.

After 1520, although the plays presumably continued, there is no further mention of them in the existing records. In addition, a second craft play had appeared in 1469, when thirty-nine of the guilds joined together to give a *Paternoster Play* on the Sunday after St Peter ad Vincula, copies being made for the different crafts. None of the *Paternoster Plays* has survived, and consequently the information given here is of some interest so far as the content of such plays is concerned. Apparently the one at Beverley consisted of pageants of the Deadly Sins, and the guilds responsible for the different scenes are given:

Viciose: the gentilmen, merchands, clerks and valets.
Pryde: the shomakers, goldsmiths, glovers, glasiers, skynners and fyshers.
Luxuria: the litsters, walkers, wevers, pynners, cardmakers, wire-draghers.

Sleweth: the watermen, husbandmen, laborers, sadlers, rapers, crelers, mylners and furbishours.
Glotony: baxters, vinters, coupers, innkeepers, cooks, tilers.
Invy: bochers, wrights, coupers, fletchers, patyners.
Avaryce: taileors, masons, braciers, plummers, and cutellers.
Ire: tanners, barbers, smiths, and painters.

An alderman was appointed for each pageant except the first, which had two.[1]

At Durham a weavers' ordinance of 1450 requires them to go in procession on Corpus Christi day, and 'playe and gar to playe the playe yat of old time longed to yaire craft'. Similar rules appear in the ordinances of the cordwainers (1463) and the barbers (1468), and as late as 1567 there is mention of the players of Durham acting at Newcastle. Possibly all that now remains of these Durham plays are thirty-six lines in a fifteenth-century hand on the dorse of MS. Archid. Dunelm. 60 in the Chapter Library of Durham. This is evidently part of the prologue to a play, and begins:

> Pes, lordyngs, I prai ʒow pes,
> And of ʒour noys ʒe stynt and ses;
> Oure gamen to lett ner cry in pres
> For ʒour courtasy.
> þat we ʒow play it is no les
> Godmen, sikirly.[2]

From 1394 onwards the accounts of Wells Cathedral show expenses in connexion with plays, but there are few indications which would allow the identification of any of them.[3] The accounts for 1423–4 of the sacrist of Worcester Priory include gifts to actors in the Corpus Christi play, and in 1467 pageants are mentioned in the craft ordinances of the town, though whether these included plays remains doubtful.[4] From Doncaster come sixteenth-century references to the Fishers' play (1540) and the Glovers' play (1582),

[1] A. F. Leach, *Beverley Town Documents* (Selden Society xiv), pp. 45, 33, 37, 36, 34, 99; *An English Miscellany presented to Dr. Furnivall* (Oxford 1891), pp. 205ff.
[2] *Archaeologia Aeliana* xi, 36, 47; *RES. NS.* x, 172–3.
[3] *HMC., Dean and Chapter of Wells* ii, 29ff.
[4] *MLN.* lv, 83–95; T. Smith, *English Gilds* (EETS. 1870), pp. 385, 407.

but with nothing to show whether these were spoken or dumb-show.[1]

There is no record of any Corpus Christi plays at Canterbury before the end of the fifteenth century, though there is some indication that they had previously been acted fairly regularly but had fallen into disuse. An inventory of the church goods of St Dunstan's, drawn up in 1500, includes various copies of the Corpus Christi plays, but by this date the crafts had become reduced in numbers and the plays were in danger of disappearing. An attempt was made to restore them by a Burgmote order, though with what success is unknown. In 1503 the corporation paid for a play of *The Three Kyngs of Coleyns* in the Guildhall, after which, apart from references to a 'pageant of St Thomas' which may have been a dumb-show, nothing more is heard of plays at Canterbury. In addition, during the fifteenth century a play of *Abraham and Isaac* appears to have been given by the guild of St Dunstan, but it had been discontinued as early as 1491.[2]

The evidence for the existence of plays at Hereford is slight. In 1286 a letter from Bishop Richard de Swinfield to the Dean threatens action against those consorting with Jews, 'whether in eating, drinking, or in the production of plays', but nothing more appears until 1440 when John Hauler and John Pewte sue Thomas Sporyour 'because of the detention of a book of plays worth 2s. 4d.' In the Corporation Register, under the year 1503, is a list of 'the paiants for the procession of Corpus Christi', which read more like dumb-shows than plays.[3]

At Ipswich the former Guild Merchant was reconstituted as a guild of Corpus Christi in 1325, but the extant constitution provides only for a procession. In 1491 an order was made 'Howe euery occupacion of Craftsmen schuld order themselves in the goyng with their pageantes in the procession of Corpus Christi', but the subjects of the pageants are not given, and we cannot be

[1] H. C. Gardiner, *Mysteries' End* (Yale U.P.), p. 123. It is doubtful whether Chaucer's Absolon, who 'pleyeth Herodes upon a scaffold hye' (*Miller's Tale* 3384), can be taken as evidence for the production of plays at Oxford during the fourteenth century.

[2] *Archaeologia Cantiana* xvi, 312ff.; xvii, 147, 80; *HMC., 9th Report,* Appendix, p. 147.

[3] W. W. Capes, *Registrum Ricardi de Swinfield* (Canterbury and York Society 1909), pp. 121ff.; *HMC, Rye and Hereford*, pp. 300, 288.

certain that they included plays. However, in 1504 the 'collectors for the play of Corpus Christi' were allowed to 'make a free burgess for their expenses at the Corpus Christi play'.[1]

There were certainly plays at Leicester during the fifteenth century, since in 1477 it was debated whether the Passion Play 'shulbe put to craftes to be bounden or nay', but little more is heard of them, and although during the last decades of the century the accounts of the churches of St Mary and St Martin include payments for plays and players, no titles or subjects are given.[2]

At Lincoln there appear to have been two main sources of drama, the cathedral clergy and the guilds. So far as we can tell, these produced their plays independently until the fifteenth century, when they apparently began to cooperate. The earliest mention of plays comes from the cathedral accounts of 1317–18, where there is a note of expenses in connexion with a play of *The Three Kings of Cologne*,[3] while in 1321–3 one on *St Thomas* appears. These two continue to be given until the end of the fourteenth century, though the performances do not seem to have been at all regular. They are then supplanted by a *Salutation of the Virgin*, given at Christmas matins, which is performed until 1465. During the fifteenth century an *Assumption* or *Coronation of the Virgin* is also established, and appears regularly until the Reformation. In the reign of Henry VIII a play of *St Anne* took the place of both the *Corpus Christi* and the *Paternoster Play*, and the various references to it suggest that it may have been very similar to the first of these. In addition, the town apparently had its own dramatic performances, though nothing is heard of them until the end of the fourteenth century. In the Bishop's Registry, among the rolls of Bishop Lexington's episcopal register, is one which 'belongs to me Thomas Poornay, gentleman, which I have written', apparently in the reign of Henry VIII. It is essentially a list of the mayors and bailiffs of the town, but includes also occasional notices of notable events, among them various references to the performance of plays. Thus a *Paternoster Play* is noted for 1398, 1411, 1425, 1457; plays on St Laurence (1442), St Susanna (1448),

---

[1] *HMC., 9th Report*, Appendix, pp. 241ff.

[2] M. Bateson, *Records of the Borough of Leicester* (London 1901) ii, 297.

[3] There is apparently no foundation for the suggestion that in 1316 a certain William Wheatley, master of grammar at Lincoln, composed a play of St Hugh. See *MLN.* lxix, 31–4.

King Robert of Sicily (1453), St Clara (1456), and a Corpus Christi play (1472, 1474), while apparently from the same document comes a reference to a *Ludus de Sancto Iacobo*. The Chapter *Curialitates* for 1478-80 include expenses in connexion with a Corpus Christi play, and in 1521 the corporation agreed 'that Paternoster Play shall be played this year'.[1]

After the incidental reference by William FitzStephen, little further is known of plays in London before the fourteenth century, though Richard of Devizes (c. 1193) tells of a Jew who sent a Christian boy to England, giving him a letter which urged him to hurry through London because of its temptations, and among these are *theatrum, histriones, mimi,* etc.[2] A petition (c. 1300) from the prioress of St Mary, Clerkenwell, complains of damage to the crops and fields of the convent caused by people attending miracle plays and wrestlings. It is endorsed with a direction that the constable of the vill should take action to prevent damage being done, but he appears to have been negligent, since a writ was issued in the following year against the 'wrestlings and miracle plays' at Clerkenwell.[3] According to Dodsley, the scholars of St Paul's presented a petition to Richard II in 1378 'to prohibit some unexpert people from presenting the History of the Old Testament, to the great prejudice of the said Clergy, who have been at great expence in order to represent it publickly at Christmas'.[4] Under the year 1384 John Malvern's continuation to Higden's *Polychronicon* refers to a play, lasting five days, given by the clerks of London at Skinnerswell, while in 1391 they produced another at the same place which lasted for four days 'in which was displayed much of the Old and New Testaments'. On the occasion of Richard II's expedition to Scotland in 1385 a proclamation by the Mayor and Aldermen forbids the play that customarily took place at 'Skynneres well'.[5] In 1392 the *London Chronicle* mentions a play 'of seynt Katerine'; in 1409 it notes a play at Skinnerswell 'which endured Wednesday, Thorsday, Fryday, and on Soneday it was ended'; and an even longer play in 1411, lasting seven days,

---

[1] *PMLA.* lii, 946ff.; *An English Miscellany presented to Dr Furnivall* (Oxford 1891), pp. 222ff.; C. Wordsworth, *op. cit.* ii, 139.

[2] Richard of Devizes (RS. 82) iii, 437.   [3] *MLR.* xxxiii, 564.

[4] R. Dodsley, *A Select Collection of Old Plays* (London 1780) i, xxxix. But the source for this statement cannot now be traced.

[5] Higden ix, 47, 259; *MLR.* xxxiii, 564.

is recorded in the *Chronicle of the Greyfriars*.[1] The Wardrobe Accounts for 1408–9 refer to a great play at Clerkenwell, 'showing how God created Heaven and Earth out of nothing and how he created Adam and on to the Day of Judgment'.[2] After this there is nothing until 1508,[3] apparently due rather to gaps in the records than to any interruption in the production of plays. Certainly the long Passion Play was still being produced in the sixteenth century, since Henry Machyn mentions one at the Greyfriars in 1557 in terms which suggest that it lasted for more than a single day.[4] Apart from these longer plays, given apparently by the clerks in minor orders, the churchwardens' accounts of some of the London churches contain references to other plays, but the notices are usually vague and no titles are given.

Most of the extant plays date from the fifteenth century, and where there is evidence for the earlier production of plays at the particular town, it is impossible to say whether these are simply modernizations of the earlier ones, or whether they are completely different. More or less complete cycles remain from York, Chester, and Wakefield. The first of these contains forty-eight plays, but a blank has been left in the manuscript for the Ironmongers' *Visit to Simon the Leper* which was never copied into it. Similarly, only the first line appears of the Vintners' play of the *Marriage at Cana*; at the end of the manuscript only forty-seven lines survive of the Innholders' play of the *Coronation of the Virgin*; and there is no trace at all of the play of *Fergus*, which fifteenth-century records show to have once been acted by the Linenweavers. In the later *Ordo*, the Masons seem to have been responsible for it, but in 1431 they complained that the play 'caused rather laughter and blows than devotion', and in consequence they were given *Herod*, one of the Goldsmiths' plays. In 1476, however, the Linenweavers were again undertaking *Fergus*, though in 1485 its production is under consideration by the Corporation, who decree that 'the mater hanging in travaux betwix the sawers and wrightis concernyng the bringing furth of the pageant of Fergus' be deferred. In the same year it is ordained that the tapiters, cordwainers, and linen-

---

[1] N. H. Nicolas and E. Tyrrell, *A Chronicle of London* (London 1827), pp. 80, 91; *Monumenta Franciscana* (RS. 4) ii, 164.

[2] J. H. Wylie, *History of England under Henry IV* (London 1884–98) iv, 213.

[3] *Annales Henrici VII* (RS. 10), p. 121.

[4] J. G. Nichols, *The Diary of Henry Machyn* (CS. 1848), p. 138.

weavers should together produce the pageant of the tapiter craft
and cardmaker craft, 'soo that the padgeant called Fergus late
broght furth by the lynweves be laid apart'. There is no record
that *Fergus* was ever played again, and this may account for its
omission from the late fifteenth-century manuscript of the plays.
These four plays have been almost completely lost, and other records
show that at one time or another there were independent ones on
The Washing of Feet, The Casting of Lots, The Hanging of Judas,
and *The Burial of the Virgin,* which no longer exist as such, though
parts of them may have been incorporated in some of the remaining
plays.[1]

In addition, two other plays once produced at York, the *Paternoster Play* and the *Creed Play,* have completely disappeared. The
earliest reference to the former occurs in the English version of
Wyclif's *De Officio Pastorali* (1378):

> & herfore freris han tauȝt in englond þe paternoster in engliȝsch
> tunge, as men seyen in þe pley of ȝork.[2]

The next information comes from a certificate or return sent by the
York Guild of the Paternoster to the King's Council in 1389, giving
an account of the foundation, constitution, customs, and property
of the association. From this it appears that the primary function
of the guild was to perform a play representing the merits of the
Lord's Prayer, including pageants of the vices and virtues; and that
the guild owned no property apart from the equipment for the play
and a wooden chest for storage.[3] One of the scenes is mentioned
in some accounts for 1399, in which John Downom and his wife
are said to owe 2s. 2d. for their entrance fee to the guild, 'but the
aforesaid John affirmed that he had contributed 2s. 1d. towards the
expenses of the play Accidie'.[4] In 1464 William Downham leaves
to William Ball 'all my books of the Pater Noster play', and by that
time it seems to have been in the hands of the Merchants' guild,
since an entry in their records 'on the election daye of Thomas
Scawsby, being master', ordains that four pageant-masters shall be
chosen who shall be responsible for the production of the Pater-

---

[1] *PMLA.* lxv, 866–76; L. T. Smith, *York Mystery Plays* (Oxford 1885),
pp. xviiff.; SS. cxxv, ii, 124.
[2] F. D. Matthew, *The English Works of Wyclif* (EETS. 1880), p. 429.
[3] *Speculum* vii, 540–6.   [4] L. T. Smith, *op. cit.,* p. xxix.

noster Play.[1] Thomas Scawsby was master of the guild in 1462, but the pageant-masters were apparently seldom if ever chosen before 1488. In the sixteenth century the play was substituted for the Corpus Christi plays, and by 1558 it is in the hands of St Anthony's, the master of which is ordered to 'provyd for the playing of one play callyd Pater Noster play this yere'. This particular performance apparently took place, but in April 1572 the council agreed that

> my Lord Mayor shall send for the maister of Saint Anthony's, and he to bryng with hym the booke of the play called the Pater Noster play, that the same may be perused, amended and corrected, and that my Lord Mayor shall certifie to theis presens at their next assemblee here of his pleasure to be taken therin.

The Lord Mayor evidently gave his approva, since in the following month the council directed that 'the Pater Noster play shalbe played this yere on the Thursday next after Trynitie Sonday next comyng'. But a few months later the Lord Mayor informed the council that

> my Lord Archebisshop of York requested to have a copie of the bookes of the Pater Noster play, wherupon it was aggreed that His Grace shall have a trewe copie of all the said bookes even as they weare played this yere.

They were accordingly delivered to the archbishop and nothing more is heard of them. Nor is there anything to show that they were ever returned, either by him or his successors, or that the play was ever performed again.[2] Its exact nature is unknown; plays of the same title were apparently given at Beverley and Lincoln, but none has survived, and the records have little to say of it beyond the bare fact of its presentation.[3]

The Creed Play is first heard of in the will of William Revetour (1446), whose bequests include a copy of the *Pricke of Conscience*, an English version of the Bible, and, to the Corpus Christi guild of York, 'a certain book called *Le Crede Play*, along with the books and standards pertaining to it', the play to be performed every tenth year 'in various places of the said city'. In 1455 the original

[1] SS. xxx, 268; SS. cxxix, 81.
[2] R. Davies, *Extracts from the Municipal Records of the City of York* (London 1843), pp. 265–72.   [3] *PMLA.* xxxix, 789ff.

manuscript was so worn that it had to be transcribed, the transcription being included in an inventory of 1465; since it is said to have contained *xxij quaternos*, the play must have been of some length.[1] Various performances are recorded, usually on or about August 1. In 1535 the Corpus Christi plays were omitted, and the crafts contributed 'pageant silver' to the *Creed Play*, but they refused to give way again in 1545. The guild was suppressed in 1547, the play passing into the hands of the hospital of St Thomas. In 1562 the corporation proposed the *Creed Play* on St Barnabas Day as an alternative to 'thystories of the old and new testament'. In 1568 they again wished to replace the regular Corpus Christi plays by the *Creed Play*, but first submitted it to Matthew Hutton, dean of York, who advised that,

> thogh it was plawsible to yeares ago, and wold now also of the ignorant sort be well liked, yet now in this happie time of the gospell, I knowe the learned will mislike it, and how the state will beare with it, I knowe not.

Consequently, the play was 'delyveryd in agayn', and nothing more is heard of it. However, an undated letter of Henry VIII speaks of a riot which took place 'at the acting of a religious interlude of St Thomas the Apostle', and it has been suggested that the *Creed Play* may have included scenes dealing with the various apostles, of which this was one, but apart from this possibility we know nothing about the subject of the play.[2] Nor is anything known of the *ludum oreginale Sancti Dionisii* which, in 1455, Robert Lasingby left to the church in York dedicated to that saint, though at that date it may be assumed to have been in English.[3]

Various plays are, for one reason or another, missing from the text of the York cycle as we now have it, and the same is true of some of the other so-called complete cycles. In the Towneley manuscript twelve leaves are missing between the first and second of the plays, suggesting the loss of one or more plays on the Temptation and Fall and on the Expulsion from Eden. In addition some

---

[1] SS. xxx, 117; lvii, 293-4.
[2] E. K. Chambers, *The Mediæval Stage* (Oxford 1903) ii, 404-6; J. O. Halliwell, *Letters of the Kings of England* (London 1848) i, 354.
[3] SS. xxx, 117, n.

of the plays are incomplete, while the 1500 lines missing between XXIX and XXX perhaps indicates the loss of plays on Pentecost and on the Death and Assumption of the Virgin. Similarly the bans of the Chester plays refer to one on the Assumption by the 'wyffys of this towne' which has apparently not survived:

> The wurshipffull wyffys of this towne
> ffynd of our Lady thassumcion.
> It to bryng forth they be bowne
> And meytene w^t all theyre might.[1]

In addition to the extant cycles, plays have also survived from Coventry, Newcastle and Norwich. The earliest reference to Coventry plays occurs in a document of 1392–3 in which a certain tenement is described as between that 'of the prior and convent on one side and between the house for the pageant of the weavers of Coventry on the other'. During the fifteenth and sixteenth centuries references to the cycle are frequent in the municipal records and in those of the different crafts. The number of crafts in the city appears to have been small; an act of the leet shows that in 1445 there were only seventeen, and although no doubt there were changes later, there never seems to have been many of them. Of these seventeen crafts only ten can be shown to have supported pageants, the remainder either being contributory to those charged with the plays, or else contriving to evade the duty altogether. Moreover, each play appears to have included a whole group of subjects, and this is certainly true of the two extant ones, that of the Shearmen and Tailors and that of the Weavers:

> Shearmen and Tailors: the Annunciation, the visit to Elizabeth, the Nativity, the Shepherds, the Kings of Cologne, the Flight into Egypt, the Massacre of the Innocents.
> Weavers: the Purification, the Doctors in the Temple.

It is fairly certain that the remaining plays also consisted of similar groups, and references in the municipal records make it possible to deduce the subjects of seven of them:

> Smiths: Christ before the High Priest, Pilate and Herod, the Denial, the Repentance of Judas, the Crucifixion.
> Pinners and Needlers: the Death of Christ, and the Burial.

[1] *The Malone Society Studies*, 1935, p. 137.

Cappers: the Descent into Hell, the Resurrection, Peter and John at the Tomb, the Appearance of Christ to Magdalene and to the Travellers.

Mercers: the Death and Assumption of Mary, the Appearance of Mary to Thomas.

Drapers: Doomsday.

No light is thrown on the play or plays presented by the Tanners, Whittawers, and Girdlers. Consequently, of this cycle of at least ten plays, one of the most important of the period, only two are now extant, though all must have been written down since the records show frequent payments for copying or correcting them. Local annals occasionally record other plays, such as one on St Catherine in 1491 and 1504, and three pageants ending 'with a goodly stage play' before Henry VIII and his queen in 1510.[1]

The Newcastle cycle is represented by the Shipwrights' play of *Noah*, now known only from an eighteenth-century edition. The earliest mention of Corpus Christi plays there occurs under the year 1426 in an 'ordinary' of the Coopers, and fifteenth-century references are not infrequent. It is clear that a complete cycle formerly existed, and the subjects of twelve of the plays, together with the crafts responsible for them, are known:

Bricklayers and Plasterers: the Creation of Adam.
Shipwrights: Noah's Ark.
Slaters: the Offering of Isaac.
Millers: the Deliverance of the Children of Israel.
Goldsmiths, Plumbers, Glaziers, Pewterers, and Painters: the Three Kings of Cologne.
Bricklayers and Plasterers: the Flying of Our Lady into Egype.
Barbers and Chirurgeons, with Chandlers: the Baptizing of Christ.
Fullers and Dyers: the Last Supper.
Weavers: the Bearing of the Cross.
House Carpenters: the Burial of Christ.
Tailors: the Descent into Hell.
Masons: the Buriall of Our Lady Saint Mary the Virgin.

The Merchant Venturers were also responsible for five plays, one of which was performed by the Ostmen and paid for by the town, but the subjects are not known, and this is also the case with the

---

[1] H. Craig, *Two Coventry Corpus Christi Plays* (EETS. ES. 1902); M. D. Harris, *The Story of Coventry* (London 1911), p. 296.

plays of the remaining six guilds. A joiners' 'ordinary' of 1589 would suggest that they themselves had no particular play, but assisted generally in the performances. As for the other five, they may have had a play each, some of them may have joined to produce one, or some may have given more than one. The saddlers' play, whatever it was, was apparently still in existence in 1730 when, according to a local historian:

> This company has belonging to it an ancient Manuscript, beautifully wrote, in Old English Rhime; it relates to our Saviour's Sufferings. I take it to be the play they were obliged by their Ordinary to maintain on the Feast of Corpus Christi.

However, it had apparently disappeared when search was made for it by another local historian fifty years later. The plays were still being given regularly in 1568, but ten years later were acted only occasionally and at the special command of the mayor and corporation, the last reference to them appearing in a masons' 'ordinary' of 1581. It seems clear that the whole cycle, when complete, must have included somewhere between twenty-two and twenty-seven plays.[1]

Of the Norwich cycle only the Grocers' play of *The Creation of Adam and Eve and the Fall* now survives. This had been copied into the *Grocers' Book*, since lost, and we are now dependent on an eighteenth-century transcript. The earliest reference to plays at Norwich dates from 1478, in which year J. Whetley writes jocularly to Sir John Paston of 'my Lord off Suffolk' that 'ther was never no man that playd Herrod in Corpus Crysty play better and more agreable to hys pageaunt than he dud'.[2] The first mention of the Corpus Christi procession occurs in 1489, when the order is given in which the thirty-one guilds of the town shall go in procession before the pageants, but nothing more appears before 1527. Up to that time the management of the plays, and the expenses in connexion with them, had been in the hands of St Luke's guild which, as a result, found itself almost bankrupt, and petitioned the corporation to divide the responsibility and expense amongst the various guilds. The following division was then made, and recorded in the *Assembly Book* of the Corporation:

[1] O. Waterhouse, *The Non-Cycle Mystery Plays* (EETS. ES. 1909), pp. xxxvff.; *Archaeologia Aeliana* xi, 31–64.

[2] N. Davis, *Paston Letters* (Oxford 1958), pp. 113–14.

Mercers, Drapers & Haberdashers: Creation off the World.

Glasiers, Steyners & Screveners, Parchmynters, Carpenters, Gravers, Caryers, Colermakers with Whelewrights: Helle Carte.

Grocers & Raffemen: Paradyse.

Shermen, Fullers, Thikwollenwevers, Coverlightmakers, Masons & Lyme brenners: Abell & Cayn.

Bakers, Bruers, Inkepers, Coks, Millers, Vynteners & Coupers: Noyse Shipp.

Taillors, Broderers, Reders & Tylers: Abraham & Isaac.

Tanners, Coryors & Cordwaners: Moises and Aaron with the Children of Israel & Pharo with his Knyghts.

Smythes: Conflict off David & Goleas.

Dyers, Colaunderers, Goldsmiths, Goldbeters, Sadelers, Pewtrers & Brasyers: The Berth off Christ with Sheperdes & iij Kings of Colen.

Barbours, Wexchandelers, Surgeons, Fisitians, Hardewaremen, Hatters, Cappers, Skynners, Glovers, Pynners, Poyntemakers, Girdelers, Pursers, Bagmakers, Sceppers, Wyerdrawers & Cardmakers: the Baptysme of Criste.

Bochers, Fishmongers & Watermen: the Resurrection.

Worsted Wevers: the Holy Gost.

This appears to have been the complete cycle in the sixteenth century, and it is exceptional only in its inclusion of a play of David and Goliath, and in the comparative absence of subjects from the New Testament. However, it seems rather short and may have been longer in earlier times.[1]

The provenance of some of the extant plays is unknown, and it is not impossible that they may be identical with plays which are assumed to have been lost, though evidence is lacking. One complete cycle survives in the forty-two plays of the so-called *Ludus Coventriæ* which probably had nothing to do with that town. The only indication of provenance is a mention of 'N. towne' in the prologue. This has led to the ascription of them to Northampton or Norwich, but the term may simply be common form, and Lincoln has also been suggested. Similarly, the Dublin *Abraham and Isaac* is so-called because the manuscript is in the library of Trinity College, Dublin. In the same hand as the play is a list of the mayors and bailiffs of North[ampton] up to 1458, and a brief chronicle in which N[orthampton] is often mentioned. Connexion with that town therefore seem possible, though nothing is known

[1] O. Waterhouse, *op. cit.*, pp. xxviff.

from any other source of the existence of plays there. The Brome *Abraham and Isaac* is preserved in a commonplace book of 1470–80 belonging to the owners of Brome manor in Suffolk. Again, nothing is known of its original provenance, and there is no indication that it ever formed part of a cycle, though in origin it is clearly a revision of the Chester play on that subject. The prologue to the Croxton *Sacrament* says that it was performed at a place of that name, and local allusions in the play would point to the vicinity of Bury. The four *Digby Plays* appear to have no connexion with each other, apart from the fact that they have been copied into the same manuscript, and in none is there any hint of the provenance. The *Burial and Resurrection* is quite anonymous, and the only connexion of the *Shrewsbury Fragments* with that town is their presence in a manuscript belonging to the school.

No plays have survived from Ireland or Scotland, though there is some evidence for their former existence in both countries. In Dublin, the *Chain Book* of the city contains a memorandum of the Corpus Christi pageants, apparently written in 1498, though whether these were plays or only dumb-shows is uncertain. In 1528 a mixture of plays was presented before the earl of Kildare:

the taylors acted the part of Adam and Eve; the shoemakers represented the story of Crispin and Crispinianus; the vintners acted Bacchus and his story; the Carpenters that of Joseph and Mary; Vulcan, and what related to him, was acted by the Smiths; and the comedy of Ceres, the goddess of corn, by the Bakers.[1]

More definite evidence of Corpus Christi plays comes from Kilkenny. From a corporation record it is clear that a definite cycle, possibly consisting of five plays only, was acted there, the book containing them being still in existence as late as 1637.[2]

In Scotland the earliest reference comes from 1440, when an entry in the *Aberdeen Council Register* mentions 'a certain play of *ly haliblude*', presumably a passion play. It is referred to again in 1445, and in 1449 Walter Balcancole, notary public, received 5s. for writing a Corpus Christi play, though whether he was simply

---

[1] J. J. Webb, *The Guilds of Dublin* (London 1929), pp. 53–5; E. K. Chambers, *The Mediæval Stage* (Oxford 1903) ii, 365.
[2] *Proceedings of the Royal Irish Academy, Section C,* xli, 206.

recopying the old *haliblude* play, re-arranging it, or composing an entirely new one does not appear. In 1471 a play of *bellyale* is mentioned, and in 1479 it was ordained that the expenses for the 'arayment & vþiris necessaris of þe play to be plait in the fest of corpus christi nixt tocum' were to be defrayed from common good funds. It is not before 1512–13 that there is any evidence for the association of the crafts with the Corpus Christi celebrations, nor are pageants definitely mentioned in connexion with these before 1530. The pre-Reformation craft records of Aberdeen have been lost, and it must remain doubtful whether a cycle of religious plays was ever performed there. The references to the pageants would suggest that they were no more than dumb-show accompaniments to the religious procession.

The earliest records of Dundee date from the sixteenth century, and there is mention of a play there in 1553, but no details are given. So far as Perth is concerned, in 1485 payments were made for a Corpus Christi play, and similar items recur in 1486 and 1487–8, but in no case is the name of the play given. A list of 'the playaris on corpus christie day and quhat money sall be payt till þame', in the craft book of the Hammermen under the year 1518 appears to indicate two plays, one on the Creation and Fall and another on St Erasmus. The two apparently continued until 1553, when the play of St Erasmus disappears from the records leaving only the Old Testament one. The Wrights' craft book has items of expenditure in 1530 for repairing the play-gear, and it is not unlikely that there may have been at Perth a regular cycle of plays, though there can be no certainty of this. At Lanark a Corpus Christi play is mentioned in 1503, and *The Kingis of Cullane* in 1507. From Edinburgh there are no references to religious plays before the middle of the sixteenth century, though they may well have existed previously, since the records are incomplete and give little information on the subject. So far as the court is concerned, Patrick Johnson was paid £6 'for his plays' in 1475–6, and in 1477 for 'certain amusements and plays' and 'for certain plays and interludes', while in 1488 he and 'the playaris of Lythgow that playt to the King' received £5, and there seems no reason to doubt that these were genuine plays. Various items in the accounts of the Lord High Treasurer from 1473 onwards suggest a play of St Nicholas, while at the University of

231

Glasgow the regulations for the annual celebration of the feast of the translation of St Nicholas mention an *interludium*.[1]

It seems clear that an immense amount of religious dramatic literature from the medieval period has been lost. References to many single plays appear, and it is possible to reconstruct the outlines of some of the lost cycles. The evidence perhaps suggests that these craft cycles may have been confined to the north and east, but even so there are important towns there which we should expect to have had such cycles whose municipal records do not begin until much later. The Passion Plays seem to have been characteristic of the south, and it is possible that had any of these survived many of our present conceptions of the nature of the religious drama might be changed. No doubt most of the lost plays were very similar to those that still remain; yet the plot of the Towneley *Secunda Pastorum* is a warning that a play should not be judged from the title alone.

Side by side with the religious drama there are some slight traces of secular plays. The earliest example of these is a fragment, written in an early fourteenth-century hand, on a narrow strip cut from the margin of an assize roll of Norfolk and Suffolk for 1250–1300. It contains 268 verses, the consecutive speeches of a single person in a play to which the title *Dux Moraud* has been given. It was evidently a version of the theme of the Incestuous Daughter, and though frequently cited as the earliest example of secular drama, it could equally well have been a miracle play.[2] If so, the remaining eighty-four lines of the interlude *De Clerico et Puella*, dating from the end of the thirteenth century, would be the first non-religious play in English. The interlude evidently dealt with a similar story to that of the somewhat earlier fabliau *Dame Siriʒ*. Apart from this, only very general references to the secular drama appear. In 1352 Bishop Grandisson of Exeter denounces a 'certain noxious and blameworthy play, or rather buffoonery, [composed] in scorn and insult of the leather-dressers [of that city] and their art'.[3] In 1444 a London chronicle notes a play of *Eglemour and Degrebelle* at St Albans, and one of a *Knight cleped Florence* at Bermondsey, which were presumably dramatic

---

[1] A. J. Mill, *Mediæval Plays in Scotland* (Edinburgh 1927), passim.
[2] *Anglia* xxx, 180ff.
[3] G. G. Coulton, *Social Life in Britain* (Cambridge 1918), p. 494.

versions of the romances of *Sir Eglamour of Artois* and *Le Bone Florence of Rome*.[1] In a fifteenth-century manuscript, written on what was once the upper half of a large folio leaf standing at the end of a volume, are forty-two lines of a play on *Robin Hood and the Sheriff of Nottingham*, beginning:

> Syr sheryffe for thy sake
> Robyn hode wull y take.[2]

No doubt this is to be connected with the reference to a play of Robin Hood in the *Paston Letters*. Numerous sixteenth-century references bear witness to the popularity of a play on the same subject in Scotland, but nothing of it has survived.[3]

This is all that we know about the secular drama, and the evidence is much too slight for any conclusions to be drawn concerning the extent of such literature during the Middle English period. The date of the references would suggest that it was a comparatively late development, and the overwhelming importance of the religious drama may have prevented it from becoming extensive. In any case, these fragments and allusions are all that now remain of a type of medieval literature of which no complete example has survived.

---

[1] E. K. Chambers, *English Literature at the Close of the Middle Ages* (Oxford 1945), p. 65.

[2] *Malone Society Collections* 1, 2, 117ff.; see also pp. 129–30 above.

[3] A. J. Mill, *op. cit.*, p. 24.

12

CONCLUSION

'Yet it is safe to say that if the lost poetry had been preserved, the whole history of English literature, prior to Chaucer and Langland, would appear to us in a different light. The homilies and lives of saints, which bulk so largely in Medieval English verse and prose, would subside till they occupied a just, and a small, proportion of our attention.'[1] This was the opinion of one of the first scholars to emphasize the fact that any attempt to estimate the achievement of medieval English literature must take into account that which has been lost as well as that which has survived. An attempt has here been made to discover how far the statement can be justified.

The plan of this survey intentionally follows that of the usual histories of Old and Middle English literature, so that comparison of what remains with what has been lost can the more easily be made. Such a method inevitably has its dangers; more particularly it tends to conceal the very uneven value of the evidence for the former existence of some of the lost literature. Occasionally the evidence is so strong that the one-time existence of a particular work may be taken for granted; at other times it can suggest little beyond the bare possibility of current works on the subject; and more often than not the evidence falls somewhere between these two extremes. Moreover, in all probability much of the lost literature never had a written existence, but there seems no good reason for restricting the term 'literature' to what has been written down, more particularly during the early Middle Ages when oral composition may have been quite as important as written.

If this wider definition of 'literature' is accepted, the most obvious result of comparing the histories of the extant and the lost literature is to strengthen the impression that neglect of the latter has distorted the outline of medieval English literature. And this

[1] *Trans. Bib. Soc.* v, 294.

distortion is due more particularly to the fact that a chapter on the Historical Narrative usually finds no place at all in the textbooks. So far as the heroic literature is concerned little emerges that is new. It has long been recognized that the extant remains of it are only a small part of that which formerly existed, and in the main the chapter on the subject does little more than provide further evidence for this. It shows, too, that many of the heroes were still known during the Middle English period, though probably it usually happened that little remained beyond the name. On the other hand, the available evidence gives no support whatever to the usual assumption that the heroic poetry was gradually ousted by romance. In Old English there are signs that the place of the heroic poetry was gradually being taken by subjects from later Anglo-Saxon history; and it is these subjects, frequently it would appear treated in the heroic manner, that were more immediately fatal to the older epic and heroic themes. The chapter on historical narrative makes it clear that the usual restriction of the title in textbooks to the extant historical poems has resulted in the neglect of what was in fact the most important type of narrative during the Old English period. No doubt this is mainly due to the fact that, whether in prose or verse, it was essentially an oral literature of which little beyond the general outline now remains, so that any critical appreciation of it is largely impossible. The distortion of the history of the early literature is, moreover, exaggerated by the stress on religious epic, a type of poetry which usually occupies much more space than is warranted by its importance or influence. It appears to have been essentially a literary development due to ecclesiastical influence; an attempt to substitute religious subjects for the suspect heroic or historical narrative, and there is little reason to believe that it met with much success outside such circles. So far as we can tell it exerted little influence on later literature, and its place was soon taken by the vernacular lives of the saints, which had no need to ape heroic legend but depended for their appeal on the accumulation of marvels from apocryphal stories. Signs of such a change are already apparent in some of the works of Cynewulf, where the heroic atmosphere is becoming less conspicuous. The investigation suggests, too, that comparatively little of importance in Old English religious or didactic prose has been lost, most of the references being to versions of works of which other copies are still in existence. Had the entire output of this prose survived, it is improbable that much would need to be added to modern accounts. The lives of the saints were, of course, always a popular subject, and any complete account of medieval literature must allot to them a comparatively large amount of space. In addition, it should note that, side by side with the written lives, there existed a flourishing oral literature, centred more particularly in the persons of the native saints – a literature which was in fact simply a special branch of the historical narrative.

In the Middle English period little seems to have been lost from the three great Matters of romance. Here again it is clear that the extant romances on these subjects were essentially part of a written literature, and in all probability the analogous Matter of England, which was mainly oral, was more popular than any of the romances of the more conventional Matters. On the other hand, it is possible that these lost oral narratives had little in common with the extant romances of the Matter of England, since these are in the main translations from earlier French versions, and they have been considerably influenced by the written romances. As far as the shorter narrative is concerned, there is reason to believe that it was formerly much more extensive; that, for example, the few extant examples of the fabliau and the beast tale are no trustworthy guide to the real popularity of such subjects during this period. The religious and didactic literature occupies a similar position to that in Old English. It is clear that a chapter dealing with it must be important and lengthy; but it is equally clear that few important works have completely vanished, the most frequent losses being other copies of still extant works. It has long been recognized that comparatively little of the secular lyrical poetry has been preserved; but it has not always been fully appreciated that the lyric was at home in England much earlier than might have been supposed. The earliest complete examples date from the late thirteenth century, and their perfection and technical excellence would suggest that they are far from the beginnings of such literature. In fact, the references make it clear that the lyric was well-established in England at least as early as the first half of the twelfth century. In dramatic literature, apart from the possible existence of a secular drama towards the end of the period, little of interest emerges. It is obvious enough that some complete cycles of craft plays, and numerous single plays, have vanished, but there is little to suggest that these lost plays differed much if at all from the extant examples, though the discovery of one of the long southern Passion Plays might change our opinions.

It is, of course, not beyond the bounds of possibility that some of the works mentioned in the preceding pages may eventually turn up. The only surviving manuscript of Malory was found in 1934 among the books in the Fellows' Library of Winchester College, where it had long been lying unrecognized. In the same year the *Book of Margery Kempe*, hitherto known only from a few uncharacteristic extracts from it printed by Wynken de Worde, was identified in the library of Colonel Butler-Bowden. An astronomical treatise, *The Equatorie of the Planetis*,[1] which quite evidently had a close connexion with Chaucer and may quite possibly be in his own handwriting, was discovered in 1951 in the library of Peterhouse, Cambridge. Such discoveries, though rare today, are by no means unknown, and medieval manuscripts of different kinds have turned up in all kinds of curious places. A cartulary from the Augustinian priory of Fineshade recently re-appeared among the records of the Court of Arches, where it had lain unnoticed since its deposit there in the course of a lawsuit in 1670, and another from Coxford (BM. MS. Additional 47784) was found during the present century in a London junk-shop. A note on an old binding, now destroyed, records that a fourteenth-century manuscript containing inventories of the muniments of the earls of Mortimer at Wigmore, was 'found in 1795 in opnning a vault in an Ruind Tower in R'.[2] Pasted inside the cover of Balliol College, MS. 384, a fifteenth-century Book of Hours, is the following note:

The Book was found in ye thatch of an old house of Atkins whose Ancestors were known to be Stewards to ye Lovetts of Astwell, an Antient family of note in these parts, but now extinct; now my guess is yt at ye beginning of ye Reformation, ys Book was committed to Atkins of Weston to be secured 'till a turn might happen; and yt ys

[1] Ed. D. J. Price (Cambridge 1955).
[2] G. R. C. Davis, *Medieval Cartularies of Great Britain* (London 1958), p. xvi.

conjecture is not forreighn may be seen in ye Calendar, where Seuerall of ye Lovetts are Register'd. I thought fitt to trouble you with y[s] account, tho to what end I know not. Pray Sr. my humble service to Mr Harris and all friends at Colledge.[1]

Similarly, a Reading Abbey cartulary (BM. MS. Egerton 3031) was discovered during the eighteenth century in a bricked-up priests' hole in Lord Fingall's house at Shinfield, while a note in MS. Harl. 4996 records that it was found between the wainscot and the wall when the west gate of Whitehall was being taken down. Even more sensational was the discovery in the nineteenth century of the charters of Newstead Priory in the ball foot of a lectern, thrown into the lake at Newstead by the monks to prevent their falling into the hands of the King's Commissioners at the dissolution of the monastery.[2]

---

[1] R. A. B. Mynors, *Catalogue of the Manuscripts of Balliol College, Oxford* (Oxford 1963), p. 362.
[2] *The Year's Work in Librarianship* xii, 406.

INDEX

239

Titchfield Abbey, catalogue, 92, 127, 153
Tobias, bishop of Rochester, 65
Tobit, Lollard version, 140
Tolsey Court Book, 178
Torrent of Portyngale, 14
Toure of all Toures, 138
Towneley, Christopher, 141
Towneley Cycle, missing plays, 225–226, *Secunda Pastorum,* 232
Tracts, heretical, 139–40
Trailbaston, statute of, 190
Trewman, Jacke, epistle of, 197
Tristram, 108, 127, works on, 107, 108–9
Trollopp, Richard, 216
Tuck, Friar, 130
Tuisto, 1
Tupholme Abbey, 83
Tyndale, William, 84

Ubba, Ubbo, Hubba, son of Ragnar Lothbrog, tales of, 34–8
'Vbbelaue', 38
Uesseden Passion, boke of, 147
Uhtred, earl, death of, 52
Unwine, Unwen, 4, 7–8, 15
Unwona, a priest, 86
Ursewyk, Sir Thomas, books of, 147–8, 150

Vandals, king of, 14
Varini, king of, 26
Vaudreuil, castle of, 188
Vegetius, English version, 154
Venables, Piers, 130
Venantius Fortunatus, 1
Vercelli Book, 60, 61, 86
Vézelay, monk of, 131
Vices and Virtues, 146
Vidigoia, 7
Viking Invasions, 19, tales of, 34–41
Vilkinus, King, 14
Visigoths, 21
Vision of Earl Leofric, 95
Visit to Simon the Leper, play of, 222
Vita antiquissima S. Gregorii, 27
Vita et Passio Waldevi, 57
Vita Haroldi, 56, 58
Vita Oswaldi, 48, 49, 82, 102
Vitae duorum Offarum, 9, 32, 33, 97–8

Vitas Patrum, 160 n. 1
Volfe of the varldis end, the tayl of the, 120
Vǫlsungar, 28
Vǫlsunga saga, 18, 23
Vǫlundarkviða, 11, 14
Vox and the Wolf, 124

Wace, *Brut,* 112
Wacherius, 131
Wade, Wada, 8, 11, 19, magic boat of, 15, 16, tales of, 14–16
Wakefield, YW, plays at, 222
Wald, 23
Waldef, 108, 112–13, English source, 113, Latin version, 8, 113
Waldere, 1, 6, 8, 13, 18
Waldere, 6, 8
Wales, 40, 95, 106, 108, 118, 134
Wallace, Sir William, songs of, 205, 207
Wallingford, Brk, 31
Wall-paintings, poems on, 176–7
Walter, archdeacon of Oxford, 73
Walter, Brother, works of, 136
Walter de Bibbesworth, 127
Walter Espec, 73, 105
Walter of Guisborough, *Chronicon,* 117, 190
Waltham Abbey, 58, inventory, 83–4
Waltheof, 7, 113 n. 1, tales of, 57
Wanley, Humphrey, 91
Wardrobe Accounts, 222
Warenne, earl of, 190
Warmundus, king of the West Angles, 9
Warocher, 131–2
Warwick, 9, earl of, 194
Washingborough, Li, 73
Washing of Feet, play of the, 223
Wassingburc, liuere Engleis de, 73–4
Waterford, 199, book of, 199
Weland, 6, 7, Middle English references to, 14, tales of, 11–14
Welbeck Abbey, library of, 215
Welles, Lord, books of, 148
Wells, So, books at, 83, Cathedral accounts, 218, plays at, 218
Wereham, Nf, 163
Werfrith, bishop of Worcester, 71, version of Gregory's *Dialogues,* 71, 75, 78, 81–2, 83